2

BRAVING HOME

D0107566

FIRST MARINER BOOKS EDITION 2004

For information about permission to reproduce selections from this book, write to Permissions, Houghton Mifflin Company, 215 Park Avenue South, New York, New York 10003.

Visit our Web site: www.houghtonmifflinbooks.com.

ISBN-10 0-618-15548-1
ISBN-13 978-0-618-15548-4
ISBN-10 0-618-44662-1 (pbk.)
ISBN-13 978-0-618-44662-9 (pbk.)

*Library of Congress Cataloging-in-Publication Data*

Halpern, Jake.
   Braving home : dispatches from the Underwater Town, the Lava-Side Inn, and other extreme locales / Jake Halpern.
       p.   cm.
       Includes bibliographical references.
       ISBN 0-618-15548-1
       ISBN 0-618-44662-1 (pbk.)
   1. United States—Description and travel.   2. United States—History, Local.
   3. Halpern, Jake—Journeys—United States.   4. United States—Biography.
   5. Home—United States—Psychological aspects—Case studies.   I. Title.

   E169.04.H345      2003
   973.929—dc21      2002191262

Book design by Anne Chalmers
Typefaces: Linotype-Hell Electra

Printed in the United States of America

MP 10 9 8 7 6 5 4 3 2 1

All photographs are by the author, with the exception of those on pages 15 and 24, by Greg Halpern; 56, by Brenda Tolman; 79, by Barbara Reynolds; and 138, by Charles Wachter. Used by permission.

To protect the privacy of certain people in this book, some names have been changed.

# Braving Home

Dispatches from the Underwater Town,
the Lava-Side Inn, and Other Extreme Locales

JAKE HALPERN

A MARINER BOOK

Houghton Mifflin Company

Boston    New York

FOR MY GRANDMOTHERS —

NORMA AND ESTHER

Home is a name, a word, it is a strong one; stronger than magician ever spoke, or spirit ever answered to, in the strongest conjuration.

—Charles Dickens, *Martin Chuzzlewit*

# Contents

# Braving Home

# Introduction

The Bad Homes Correspondent

EVERY JOURNALIST has a niche—it's inevitable—and I was just a few days into my career when I stumbled upon mine. It started as a running joke at the office: I was the magazine's Bad Homes Correspondent. The production department quipped about changing my title on the masthead. I laughed it off, but some of the older writers definitely thought there was something wrong with me. "Did you grow up in some sort of dysfunctional household?" a senior editor asked. *No,* I told him. "Well, there's got to be something in your past that makes you interested in these stories—*you ought to think about it.*"

The magazine I worked for was the *New Republic,* and my co-workers were a mix of policy wonks, art critics, and political junkies. I was none of these, and instead of trying to pass as one, I set out to write a different kind of story; yet every time I did, it ended up being about some outlandish and often hellish place inhabited by a handful of stalwarts who refused to leave. Iron-willed, unfearing, and utterly immovable, these characters captured my imagination. They were the nation's toughest home-keepers, and I was their aspiring chronicler. It was an odd niche of journalism, if you could even call it that, but it grew on me quickly.

It all began my first week at the magazine when a friend from college sent me an e-mail message with a rather cryptic lead: "Looking for a story? How about an old coal-mining town in PA where the whole place is cooking like a giant BBQ?" Initially, I thought it was a joke, but after doing some research, I discovered that this bizarre little town *did* exist. Its name was Centralia, and its coal mines had been on fire for almost forty years. Sinkholes had swallowed back yards, clouds of carbon monoxide had enveloped homes, and a network of smoldering coal veins continued to warm the earth like revved-up heating tubes in a giant electric blanket. Eventually, Centralia was evacuated and the government claimed ownership of the town, but a handful of residents defied their eviction notices, and the town's aging mayor, Lamar Mervine, vowed there would be "another Waco" before he'd relocate.

The following Thursday, while the rest of the magazine's staff mused over D.C. politics at our weekly editorial meeting, I pitched my very first story, a dispatch about a burning town that nobody wanted to leave. An awkward moment of silence came over the room. Finally, an editor spoke up: "Sounds interesting!" The following weekend I was in Centralia, chatting with Lamar Mervine himself. "I have no reason to relocate at all—I like it here," he told me from the comfort of a living room that wasn't legally his, while sitting in a well-worn recliner, gazing out the window at a mist of white smoke. Lamar's wife, Lana, nodded her head in agreement. "Besides," she added, "where would we possibly move to?"

Sitting with Lamar and Lana, sipping tea from a cup resting in a chipped saucer, admiring a collection of cheerful knick-knacks and dog-eared Centralia scrapbooks, I felt oddly at home. Something about the Mervines seemed familiar, even endearing. Lamar bore a vague resemblance to my own grandfather, with his stubbly chin, thick glasses, callused workingman's hands, and that same slightly melancholy, unfocused gaze of a workaholic ill at ease with the prospect of rest. Lamar had labored most of his life in the coal mines beneath Centralia, paying off his mortgage in seven-hour shifts of unremitting darkness, and even now, without a deed or any legal claim to show for what he had earned, Lamar remained proud. His house was more than an asset or a piece of real estate, more than mere clapboard and cinderblock—it was an extension of his own life.

Later that day, as I said goodbye to the Mervines and headed back toward Washington, D.C., I tried to stay focused on the story at hand. But as I cruised south along the Appalachians and down past Gettysburg, through a forlorn landscape of zinc mines, landfills, and falling-rock zones, I couldn't help but wonder: How many other Americans held fast to this ironclad sense of home? Who else was making this stand, doggedly refusing to leave the grueling environs in which they lived?

In the weeks after my Centralia article saw print, I began to look for leads on similar stories. This process involved a lot of digging, but I didn't mind, because digging was essentially my job. My chief responsibility at the magazine was researching and fact-checking. I spent hours, days, and weeks looking for correct spellings and exact dates. Being a quick fact-checker was always a point of pride among the office grunts like myself, and though it was an obscure and largely useless skill, I found it quite helpful in tracking down information on outlandish towns like Centralia. On my lunch breaks and in between assignments I searched for clues, and gradually I found them—reports of holdouts like Lamar living on lava fields, windswept sandbars, and desolate arctic glaciers. I spent Sunday afternoons combing the Web, using a smattering of search terms like "squatter," "won't leave home," and "people call him crazy." I became friendly with the press office at the Federal Emergency Management Agency (FEMA), and I pumped them for ideas. It turned into something of a hobby. Some people collected stamps, others pressed leaves, I scavenged for strange and daring homes.

These holdouts formed a curious cast of characters—fiercely loyal, seemingly unfazed by danger—the sort of diehard Americans you'd see on the six o'clock news and promptly dismiss as nuts. Even when given an out, they refused to take it. Neither buyouts, nor threats of eviction, nor astronomical insurance rates, nor any amount of reasoning could uproot them. What was their motivation? Was it stubbornness? Was it fatalism? Or had they actually found some strange hidden paradise that the rest of us could not see? Despite the overwhelming drawbacks, home still held some transcendent value for these people, and I couldn't help but feel moved by their will to hold fast. I was impressed by their fierce pioneer spirit, clearly atavistic, yet proudly unyielding. They struck me as throwbacks to another era, when traveling of any kind was burdensome or downright dangerous and a person's world was often no more than a few miles in any direction. Home was not just a place but a way of life, a work in progress, something you built and rebuilt over the course of a lifetime, until at last, like the old-timers who went by geographic names—Francis of Middlebury or Jeremiah of Ipswich—home was simply *who you were*.

❧

I grew up in Buffalo, New York, which is best known as a place that people like to leave. This never-ending exodus has created a bleak landscape of deserted factories, boarded-up houses, and crumbling train stations. As kids, my brother and I would drive along the windswept shores of Lake Erie and sneak into abandoned buildings where green moss carpeted floors, rainwater cascaded down stairways, and busted typewriters rusted firm against dank walls. On one of our later expeditions, when I was already in college, we were caught by an ancient, toothless security guard who then handed us over to the police.

"You graduated from high school?" the police officer asked me as I sat in the back of his squad car.

"Yes," I told him.

"You in college?"

"Yes," I said again.

"Where?"

"Yale."

"Quit fucking around!" he barked. Eventually I produced my Yale ID, and this really threw him for a laugh. "What are you doing back in Buffalo?" he asked sympathetically, as if my life were clearly drifting toward ruin. "And why the hell are you over here?"

"I kind of like it here," I told him. And I wasn't the only one. The area was still inhabited by a handful of old-timers—retired factory workers and profitless shopkeepers who refused to leave. They were the ultimate Buffalonians, remnants of the city's golden era, now holding on for dear life. Their homes existed outside the realm of city hall: effectively condemned, unpoliced and unplowed (which in snow-packed Buffalo is the kiss of death). My brother was so taken with them that he took a number of photographs and covered the walls of his Boston apartment with portraits of their tough, shadowy faces. And on quiet weekends, when I sometimes visited, these faces would stare me down, reminding me once and forever: *We never left*.

I come from a family with a long tradition of leaving places. My great-grandmother emigrated to America, returned home to Hungary, then emigrated to America once again. My grandfather was so desperate to get out of New York that in 1934 he took a job chipping paint on a giant freighter bound for California via the Panama Canal. My mother is an itinerant lawyer who practically lives out of a jet and is rarely in the same city for more than two days in a row. I'm no better. In the last several years I've lived in New Haven, Boston, Washington, D.C., Israel, India, and the Czech Republic.

In many ways being rootless has become trendy. It's considered a privilege to go away to college, or better yet study abroad. Jobs that involve travel are viewed as glamorous. Ditching an office for a laptop has become the benchmark of freedom. Mobility has become an integral part of modern life, and, while not everyone is a jetsetter, the concept of a permanent home seems to be quickly vanishing. Nowadays, Americans are relocating at a staggering rate, even if it is just across town or into a neighboring county. According to the U.S. Census Bureau, the average American will move twelve times in his or her lifetime, about once every six or seven years.[1] Forty-three million people moved in 1999 alone.[2]

Perhaps none of this should be so surprising. Historically, we are a nation of people on the move: immigrants arriving by boat, settlers heading out west, freed slaves moving north, laid-off steelworkers going south, disenchanted lawyers relocating to the Silicon Valley, and displaced natives sandwiched everywhere in between. We pride ourselves as a "land of opportunity," but no one likes to acknowledge the tacit implication that we are a nation of opportunists, largely willing to pull up stakes when it is advantageous to do so. How many of us would actually stick around if things got bad? In truth, how many of us would turn down a better job, or a bigger house, or a government buyout that spared us the ravages of nature? Unless, of course, home itself offers something inherently redeeming in its permanence — something that for me has never been more than a dull phantom-limb ache, but for others holds some deep-rooted primal magic that not even the fiercest earthly torments can break.

As I continued working at the *New Republic*, word spread of my unusual journalistic niche, and soon friends and family were sending me leads on other "problem" towns from around the country. I researched many of these leads, and a few of them even developed into stories, but most of them I simply took home and filed away with my growing collection. Gradually, I filled a massive three-ring binder with hundreds of pages of research, overflowing with frayed maps and anecdotal histories. It was more than just a backlog of story ideas — it was an atlas of broken places, an inventory of the nation's most punishing landscapes.

In idle moments, I flipped through my binder and wondered which locations would be the most interesting, dangerous, and inconceivable to visit. I also wondered what the inhabitants of these disparate places might have in common. Was there a "type" of person who refused to leave home? The U.S. Census Bureau shed some light on this subject. In its "Geographic Mobility" report for the year 2000, the Bureau compared the group traits of movers versus nonmovers. As it turns out, the *least* likely types to move included the elderly, rural inhabitants, homeowners, and widows and widowers.[3] With these demographics in mind, I was soon envisioning the painting *American Gothic*, with its eerie depiction of a pitchfork-toting Iowa farmer and his daughter standing in front of a desolate farmhouse.

Eventually I turned to academia for more clues. As it turns out, ever since the 1960s, environmental psychologists have been trying to explain why certain people get so attached to their surroundings. There are a number of competing theories on this issue. Perhaps the most prominent of these is that of "place identity," originated by Harold Proshansky at the City College of New York.[4] Proshansky claimed that physical settings, and especially homes, provide people with an identity and a defining sense of purpose. Without these places, he asserted, people may feel lost or uncertain about who they really are. Unfortunately, Proshansky and his colleagues had little if anything to say about people who attach themselves to punishing places, or what *their* sense of purpose might be.

The journey chronicled in this book began as whimsy, as a pipe dream, as errant thoughts of finishing an investigation I'd barely begun. Yet it built momentum rather quickly. I made a short list of my top locations from my three-ring binder, and not long after, I bought a wall map and began tracing several possible travel routes. Next I took out a calendar and drew up an itinerary. Most of my destinations were afflicted by seasonal disasters, and I figured if I timed it well, I could hit each place in its fiercest, most defining hour. Of course the logistics of this grand journey were still extremely fuzzy—especially my means of financing it—but slowly a plan was forming.

My most immediate problem, other than money, was time. I couldn't cram any of these visits into a single action-packed Saturday. I had tried this with Lamar Mervine in Centralia, and I ended up with a one-page article that barely scratched the surface. I wanted to experience these places, not just report on them. What I really needed was a few months. Unfortunately, the best I could muster was my one week of paid vacation time. It didn't allow for the sweeping epic I envisioned, but I figured it was long enough for one good visit. It would be my trial run. My seven-day stab at the big question. And if by some chance I made a breakthrough, perhaps I would find a way to continue on my journey.

The only remaining issue was where to begin. Eventually I settled on Princeville, North Carolina, a town situated on a dangerous floodplain. This was one of the places I had already written about for the magazine. Princeville was reputed to be the oldest all-black town in America, until September of 1999, when it vanished beneath a sea of floodwater that covered much of northeast North Carolina.

Princeville was submerged for almost two weeks, and when the floodwaters finally receded, a national debate erupted over whether or not to rebuild this historic town. When I headed down south to cover this story for the magazine, it was a quick visit. I was in Princeville for just a few hours, and I didn't see a soul on any of its mud-caked streets. There were no diehards, no holdouts—just a waterlogged town rotting in the late summer heat.

Rather disappointed, I returned to Washington, D.C. Yet even then, I had the nagging feeling that I had given up too easily, that in my haste I had missed something.

# The Underwater Town
## Princeville, North Carolina

THROUGHOUT THE FALL of 1999, newspaper headlines reported that the town of Princeville was empty, completely abandoned, nothing but a "waterlogged Pompeii."[1] During my own brief visit, I had come to the same conclusion. Yet little did almost anyone know, at the far end of town, one man remained—perched on a battered recliner, wrapped in a thick wool blanket, slowly reading his Bible. Thad Knight was the town's only inhabitant. His house was gutted. His life's belongings were lost. Yet there he stayed throughout the fall and into the winter, amid a forsaken landscape of wrecked houses, a seventy-two-year-old black man sitting in the frost.

"I guess people didn't realize I was over here," Thad told me months later. Apparently, this suited him just fine. Thad claimed to enjoy the solitude. If he got bored, or his bones grew stiff, he would stand up and trudge across his small half-acre of land. He said he knew the contours of every dip, every gentle slope—he could see them even with his eyes shut—and his intimacy with the terrain gave him comfort. When he tired of walking he stood for a while in the skeleton of his house and wondered whether it could be salvaged, whether it could somehow be repaired. Most days, that seemed doubtful, and Thad returned to his chair to sit and read some more.

Around midday a relief truck from the Red Cross made a special trip to Princeville to deliver lunch to the town's one resident. It was usually something cooked, like spaghetti, and Thad savored its smell and warmth. The afternoons were especially empty. Often the only sound was that of wind groaning through the holes in his house. His most dependable visitors were the packs of feral dogs who roamed the town scavenging for scraps of food.

Thad had survived the worst, this much he knew for sure. That September, Hurricane Floyd enlarged the Tar River and sunk the town of Princeville. The river starts in the highlands north of Durham, then drops a smooth 179 miles toward the coast below. Along the way it builds momentum and grows in size, and during hurricane season it often roars out of control. Two thirds of the way to the coast, the river wraps itself around a boggy stretch of land called Princeville, where it often skids off course—pummeling the town like a runaway truck.

Princeville is situated smack in the middle of a dangerous flood-plain. By today's standards, the location is far from ideal, but during the height of the Civil War it was a safe haven for a band of freed slaves who squatted there. Their makeshift home was protected by a troop of Union soldiers stationed nearby. Every so often, the freed slaves would gather around the Union camp and listen for news from the warfront. Then one day, in the spring of 1865, a Union officer scrambled to the top of an adjoining knoll and announced that the Confederacy had surrendered. These former slaves were officially freedmen, and to honor the occasion, they hallowed the ground on which the Union officer stood, dubbing it "Freedom Hill."[2]

In compliance with federal policy, the Union soldiers advised the freedmen and -women to return to their plantations to work for their old masters, but they refused to budge, opting instead to face the floods. Twenty years later, their weather-beaten refuge was still standing. Sufficiently impressed, the state of North Carolina drew up an official charter, and Princeville became the first incorporated black town in the state and quite possibly the country.* Back then, the concept of an all-black town was novel, yet many whites in the neighboring town of Tarboro quickly accepted it as a necessity—for it kept the former slaves across the river at a safe distance but close enough that they could be hired as farm hands, servants, and artisans. For the next century these two towns functioned symbiotically, facing each other across the river like matching bridgeheads, except for those inevitable occasions when much of Princeville would simply vanish. At least once a decade Princeville's decidedly lower shores would sink beneath a deep expanse of murky river water, until 1965, when its residents finally erected a large earthen dike.[3] The dike kept Princeville dry for more than thirty years, but in the end, it was no match for Hurricane Floyd.

In early September of 1999, when Hurricane Floyd was still more than a thousand miles off at sea, weather officials were already getting nervous. With its roughly 150-mile-per-hour winds, Floyd was on the verge of becoming a category-5 storm.[4] This is the highest possible rating, in fact, only two storms of this size had ever hit the United States in recorded history.[5] Floyd grazed the Bahamas, lost a bit of momentum, then tore northeastward on a due course for Wilmington, North Carolina. Panic spread throughout the entire

---

* There is no definitive scholarship on whether Princeville is in fact the oldest incorporated black town in the United States. For a long time it was believed that Eatonville, Florida (the setting of Zora Neale Hurston's *Their Eyes Were Watching God*), held that distinction. Princeville was later believed to be older than Eatonville, and many politicians and newspapers have since heralded it as the nation's oldest incorporated black town. But there is no bona fide historical research on whether this is true, and it remains an educated guess.

East Coast, and the largest evacuation in the nation's history commenced, involving some 2.6 million people.[6]

On the night Floyd hit, Thursday, September 16, the main concern in Princeville was not the storm but the river, which had become bloated with rainwater. More than a hundred volunteers worked to fortify the dike with sandbags. Princeville's four police officers shoveled alongside local criminals whom they'd arrested many times before. Sometime after midnight, they received orders to stop. "The dike is about to break," yelled Captain Fred Crowell of the Princeville Fire Department. "Everyone has to leave as of now!" Crowell then got into the town's fire engine and made one last drive through town. In some places, where the dike was already crumbling, Crowell encountered more than four feet of water. "If I had opened my door, water would have rushed in," he later told me. Still he plodded onward, navigating his half-submerged fire engine through the town's murky streets, blaring his siren and honking his horn as he went. It was a last warning—like a sinking ship, Princeville was about to go under.

Thad Knight woke to the sound of his daughter knocking on his bedroom door. Frantically she told him about the dike, and together they stood for a moment on his front porch, listening to the distant clamor of the fire engines. As the sirens receded, their low-pitched yawns gave way to a steady hissing. At first Thad mistook this sound for the rustle of strong wind, but soon it grew fuller, like the distant roar of a waterfall. Then he felt it—a sweet, misty chill in the air. Finally he knew without a doubt: The river was coming. Princeville was about to flood. Not knowing how to swim, Thad quickly got into his car and drove toward higher ground.

As floodwater crested the top of the dike, Mayor Delia Perkins remained in the town hall, telephoning officials at the National

Weather Service, pumping them for every last detail about the storm. Sometime between eleven P.M. and midnight, the phone went dead. A short time later, Mayor Perkins drove down to the river and saw that it was hopeless. The town was going to flood. Wearily, she returned to the town hall for a few more hours to coordinate a final evacuation effort. At last, she could stall no longer. Perkins got into her car and drove toward dry land. Eventually she pulled into a parking lot and killed the engine on her car. It was a moment of realization, Perkins later told me. Finally she allowed herself to think of all the things she had not done—like grabbing her family photo albums, her collection of jazz records, or any of many things she had accumulated over several decades in Princeville.

Soon heavy black water was roaring into town, crashing through people's windows and bowling over tin trailers. Those who missed the fire engine's warning climbed into their attics, and when the water met them there, they punched holes between the rafters and climbed onto their roofs. Even as the water lapped against the rain gutters, some people refused to budge. One old man had to be hoisted out through a hole that rescuers drilled in his ceiling. By the following day, Princeville lay beneath twenty feet of water. Giant, frothing whirlpools spun through town, and rescue boats sped across them, looking for survivors.

Many of those who escaped gathered in the parking lot of the Tarboro Kmart, and there they waited through the night. Shortly after sunrise, one of the town's commissioners, a woman named Anne Howell, contacted the police to see if it was safe to go back. "What's going on in Princeville?" she asked. "Commissioner Howell," said the officer awkwardly, "I don't know how to tell you this, other than . . . there is no more Princeville."

The town had all but vanished. One of the only remaining traces was the top of a church steeple, the tip of which poked through the surface of a sprawling river. Initially, many local residents speculated that Princeville would remain under water forever, slowly decomposing among the fish. Thad Knight, who was staying at his daughter's house during this time, doubted he'd ever see Princeville again. "I know how high the churches are in this town," he later told me. "And when I turned on the TV and saw that one steeple just barely coming through the water, I figured Princeville was gone." Yet just eleven days later, the Tar River receded and uncovered its damage. Houses were destroyed, as if whipped apart in a blender. They were cracked down the center, hemorrhaging limp, soggy strips of insulation and severed electrical wires. Many were swept entirely off their foundations, and one had actually been dumped onto the hood of a car. The insides were gutted; furniture, clothing, appliances, pic-

*Thad Knight inspecting the steeple of the Saint Luke Church of Christ, one of many structures destroyed in the flood of 1999.*

tures, and books were strewn over lawns and across bushes. Even the air was marked, hung with the stabbing odor of rotting pig carcasses and busted septic tanks.

When Thad finally returned to his house, he found a dozen or so unearthed coffins sitting on his front lawn. They had been uprooted from the local cemetery, a wildly overgrown place where freed slaves were buried. Thad's house was also wrecked, coated in mud and bits of debris from other houses. Moving back was not an option, yet Thad hated the thought of burdening his daughter any longer, so he joined the rest of the town's survivors in a giant displacement camp twenty-five miles west of town. There, several hundred trailers were assembled on an enormous field of gravel next to a women's prison. Thad agreed to sleep there, but not to live there, and each day he awoke before dawn and drove through the darkness back to Princeville. There he sat, alone beside the remains of his destroyed house—through October, November, and December—starting each day by watching the sun rise like an orange pyre over the town's broken rooftops.

As Thad single-handedly manned the town of Princeville, the town's officials bickered over a massive buyout proposed by the Federal Emergency Management Agency (FEMA). It was an all-or-nothing arrangement: Everybody stayed, or everybody left. There were to be no partial deals. If FEMA was going to spend millions of dollars, it wanted the situation fixed once and for all. In this case, "fixed" meant bulldozing the town into a series of softball fields or something similar. For many former residents, this was an abhorrent thought. As one of the oldest black towns in America, Princeville was more than just a place, it was a piece of history. But in truth, it was a calamitous history, and now the government was offering an end to the town's torments.

The decision was left in the hands of Mayor Perkins and

Princeville's four town commissioners. Each of them had a vote. Usually the decisions they made were routine matters of civic life: whether to adjust property taxes, approve a town fair, or test a sewer line for leaks. Suddenly the very fate of Princeville was on their agenda.

From the start, Commissioner Anne Howell wanted to rebuild Princeville, but she knew it wouldn't be easy. If the town accepted the buyout, FEMA would write everyone a check for the market value of their property; if they turned the money down, they would get nothing but a lot of dirt with which to rebuild the dike, one more time. The seriousness and finality of this decision weighed on Anne greatly. Sometimes in the evenings, as she stepped out onto the sprawling gravel parking lot of the displacement camp, she stopped for a moment to look eastward. Strange as it seemed, Princeville was just twenty miles away. If she could climb the roof of the nearby prison she might even be able to see it. The flood had washed away almost everything, but Princeville itself remained a fixed point on the horizon.

Meanwhile, back in town, Thad Knight continued to sit patiently beside his ruined house. He was the town's sole keeper, and it seemed like a strange role for him to be playing. Thad had lived an inconspicuous life, attending church, providing for his family, just trying to get by. As a young boy he once stole a quick drink from the "white" water fountain, eager to see how delicious it might be, but was quickly disappointed by the familiarity of its taste. Almost from then on, Thad did what his family expected him to do: He dropped out of school to help his father break even as a sharecropper, and he continued tilling the fields even as all eleven of his brothers and sisters moved away. "I just want one Knight by my side," his father had said. And so Thad stayed, building a small house next to his father's on the edge of town.

As time passed, everyone seemed to slip away. Thad's seven children grew up, his marriage dissolved, and his father died early one
winter morning. Now Thad was seventy-two years old and alone. No
one was counting on him anymore, and he found himself following
some strange inner compass. He would *not* live in a parking lot next
to a women's prison. He would *not* be forced to leave his home.

⚡

I first met Thad while looking for a place to sleep. I'd spent the day
walking around town, creeping through dank abandoned houses and
wildly overgrown yards, trying to get a better feel for the place. Very
little had changed since my first visit for the magazine. Debris still
hung from the trees like strange ornaments: the head of a doll, a
washboard, even a snorkel and mask dangled from twiggy limbs. It
was now April of 2000—roughly half a year had passed since the
flood—and still the town lay in ruins.

My plan was to find a dry stretch of flat ground and pitch a tent
amid the vacant houses. Technically I was on vacation, and I figured
that a bit of the outdoors would be both a cheap and refreshing reprieve from my cubicle life. Of course, my coworkers were baffled.
"Princeville? Didn't you already cover that story?" someone asked
me. "You're vacationing in a ghost town?" another inquired. In truth,
I had been catching flack over Princeville ever since my first visit.
Back then, my editor couldn't understand my reluctance to endorse
the FEMA buyout. "Why should they rebuild, if they're just going to
get washed away?" he asked me rather exasperatedly. This was a good
question, and though I failed to come up with a decent answer and
did not even know if there was one, I remained determined to have a
closer look.

So one Friday afternoon in mid-April, I left my office in Washington, hastily packed a bag full of camping gear, and headed south to-

ward Princeville. I could hardly wait to get going, though in my haste I had forgotten a few things. I had a tent but no ground tarp or sleeping mat. I brought books to read but no flashlight to read them with. Most regrettable was my food situation. By the time I reached Princeville, all I had left was a mangled piece of beef jerky and half a bottle of Hawaiian Punch. It was a sorry set of supplies, but the way I figured it, I needed some toughening up. How else was I going to make a good impression on all the diehards I wanted to meet?

Now dusk was approaching, and I still hadn't spotted a single decent campsite. Most of the ground was shrouded with dense vegetation, so thick I'd need a machete to clear the way. The few open spaces were nothing but rich beds of black mud. So I kept going, and eventually I came upon a trailer next to a giant rubbish fire. Twenty paces away sat an elderly man in his carport, thumbing through a book, apparently waiting out the last bit of light. He wore a thick pair of reading glasses, and their plastic arms flexed around the sides of his gleaming bald head. Even from a seated position, it was clear that he was a large man with a powerful build. His dress was formal: polished shoes, pressed slacks, a button-down shirt, and a pair of suspenders that barely fit around his barrel chest. As I made my way down his driveway he gave me a welcoming wave.

"How are you?" I asked awkwardly.

"Well, I'm still here," he said with a quick flick of his eyes—two enormous pupils, greatly enlarged by the thick warp of his lenses. "At least for now," he added, carefully prying off his glasses, then gently massaging the marks they'd left.

"You're just about the only person I've seen all day," I told him. This brought a smile to his face.

"Oh yeah? Well, sometimes folks ask me why I'm here. They say: 'What are you doing over here? It isn't going to change anything.' And then I remind them: *I'm enjoying myself.*" He paused to wipe his

brow of sweat. "Here, hand me my stick," he said, pointing toward a
rusted three-footed cane sitting on the chair next to him. I handed it
to him. "Good," he said. "Now you can sit down." Then he patted me
once on the shoulder in lieu of a handshake and told me his name
was Thad Knight.

I took a seat in the green plastic lawn chair next to him, and he
took off his baseball cap, as if to be polite. It was a blue denim hat
with a large piece of duct tape across the front. Later, Thad explained
that he'd gotten it free of charge from a lumber store in the neighboring town of Rocky Mount. The store's name was stitched across the
front, so Thad had covered it with duct tape because he didn't want
people to know that he'd been shopping "out of town." He liked to
keep his money within the community, but the flood had limited his
options.

Together Thad and I sat in his carport and gazed out on a collection of pulverized houses, which were surrounded by sprawling beds
of sludge that used to be lawns. The front of each house was now
marked with a giant spray-painted "X," indicating that it had been
searched for dead bodies. For good measure, stapled to the front of
each door was a sign reading, THIS BUILDING IS UNFIT FOR
HUMAN HABITATION. THE USE OR OCCUPANCY OF THIS
BUILDING FOR HUMAN HABITATION IS PROHIBITED AND
UNLAWFUL.

"Are you thirsty?" Thad asked me.

"Sure," I said.

Thad pulled himself up, walked down to the end of his carport,
and picked up a container of bottled water. Apparently tap water was
still not an option. During the flood more than a hundred thousand
dead hogs and nearly a million dead chickens and turkeys had sat for
weeks in a sea of stagnant water, and even now the groundwater

wasn't reliable.[7] Thad uncapped the canister and filled both of our glasses with water.

As we sipped our drinks, I asked Thad why he wasn't in the displacement camp with everyone else. He looked at me like I was crazy. "That's no place to pass time," he said. Thad explained that the camp was so jam-packed with people that there wasn't a moment's rest. The noise was ceaseless. At night, strangers strolled and chatted outside his trailer, right beside the window where his head was resting. "I didn't do much sleeping there," he told me. During the day the camp buzzed with a din of quarreling over food handouts, secondhand clothing, and government-issue propane tanks. Thad said he had worked his entire life to escape this sort of squalor; in fact, so had generations of Knights before him. His great-grandparents had grown up in the cramped, dingy cabins of the slave quarters, which were somewhat infamous in this region. When Frederick Law Olmsted made his tour of the South for the New York Times in the 1850s, he described some typical quarters in the Carolinas: "The Negro-cabins, here, were the smallest I had seen—I thought not more than twelve feet square inside. They stood in two rows, with a wide street between them. They were built of logs, with no windows—no opening at all except a doorway." The more luxurious dwellings (e.g., the sort that poor whites might also use) offered better ventilation, but the cost was privacy: "Through the chinks, as you pass along the road, you may often see all that is going on in the house; and, at night, the light of the fire shines brightly out on all sides."[8]

When slaves of this region finally won their freedom, almost nothing was sweeter than the right to own their homes. In 1865 the head of North Carolina's Freedmen's Bureau wrote about this phenomenon: "To be absolute owners of the soil, to be allowed to build upon their own lands, however humble, in which they should enjoy the sacred privileges of a home, was more than they had ever dared to pray for."⁹ Buying land did cost money, something most freed slaves didn't have, and again Princeville proved itself to be an oddly auspicious location—flood-prone land is cheap. Almost overnight, the old slave encampment began to resemble a fledgling town. Cabins were built along spacious streets, and they often had windows and wood floors.¹⁰ But even in Princeville many freedmen lived as tenants and squatters. For the Knight family, ownership would remain an elusive dream for the next century.

Thad grew up in a rickety sharecropper's house, in which he could see the ground through the floorboards, and sometimes even a pack of hogs that came looking for shelter on cold winter nights. "My father tried to keep the hogs out," Thad told me. "But it was difficult, so we got used to living with them." As Thad got older, he dreamed of doing better for himself. "I used to drive by the houses where the white people lived and I would hope that one day I had a house with central heat and a bathroom," he recalled. Eventually, Thad realized this would never happen unless he quit sharecropping. So, at the age of forty-two, with a wife and seven kids, Thad looked into a new job at the local textile mill. Initially his landlord forbade him to take the new job, but after consulting with a local justice of the peace, Thad determined that he was within his rights to take whatever job he wanted. He soon began working at the mill, where he did the night shift, from eleven P.M. to seven A.M. Then he worked a second job hauling cucumbers from eight A.M. to four P.M. He traded in his vacation for overtime work, and he got by on just four or five hours of sleep a night. After a few years he had saved enough money to take out a mortgage on a house. It was a modern house with central heat, indoor plumbing, and carpeted floors. When the builder asked Thad if he wanted a fireplace, the answer was immediate: *No way.* "I had central heat," explained Thad proudly. "Why would I want a fireplace? I never wanted to chop wood again."

Together Thad and I leaned up against his house. It was oddly conventional in its appearance, the sort of one-story prefab you'd expect to see in just about any suburban community. Yet the carport really distinguished Thad's house. Here he had assembled a hodge-podge of odd furnishings—lawn chairs, doormats, blankets, a few rickety tables, and a massive wooden radio that no longer worked—all of it cluttered but lovingly arranged, like the parlor of a tidy castaway. In the carport Thad held court and received guests with elaborate formality, dusting off chairs, filling cups of water, flipping through the Bible for an appropriate passage to set the mood. Thad had transformed this mere parking space into a makeshift home, and together we enjoyed its simple amenities.

Home-keeping had become the driving force in Thad's life. Thad told me that after the floodwaters receded he woke each morning before sunup and drove through the darkness toward Princeville. There was no self-pity, no blaming the dike or the government, no hopeless mornings when he hit the snooze button again and again. "I was there every day, rain or shine, watching the road and reading the Bible, like it was my job," he recalled. Of course, there were unpleasantries. His toilet, for example, was just a five-gallon plastic bucket that he brought with him each day. But according to Thad, anything was better than sitting in that cramped gravel parking lot of the displacement camp, staring glumly out the window, waiting for the next Social Security check to arrive.

After a week of sitting beside his destroyed house, Thad became convinced that he could handle more. He sought out the government official managing the displacement camp and asked him, "Can you move my trailer back to Princeville?"

"There's nothing in Princeville," the official told him.

"There is for me," said Thad.

"I'll think about it," said the official.

Thad came back almost every other night to inquire about his request. He would drive back from a long day in Princeville and head directly for the manager's trailer. "You should move your bed in here," the manager told him jokingly.

"If you don't get me back to Princeville, that's exactly what I am going to do," replied Thad. The manager turned him away some

*In a trailer park near the dike, all that remains are the cement steps to a house that was washed away.*

twenty times, but with each rebuff Thad only became more confident that he could really do this. Then one evening in late November, the beleaguered manager finally gave in. He promised to tow Thad's trailer back to Princeville but warned him that from then on he would be largely on his own. It was an odd victory, a go-ahead on a self-inflicted sentence of exile, but it would also be a homecoming, and Thad said he wanted to see it through.

The night of the move, Thad's children drove in from all across the county to help him settle in. A government truck pulled into the driveway, parked the small trailer in the shadow of Thad's wrecked house, and then motored away. The trailer's scant battery-powered lamp was one of the only lights in town. It would be another week before Thad had any real utilities. Eventually, he and his family lobbied their local power company (Edgecombe-Martin County Electric) to put Thad's property back on the grid. Getting running water was even trickier. First Thad had to convince the town of Princeville to turn his water back on, and when it finally came, the pipes at his house were so leaky that the whole building shot off spray like a giant sprinkler. Finally Thad called a plumber to put in new pipes so he could at least have use of his garden hose. On that first night in Princeville, however, he was essentially camping.

"Dad, I don't like this," one of his sons told him finally. His other children quickly agreed that it felt all wrong. "Are you sure about this?" his son asked him again.

"I'll be just fine," he told them. The moment had taken on the semblance of an impromptu ceremony, though no one knew what to do next. "Don't worry," Thad said finally. "Just go on home."

Reluctantly, the members of the Knight family said their good-byes. As they readied to leave, Thad stepped into his trailer and locked the door behind him. Moments later, a small convoy of cars backed out of Thad's driveway and made its way down Greenwood

Boulevard toward the bridge leaving town. From his trailer window, Thad watched the many taillights trace a road through the night. Soon a strange uneasiness came over him, Thad recalled, and he could not help but wonder what he had gotten himself into.

Hours later, as he lay in bed, Thad listened to the strange workings of the night—packs of stray dogs rummaging for food and a distant clatter that he feared was the sound of looters pillaging the town's empty houses. To calm himself, he recited one of his favorite psalms. He didn't have much of a singing voice. He rarely sang, even in church, with the support of a full choir—but tonight he sang to himself:

> *Come by here good Lord,*
> *Come by here.*
> *Somebody needs you Lord,*
> *Come by here.*
> *It's praying time Lord,*
> *Come by here.*
> *Oh lord, come by here.*

Thad repeated it over and over, until he finally fell asleep.

Thad was raised as a strict Baptist, but he wasn't always so observant. "I used to drink a lot of whiskey," he told me, with a shy chuckle. "I mean, *a whole lot* of whiskey." Apparently, in his younger years, Thad was something of a wild man. "Once I got into a car wreck and they charged me for driving while under the influence," he admitted. "But with the help of the Lord I got past that." Basically, he gave up drinking, attended church more regularly, and eventually became a deacon. Yet his biggest religious transformation came after the flood, when he moved back to Princeville.

"Somehow I felt closer to God over in that trailer," he told me. Its cramped tin walls formed a dark, intimate space, like a cave or a crypt, and its hot, breathy air was thick with an unending litany of prayers and psalms. When Thad awoke in the predawn hours he would often talk aloud, casually chatting with God, something he'd rarely done before. Now, in the most unexpected of places, Thad eased his way into a new form of observance, and it heartened him to think that an old man could change.

During the day Thad sat in his carport, reading a thick, large-print version of the Bible. He knew much of it by heart. He savored his favorite passages: the story of Daniel and the lion, and that of Noah and the flood. Again and again Thad pictured the image of the dove returning to the ark with a freshly plucked olive leaf in its mouth— promising that a new life, on dry land, was just ahead.

As winter approached, the ground became covered with frost, and later with snow. One morning the door to Thad's trailer froze shut and he had to boil a pot of water to get it open. Another morning he opened his door to find a pack of dogs begging for food. He said he soon felt like a hermit, alone in the wilderness, battling the elements. Dusk became an eerie, unsettling time when the woods seemed to creep noticeably closer. Nights were long and often filled with claustrophobic dreams. Yet all was set right by those first frosty rays of orange light that reminded him with resounding certainty that he had done it—he'd made it through another night—and it gave him a pioneer's rush.

Thad spoke in long, rambling monologues, often losing himself in the details of specific memories, then tapering off into silence for a moment or two before starting again. During one such pause I interjected: "It's hard for me to imagine feeling this way about any of the apartments that I've lived in."

This set Thad off on a laugh. "Well, where'd you grow up?" he asked finally. "Where's your real home?"

"Buffalo, New York," I told him.

"Don't you want to go back?"

"Sometimes—but mainly just to visit." Thad nodded his head; it was clear I was quite a curiosity to him.

"So you travel around a lot, do you?" he asked.

"Yeah, quite a bit. This time last year, I was living in Israel."

"You've been to Jerusalem?"

"Yes," I said.

"Let me ask you," he said cautiously. "Do people in Jerusalem still walk around in robes, like they do in the Bible?"

I thought for a moment. "Yes, some of them do—especially the Bedouin."

"Oh," he said with a nod of his head. He seemed pleased.

From the distance came the groan of a giant flatbed truck, and its headlights revealed the flat, dry terrain of Thad's lawn. It was the best ground I'd seen all day. Before I had a chance to second-guess myself, I asked him, "Thad, would it be okay if I pitched a tent in your back yard and slept out here tonight?"

"Sure," he said. "That'd be just fine."

So I grabbed my backpack and set out to pitch my tent before it got too dark. As I rounded the back of the carport, I noticed something that brought me to a dead halt—graves, hundreds of them. Thad's back yard spilled directly into the town cemetery. There was not even a fence separating the two. Some graves were just a few paces from the house. I now understood why the flood had left so many coffins on Thad's lawn.

The far part of the yard turned into what looked like a marsh, so I stuck close to the house and found a nice flat spot. I'm not a terribly superstitious person, but as I raised my tent, driving stakes into the ground just a few yards from the first row of nearby graves, I had to suppress a creepy feeling. *Who camps between a swamp and a grave-*

*yard?* I felt like the clueless guy who gets gored in the opening scene of a B-grade horror flick.

Back on the carport, Thad and I continued talking about the flood and many other details of his daily life—from tips on avoiding snakes to the recipe for his favorite bean-based dish called "dandoolies." Thad was very good-natured about all the questions I threw his way; in fact, all the attention seemed to amuse him. "Do you do this often?" he asked me quizzically.

"Do what?" I asked.

"Camp out in people's back yards and ask them questions."

"No," I said. "You're the first one."

Thad shook his head and chuckled. "You know," he said, "there *are* other folks you can talk to." Of course, he was right. The story of Princeville was not his alone, and neither was the decision to stay or go. It was a town matter, a question of accepting or rejecting a FEMA buyout, and when it came down to it, Thad was as much a spectator as I was.

⚡

The question of the buyout was resolved on a Monday night in late November of 1999, roughly four months earlier. It was an emotional time; the flood was still fresh in everyone's memory. Thanksgiving was just three days away, Christmas was around the corner, and the bite of being homeless was starting to make itself felt. Above all, people were tired of waiting. They wanted to know, once and for all, whether Princeville was for sale.

The vote took place in a parking lot across the river in Tarboro. Here stood a small trailer that served as Princeville's temporary town hall. Inside was a conference table, a handful of chairs occupied by local officials, and a jumble of reporters and politicians packed in like commuters on a rush-hour train. By the time Commissioner Anne Howell arrived, the parking lot was swarming with television crews and spectators from across the county. In the weeks since the flood, Princeville had become the local media's favorite human-interest story, and now everyone had gathered to watch the dramatic closing act. As Anne approached the front door of the trailer, people stepped aside. She was a large woman, consummately maternal. For her, the vote came down to family, simple as that. Princeville had always been a special place, not only because it had offered freed slaves a chance to own their own land, but because it became a place where families could finally stay together. "My family has been here for four generations," Anne later told me. "Princeville holds us together." It was clear in her mind that a buyout meant dispersion, and the prospect of reunions on freshly flattened softball fields didn't hearten her at all.

Perhaps the worst moment for Anne came several months earlier when her sister-in-law's casket was reported missing. She helped her husband fill out the seven pages of paperwork, detailing what his dead sister looked like. Miles away, in a warehouse filled with washed-up bodies, officials worked all day to find matches based on distinctive features: missing fingertips, a gold tooth, green shoes, a left breast prosthesis, a butterfly brooch, even the serial number on a pacemaker.[11] When nothing turned up, Anne tried to remain thankful that her eldest son was still buried. Several years back his coffin had partially unearthed in another storm, but somehow it had managed to remain buried during Floyd. Determined to focus on the positive, Anne snapped a picture of his intact plot.

As it neared time for the vote, Anne took a seat around the conference table with the mayor and the town's three other commissioners. "I was sitting there and sweating," she later told me. "Even in the depth of winter that trailer was hot, and I think everybody was very tense." There was a great deal of speculation about the vote. Nobody knew exactly how it would go. Anne felt most certain about Commissioner Linda Worsley, who was a telephone worker at Sprint and a lifelong resident of Princeville. "I felt very confident that she was with me," recalled Anne. She suspected that the two other commissioners, Milton Johnson and Frank Braswell, were going to vote for the buyout. This left Mayor Delia Perkins. "I knew she would have to be the tiebreaker," said Anne.

Mayor Perkins sat at the far end of the conference table, a small woman with a broad, serious face. So much had happened since that night when she sat in the town hall, talking with officials from the National Weather Service until the line went dead. When Perkins first returned to Princeville, it was by helicopter, hovering above a maze of flooded streets. It was a surreal experience, Perkins later told me. From her airborne perch she watched the Coast Guard round up a small navy of floating coffins. Days later FEMA offered its massive buyout, and this appeared to be Princeville's coup de grâce. But then, most unexpectedly, Princeville's history finally started to do the town some good. Local and regional newspapers began to pick up on this story of history verses nature. Soon even the *New York Times* was running headlines like "Landmark for Ex-Slaves Felt Brunt of Storm" and "Town with Fabled Past Facing Uncertain Future."[12]

Around that time, Princeville was visited by an assortment of public figures. First was Jesse Jackson. He ushered a large entourage into the waterlogged town hall, hoisted a dank American flag, and publicly demanded money for the town. The next day a photograph of Jackson hugging Delia Perkins hit the newspapers. Not long after, Al Sharpton arrived and alleged that the FEMA buyout was a racist sham. "If this was Valley Forge, imagine what America would be doing," declared Sharpton.[13] Soon there was a steady stream of visitors, including delegations from the Congressional Black Caucus, the NAACP, and the Nation of Islam. Money poured in from celebrities like Prince, Evander Holyfield, Tom Joyner, and Queen Latifah, not to mention sports teams like the Charlotte Hornets and the Carolina Panthers. President Clinton visited and formed the President's Council on the Future of Princeville, chaired by the secretaries of defense, agriculture, commerce, labor, health and human services, and transportation.[14]

Despite all of this support, Mayor Perkins still had one major concern. The Army Corps of Engineers had made it clear: Dike or no dike, at some point in the indefinite future Princeville would flood again. This was the unavoidable reality of living in a floodplain. Now it was up to Perkins to weigh all of these factors. Finally, she called for the vote, asking all those in favor of rebuilding the dike to raise their hands. Milton Johnson and Frank Braswell sat motionless. Anne Howell and Linda Worsley raised their hands, and, a moment later, so did the mayor. It was settled: Princeville was rebuilding. There was a great deal of commotion, followed by a barrage of questions from the press. Mayor Perkins kept her comments brief. "Rebuilding is staying with your heritage," she told one reporter from the *Atlanta Journal and Constitution.* "We plan to stay."[15]

Outside, in a quiet corner of the parking lot, Sam Knight, Thad's oldest son, dialed the number of the cell phone that they'd insisted Thad get. It was odd happenstance that Thad was whisked into the world of global communication out of his stubborn desire to live in utter seclusion. On that night, however, it came in handy. Excitedly, Sam told his father the news: *They voted for the dike—it's all settled.* Thad was greatly relieved, though even then he had worries. His house lay in ruins. He had very little money saved and no income to count on other than Social Security. Perhaps most daunting of all, a very long winter lay ahead. Thad braced himself for the worst, and within just two weeks, it came.[16]

❧

In the days that followed the vote, the Army Corps of Engineers hurriedly assembled a crew to rebuild the dike. Every moment counted. By June another hurricane season would be under way, and the town of Princeville lay unprotected. The decision to turn down the FEMA buyout was pivotal, but now two equally important questions were on the table: Was it possible to build a better dike? And could it be finished on time?

The answers soon rested in the hands of a man named Prentice Lanier, the young builder who won the contract to rebuild the dike. In the world of government contracting, the dike was a modest project with a limited budget of roughly $768,000, little of which Lanier would see himself. Essentially it was a repair job. FEMA said it would pay only to restore the dike to its preflood level. The old dike was just a wall of red clay, roughly two miles long and on average twenty feet high. It had worked well enough for thirty years—then came Hurricane Floyd, topping the dike by a solid three feet. Floyd was a massive storm—some even called it "the storm of the century"—yet it cleared the dike with ease, proving that there was plenty of leeway for a lesser storm to do the same.*

Determined to make the best of a bad deal, town officials began exploring ways to raise the dike further. Eager to help, the Army Corps of Engineers petitioned Congress for money to conduct preliminary tests on the benefits of a higher dike. Meanwhile, at the edge

---

* The U.S. Army Corps of Engineers (Engineering & Planning Branch) notes that the old dike stood forty-nine feet above mean sea level. During Hurricane Floyd, the river reached fifty-one feet above mean sea level. According to Doug Greene, an engineer in the Wilmington District, that's a "huge amount of overtopping."

of town, Prentice Lanier began a double-speed effort—bringing in truckload after truckload of red clay—trying to reach a base level of thirty-seven feet by the first of June, in time for the hurricane season.

Several miles to the south, at the opposite end of town, Thad Knight was dealing with pressing concerns of his own. One day in early December, as Thad sat in his carport, he started to feel his feet swell and his chest tighten. "I didn't think much of it," he later told me. "I just figured I'd gotten too much fresh air." But that evening, as he undressed for bed, Thad discovered that his feet were so swollen that he couldn't take his shoes off. The tightening in his chest had also gotten worse, so he called his daughter Cynthia and told her that he was a little worried.

One of Thad's sons soon picked him up, and together they met the rest of the family in the emergency room of Heritage Hospital in Tarboro. Thad waited to be seen by a doctor for about thirty minutes, until a nurse realized he was having a heart attack and rushed him into an examining room. His circulation was merely trickling, and his heart was skipping beats. The doctor quickly put him on blood thinner and sent him to the hospital's intensive care unit, where he stayed for the next few days.

When Thad's condition finally stabilized, his children came to the hospital to help him check out. The doctor explained that Thad needed a lot of rest and constant supervision. He was lucky to be alive, and the last thing he should be doing was struggling to survive in the wilderness. So Thad's children began discussing at whose house he would recover and how they'd move all his stuff. Finally Thad interjected and explained his intentions: He would return to Princeville. For a moment no one said anything. "We were shocked," one of his daughters later told me. "Totally shocked."

Eventually several of his children pushed him to justify his decision, but Thad was reluctant to explain himself. "He had just made up his mind," his youngest son, Dennis, later told me. "There was no talking him out of it." Finally the family reached a compromise: Thad would allow his twenty-year-old grandson, Tee, to live with him. Reluctantly, the doctor agreed. But when Tee showed up at his trailer later that night, Thad told him not to bother. Instead Tee agreed to join Thad for dinner every so often, and the arrangement became their little secret. "I'm still asking the Lord for forgiveness on that one," Thad told me with a smile.

As Thad recounted this part of the story months later from the comfort of his carport, I found myself empathizing with his children. What was he trying to prove? Was this one last gasp against the indignities and helplessness of old age? Or was it precisely the opposite? There was something undeniably moribund about Thad's vigil. Granted, he had reason to be proud. His house was a physical reminder that he had stayed by his father's side, that he had given up sharecropping, and that he had raised his family to live a better life. Yet all these things were in the past, and now even the house itself was crumbling and empty—a final and irrefutable reminder that his life was just a shell of what it once was. Thad never admitted it to me, but it had to be very depressing at times. And on quiet winter mornings, as he sat in a town that was all but dead, surrounded by several hundred snowcapped graves, wouldn't it be natural to think of letting go? Wasn't it possible that he had come home to die?

Thad assured me that this was not the case, but he conceded that during the winter death was occasionally in his thoughts, especially in February, when a work crew arrived to rebury the town's dead. Thad walked down the road behind his house to meet the crew. He offered them bottled water, and together they chatted as a backhoe dug deep holes into the frozen earth. The unearthed corpses were now entombed in giant steel "hurricane-proof" coffins. For years corpses had been popping out of the earth during bad floods, as if to express some belated desire to leave. "You don't have to worry about these things floating away," a crew member told him. These coffins were pure ballast. Thad watched the crew rebury them one by one.

That winter, the workmen were not Thad's only visitors. Occasionally, as people drove through Princeville, some of them stopped and asked Thad questions: *Are you all right? What happened to this town? What are you still doing here?* Glad to have the company, Thad would tell them his whole story, starting with the night of the flood. They would listen, and when he was done they would often hand him some money. Thad always protested, but they would insist, stuffing money into his coat pockets. By the end of the winter visitors had given him almost five thousand dollars in crumpled bills. Thad took that money and put it away. For the first time since the flood, it looked like he might have the means to rebuild his house.

By the end of winter, Thad was no longer the town's only resident. A handful of other people, including Commissioner Anne Howell, had also moved their trailers back into town. By springtime the rudiments of civilization had returned: working phone lines, streetlights on every corner, and lawnmowers trimming roadside grass. A makeshift mayor's office was even erected in the shadow of the old town hall. Slowly, life was returning to normal. Yet June was just around the corner, and repairs on the dike were well behind schedule. It rained often, and from a distance the dike came to resemble a giant, sloping pile of mud. For many it also carried an unshakable air of defeat. It was a broken fortification, a kind of earthen Maginot Line. Now, however, all anyone could do was hope that Prentice Lanier would fix it in time.

By the time I met Thad, it was already mid-April, and the air had warmed to a temperate sixty-five degrees. It was ideal camping weather; and as night finally fell, cloaking the town's landscape, I began to feel better about my tenting situation. At least the tombstones were out of sight. In the meantime I continued to sit with Thad in his carport, chatting about the flood and admiring the glimmer of unchallenged starlight.

When I had first arrived earlier in the evening, I hadn't gotten a good look at his house. The rubbish fire and Thad's government-issue trailer had blocked my view. Now that I'd committed to spending the night, however, Thad insisted on showing me around. He opened the side door to the house, and I was taken aback at what I saw—a completely restored interior. There were brand-new walls, floors, ceilings, fixtures, and appliances. The outside definitely needed a little work, but on second glance, I noticed that the windows, shingles, and rain gutters were also new.

"Isn't it amazing?" asked Thad. "Just like Noah and those Hebrew boys, I'm starting a new life."

Thad explained that the house had been restored within the last month. A group of Mennonite volunteers from Ohio and Pennsylvania had done the work. They'd used some building supplies donated by celebrities, and when those ran out, Thad had bought the remaining supplies with his own money.[17]

The rebuilding process wasn't easy, explained Thad. Just two years before the flood, he had paid to have his entire house remodeled. He'd put in new floors, a new roof, and new furnishings. On the day the Mennonites tore out the floorboards, Thad paced about restlessly. He was still repaying the bank for those slabs of wood—$250 a month—and he'd have to keep repaying this "home improvement loan" for the next few years. Eventually Thad retired to his small trailer and turned up the volume on his transistor radio, drowning out the clamor of construction.

Now Thad was once again living in his own house, but he was far from safe. Hurricane season was just a few weeks away, and Prentice Lanier was more than a month behind schedule building the dike. Thad's early decision to rebuild had clearly put him at risk, and I had to wonder why he couldn't wait just a few more months until the dike was fully restored. Thad seemed to be taking one brazen risk after another. His life was quickly taking on the epic dimensions of the Bible stories that he spent all day reading. And as everything swung precariously in the balance, Thad told me that he had begun to taste Daniel's and Jonah's gnawing fear, Job's spiraling sense of loss, and Noah's cautious hope. "They almost felt like real people in my life," explained Thad. It was an intoxicating religious experience, a crowning test of his faith in self and God, and gradually even Thad's children were won over by his fervor and his apparently unstoppable momentum. Later in my stay Thad's youngest daughter, Cynthia, explained: "Dad kept telling us that God was going to work things out for him—was going to restore everything he lost—and after a while, we just stopped worrying."

As Thad and I finished out the evening on his carport, we marveled at the strange twist of events that had brought him here. It was an odd life, filled with renewed faith and strange new curiosities— like air-conditioning, cell phones, and sneakers. Thad had only recently discovered the comfort of sneakers. Currently he had two of his favorite pairs on display on the table at the far end of the carport: a pair of Saucony running shoes and a pair of Nike Air high-tops. "I never wore sneakers before the flood," he told me. "Now I have ten pairs." Apparently, during the relief effort, the town of Princeville was inundated with donations of sneakers.

"It's hard to go back to shoes after wearing sneakers," I told him.

"Yeah," he said, "but I think I have enough to last me a long time."

A cool breeze blew across the lawn, stoking the dying embers of the rubbish fire and sending a slight shiver up my back. It was almost time for sleep, which meant my returning to the graveyard. I needed to get going, but first I had to ask, "Does it bother you living next to a cemetery?"

"Oh, I don't worry about the people in the cemetery because those folks are bygones. It's the people out here you have to worry about," he said, pointing to a passing car.

Somehow I doubted whether that would calm me later that night as I returned to my tent to sleep with those bygones. Unfazed, Thad continued talking about the cemetery, explaining that all of the deceased relatives from his immediate family were buried back there—except his son Carlton, who had killed himself a few years before and was buried elsewhere.

"One day my son just went back over there and shot himself," said Thad, pointing with his finger to almost the exact location where my tent was pitched. "The thing is, he told his mother he was going to kill himself. She called me at the mill and gave me the message, but I said that he must be joking. When I finally came home, it was around this time of night, and some of the neighbor children told me that he had gone around back with my shotgun and they had heard a noise." Thad paused. "I never did know why he did it, or why he drove the eight miles from his house to do it over here."

I wasn't sure why Carlton wasn't buried in the graveyard with the rest of the Knights, and Thad didn't offer much of an explanation. In some cultures the corpse of a suicide is deliberately buried as far away from home as possible so that its ghost might not find its way back. Suicide ghosts are considered particularly restless because of the desperate state of mind in which they leave life. The Baganda tribe of Uganda buries a suicide's corpse at a distant crossroad; the Bannaus of Cambodia bury suicides in a far corner of a forest; and the Alabama Indians simply throw them into a river.[18] No matter where Carlton was buried, however, it was clear that his choice to kill himself at home had a haunting effect. Every day, Thad couldn't help but glance at the spot where it happened, remembering the excruciating details of the day he found him, again and again, until it seemed that Carlton's ghost had also made its way home.

There were other questions I had about Carlton's death, but somehow I didn't have the heart to ask them. Instead I sat quietly for a few more minutes, listening to the crickets and the sound of cars. Finally, I bid Thad good night and trudged back toward the graveyard, wanting nothing more than to fall fast asleep. But just as I was zipping up my tent, I heard a rather unsettling screech. I poked my head back outside and noticed for the first time that there was an old barn set back about a hundred feet in the woods, with a rusty door that looked like it would be swinging all night long. Just then, I heard what sounded like a pack of dogs barking in the distance.

Before I'd left the carport, Thad had invited me to stay in his guest room if the rain or wind kicked up. But I could see from my tent's screened-in moon roof that it was pretty much a perfect night. I lay sleepless for a good hour, and then I swallowed my pride, put on my shoes, and exited my tent. Moments later I was knocking on Thad's door. To my relief, he was still up. It was clear he knew what had happened. "It is a bit chilly out there," he said casually. "Come on in. I'm just making some hog's head." He led me down a narrow hallway past a faux oil painting of Jesus, and into his guest room, where I would end up sleeping for the remainder of the week. Thad said good night, and I drifted off to the sweet, synthetic scent of new carpet and fresh paint.

The next morning I awoke to the sound of rain, and before I knew it I found myself thinking about the dike. The thought seemed to come with the weather; the two are inseparable in Princeville. It occurred to me that there should be a small gauge in everyone's house indicating the water level.

An hour or so later I was treading through a light rain to have a look at the dike for myself. On the way, I passed Glennie's General Store, one of the town's oldest business establishments. Now the two-storied building was in shambles, and a backhoe was loading wreckage into a dumpster while three men looked on idly from the street. These three men made up the building's work crew, though calling them a "work crew" is a bit misleading, as I'm not sure I ever saw them do much work. In theory, however, they were in charge of gutting Glennie's and getting it ready to be rebuilt. Throughout my one-week stay in Princeville, I stopped and chatted with the crew, usually in the mornings, on my way back from buying coffee in Tarboro. Today their only real responsibility was to ensure that the backhoe didn't tear up the gas line leading to the pump in front of the store.

"My biggest worry is that snakes could be slithering all around in the store," said William, the leader of the crew. This apparently was the wrong thing to say around Arthur, the crew's one senior citizen, who was already quite uneasy about the whole arrangement.

"If I see a motherfucking snake, William, just one of those slithering motherfuckers, I'm out of here like that." William rolled his eyes. "And if they hit that gas line," continued Authur, who was now on a roll, "I'll run the other motherfucking way, and I'm never coming back." Arthur had the highest rate of "motherfucker" usage per sentence I'd ever heard; it almost served as cadence, lending a pleasant rhythm to everything he said. Arthur talked for a while more, delivering an epic soliloquy on the dangers of the workplace and cracking us all up as the backhoe drew dangerously close to the gas pump.

When I mentioned that I was headed over to take a look at the dike, the crew seemed interested. "The dike, huh . . ." said William. "My mom is still too scared to go near the river or the dike. Doesn't trust it, and I don't blame her."

"Yeah, something about that dike doesn't look right," affirmed Arthur.

"What's that?" I asked.

"It's not motherfucking high enough."

After saying goodbye to the crew, I continued onward through a steadily intensifying rain until I reached the dike. As I climbed up its muddy side, I struggled to keep from sinking. The clay had become so damp that it was literally sucking my shoes into the ground. When I pulled them out, big chunks of the dike clung to my soles, turning my sneakers into platform shoes.

On the top of the dike I was relieved to find that it stood a good distance above the river, but as I headed down a bit farther, I soon discovered a number of giant gaps through which water could easily rush in. I continued walking until I found a parked tractor with a thirtyish-looking man in work boots and a hardhat standing next to it. I introduced myself. He shook my hand, gave me a hardhat, and told me his name was Prentice Lanier.

Reluctantly, Lanier agreed to give me a quick tour of the dike. As we continued along the bottom of a particularly long gap, Lanier told me more about the structure. He explained that in the thirty years since it was built, much of the original clay had washed away, significantly weakening the dike.

"Why don't they make the dike out of concrete or something stronger?" I asked.

"Way too expensive," said Lanier. "You know how much that would cost?"

"Why not make the dike bigger, then?"

"A lot of reasons," said Lanier. He didn't want to talk about it in detail, but later on that week I contacted a woman at the Army Corps of Engineers who gave me the rest of the story.

Apparently, members of the Tarboro Town Council got together and drafted a letter to the Army Corps of Engineers, objecting to any modifications on Princeville's dike. The council members knew that if Princeville's dike was elevated much higher, the Tar River would flood onto their shores instead. Not long after the letter, Tarboro's town manager issued a clear warning in an interview with a local newspaper called the *Daily Southerner*: "We want Princeville to rebuild its dike—we just don't want them to build it any higher."[19] And just to make this point perfectly clear, Tarboro's attorney issued a thinly veiled threat to sue the town of Princeville if it didn't heed this warning.

The threat was never acted on, but it didn't need to be. For more than a hundred and thirty years, people in Princeville had been deferring to their neighbors in Tarboro. It was deeply ingrained in their past, and that wasn't about to change now. Besides, Mayor Perkins was currently being threatened with impeachment by a band of disgruntled citizens, and the last thing she wanted was a lawsuit. She had no interest in battling with Tarboro, and to make this clear, she imposed a gag order barring any Princeville official from even discussing the idea.[20] The final blow came in the spring, when Congress denied the Army Corps of Engineers money to conduct preliminary tests on the effects of a bigger dike.[21]

By the time Lanier and I finished our tour, we were both in a sweat. I turned to Lanier. "Do you think this town is safe?" I asked him.

"Safe as it can be," he replied.

"But would you live here?"

Lanier sighed—it wasn't a fair question and we both knew it. Still, I waited for his answer. "We're building a good dike here," he said finally. "As good a dike as we can."

I headed back into town through a steady rain, letting the water wash the clay off my shoes. By the time I made it back to Thad's, a serious storm was brewing. Outside the sky was illuminated in a perpetual flicker of lightning—as if by giant stadium lights shimmering out their last bits of filament.

There would be no sitting in the carport tonight. Instead we sat in Thad's living room, watching Seinfeld reruns and waiting for the storm. It arrived with a shotgun blast of rain, which hit the roof with startling force. Only intermittent bursts of thunder, which rattled off like nearby artillery fire, broke the beating of the downpour. The bombardment of noise drowned out the conversation on TV and left Thad and me looking at each other awkwardly.

"Do you still worry about flooding?" I asked finally.

"I think God will take care of us in the home we are in, just as he always has," he told me. Thad's large, timeworn hands were shaking, and suddenly he struck me as both tired and frail. Thad knew his health wasn't good. Besides his heart troubles, he also suffered from diabetes and gout. Even when Thad spoke of events just months away he would stop to add "If I'm still around." Often his conversations drifted to talk of the afterlife, something that seemed to hearten him. "I'm hoping and I'm praying that I have a home up yonder when I leave here," he said, pointing to the sky.

Thad believed strongly in the idea of having two homes—one on earth and one in heaven, assuming everything worked out for the best. In fact, Thad didn't even use the word *heaven*; he just said "my home up yonder." Home and heaven were synonymous as far as he was concerned. This point became even clearer when he showed me his psalm book from church. I was immediately struck by the number of titles about home—"O Think of the Home over There," "O Happy Home Where Thou Art Loved," "God Give Us Christian Homes," "O Happy Home," etc. Here too the word *home* was substituted for *heaven*, a phenomenon that seemed to have two effects. On the one hand, it put the notion of an earthly home in perspective—

after all, it was only temporary. But it also reinforced the notion that there was something divine about any home, which like heaven was a reprieve from the worries of the world. As far as I could tell, for Thad, heaven was a place almost identical to his earthly home— only without the floods.

Thad stood up and turned off the TV. "I just plan to stay here the rest of my life," he told me as the rain continued to hammer against the roof.

That night as I lay in bed, I listened to the hissing of the rain and watched the tombstones flicker with the lightning in the windows. For some reason, I thought of Commissioner Anne Howell's mother, Anna Belle Brown, whom I'd met earlier in the day. I'd found her standing in the rain beside the empty lot where her house once stood, checking the one structure the flood hadn't washed away: her mailbox. Somehow Anna Belle had convinced the post office to deliver all her mail to this old box. Initially I found this somewhat puzzling, but then I thought again of Thad—sitting beside his destroyed house throughout the winter—and suddenly Anna Belle's arrangement made more sense, because I knew that sometimes home existed, even if only as a ritual.

The next day the weather cleared, and in the morning I walked up the road to a small convenience store called Darlene's. Inside I met the owner, Darlene, a plump, middle-aged white woman with thinning blond hair and a ruddy face with hundreds of burst capillaries. I picked out a carton of orange juice and chatted for a while at the counter with Darlene. She told me that she had lost a thousand cases of Budweiser in the flood and that overall she had sustained some $250,000 in damage. "Are you a reporter?" she asked me finally.

"Yes," I told her.

"Well, this town got a lot of attention because of its history," she said, somewhat accusingly. Then Darlene leaned a little closer: "But there are a lot of people who had it worse than these niggers." Just then an elderly black woman teetered into the store. "Hey there, you keeping your feet dry?" Darlene asked her sweetly. Then she waited for the woman to pass.

"You don't think it's fair, all the attention they've gotten?" I asked her.

Darlene looked at me hard. "Do *you* think it's fair?"

"But you're glad people are coming back?" I asked her.

"Look," she said, "I profit from it, so I'm not complaining."

Darlene said hello to another customer.

"Are you worried about people moving away?" I asked her.

"Tell me," she said softly, "where else these niggers gonna go?"

I paid for my orange juice and walked back toward town. In the distance I could hear the beeping of a giant tractor backing up. Down the street, several young men in work clothes were laying the foundation for a new doublewide. And across town, Sam Knight was starting to roast a pig for a busload of Air Force volunteers who were coming to town to help clean up trash.

When I arrived back at Thad's, I found him standing in front of the house, holding his three-footed cane. As usual, he was dressed in black slacks, with a collared shirt and a sturdy pair of suspenders. I held up my carton of orange juice, but before I could offer him anything to drink, he suggested we enjoy the nice weather and take a walk in the cemetery.

I agreed, and soon the two of us were strolling down the gravel road alongside Thad's house, which led into the verdant undergrowth of the cemetery. Thad's walking was slow and labored, but eventually the sound of passing cars receded and we found ourselves in the silent company of the town's deceased. Many of the tombstones were overgrown with weeds. Other plots were still freshly piled with dirt, a result of the massive reburying effort.

Thad and I stopped at a series of modest tombstones that all read, "Knight." Thad showed me the graves of his mother and father, and then he walked over to the graves of his three deceased brothers. "This one lived in New Jersey, this one lived in Jamaica, New York, and this one was in Greensboro," he said. "They all wanted to be brought home."

After I had spent a week in Princeville, Thad and I shared one last breakfast together in his cramped eat-in kitchen, and then he watched as I packed up my things. "You're always welcome back here," he told me as I disassembled the swampside tent that I hadn't slept in. Just before I left, he presented me with a parting gift: a small, creased headshot of himself. It was one of his only photographs to survive the flood. I tried repeatedly to give it back, but he refused.

Later that day, as I headed northward on Interstate 95, I pulled into a rest stop around dusk and watched the sun sink over the back of a McDonald's. My weeklong vacation was officially over. In a day's time I'd be back at the office, fact-checking the stories of people I would never meet. For the moment, however, I thought again of Thad—closing out another day on his carport, presiding over Princeville as the owls called on for night.

More than anyone else, Thad Knight launched my journey. He literally opened the door for me, and after visiting him in Princeville I was determined to keep going. Within days of returning to work, I was again flipping through my giant three-ring binder, pondering: Where would I go next? Whom else would I meet? And could I find some *common* explanations for why these home-keepers refused to budge? Yet all of these questions would have to wait. Despite my best efforts, a full year passed before I found the nerve and the means to continue on my journey. In that time, I left my job at the *New Republic*, moved into my brother's small apartment in Boston, and came upon the transportation deal of a lifetime.

The remaining places that I hoped to visit were as far away as Hawaii and Alaska. My brother had an old beat-up minivan named Bertha, but I doubted she could make it more than a hundred miles, and she certainly couldn't cross the Pacific. I would have to fly, and that would be costly. Yet before I had a chance to worry, my problem was solved by a relative who worked for the airlines. Through the family grapevine, she heard about my travel aspirations and quite generously agreed to give me her most prized job benefit—a flying pass—which allowed me to travel anywhere in the world for free as long as I went standby. Almost overnight I was transformed into an aerospace hitchhiker, a flying hobo. I just showed up at the check-in counter with my carry-on bag, flashed my driver's license, and waited for the next flight to wherever I was going.

By late March of 2001—roughly a year after I'd met Thad Knight— I was ready to recommence my journey. From Boston, I caught the last seat on a five P.M. flight to Seattle. From there I flew to Anchorage, Alaska. With layovers and one missed connection I made the trip in roughly twenty hours, which gave me plenty of time to thumb through my three-ring binder and read up on my final destination: Whittier, Alaska.

Reportedly, somewhere in the remote coves of Prince William Sound, there was a fourteen-story high-rise nestled among the glaciers. This single, snowbound building *was* the "city" of Whittier, Alaska. Almost all of the town's residents lived in this monolithic bunker, and everything they needed was just an elevator ride away. In the summer, the high-rise offered spectacular views of whales rising offshore and waterfalls plummeting off glacial crests. But in December, the sun set for several months, a punishing winter arrived, and it became clear why this city existed indoors.

Perhaps what intrigued me most was Whittier's lone entrance-way—a two-and-a-half-mile-long railroad tunnel that burrowed beneath a surrounding wall of mountains and brought a train into town several times a week. Recently, however, the state of Alaska had modified the tunnel to install an accompanying road for cars and buses. People in Whittier were miffed. From what I read in the *Anchorage Daily News*, most residents treasured their fortified isolation. They didn't want the road, and a few, including an outspoken diehard named Babs Reynolds, promised to fight it to the bitter end.[22]

# Tower of the Arctic

## Whittier, Alaska

THROUGH THE BEAMS of our headlights I could see the walls glistening, sweating streamlets of icy mountain water. The tunnel's contours were jagged like those of a mining shaft, roughly chiseled, arcing upward to a ceiling that dipped and rose along the backs of countless hanging boulders. The air had moistened to a musty cellar scent, the light thinned to an orange flicker, and my eyes strained to watch for bits of rock that were known to fall and crack windshields. We were passing through the bowels of a four-thousand-foot mountain, and slowly the car radio began to hiss with static.

My taxi driver, Kent, had timed our passage to get himself in and out of Whittier as quickly as possible. The controversial new road into town—which had just opened the previous spring—was only one lane wide. There simply wasn't enough room for a second lane in the narrow, two-and-a-half-mile-long entrance tunnel. Consequently, the road operated on a tight timetable, alternating its traffic flow every half-hour until four-thirty. At that time, two massive metal doors slid shut, sealing off Whittier for the night like a modern-day portcullis.*

Kent, a heavyset man in his fifties, was worried about getting stuck

---

* The tunnel schedule varies by day and by season. On Friday nights, for instance, it stays open until nine-thirty P.M. so that people can leave or stay out a little later.

in Whittier. It was now almost four P.M., and as the two of us drove down the longest vehicular tunnel in North America, Kent's eyes remained fixed on the dashboard clock.* "I really don't want to spend another night in Whittier," he told me for the second or third time. As it so happened, Kent was a former Whittier resident. I met him quite randomly at the Anchorage airport, and after a bit of haggling he agreed to drive me to Whittier for eighty-five dollars. This meeting was a stroke of good luck. Few if any commercial vehicles are willing to take passengers to Whittier in the winter. Kent, however, knew the sixty-mile drive well. He navigated us through the snow-packed turns of Portage Valley, alongside an imposing chain of mountains that eclipsed the sun, and past a series of small road signs that read, AVALANCHE ROAD CLOSURE INFO 273–6037.

Before entering the tunnel into Whittier, we drove past a lonely wooden tollbooth and stopped for a moment in front of a large steel A-frame that sheltered the mouth of the tunnel. Near the A-frame was a warning sign:

# AVALANCHE!

Breaking loose with savage power, snow can become an unstoppable instrument of destruction. A fully developed avalanche can attain a mass of over a million tons—this mass can hurdle downhill at tremendous speeds, pushing an invisible blast of air up to 200 mph in front of the avalanche, threatening life and property. The Portage tunnels A-frame portals are built to withstand most avalanches.

It was currently late March, prime avalanche season. I had already noticed several mountains that were scraped clean with giant skid

---

* According to the Alaska Department of Transportation and Public Facilities, the "Anton Anderson Memorial Tunnel" into Whittier is the longest "highway" or "vehicular" tunnel in North America. At 13,300 feet it is considerably longer than the runner-up, the East River Tunnel in New York, which is a mere 9,117 feet.

marks. Roughly a year before, a particularly large down-rush had cut Whittier off for days. "If we wait here long enough we'll probably see a slide or two," Kent told me. Then he steered our taxi into the darkness of the tunnel.

It was the tunnel that first brought Whittier to my attention. Back when I was still working at the magazine, when I was still pumping every living person I knew for any leads on intrepid home-keepers, I got a curious tip from an otherwise withdrawn and crusty editor about a newly built road that ran through a tunnel and led to an "indoor city" in Alaska. He claimed to have read about it in the *Los Angeles Times*. I took all such leads with a grain of salt. Early on I'd gotten quite excited about a town in Texas that was allegedly invaded each year by a horde of rattlesnakes, only to discover that it was largely a tourism gimmick used to lure reptile enthusiasts.[1] But after doing a little research I discovered that the editor was right. Improbable as it seemed, this indoor city did exist.[2]

Whittier owed its existence to the United States military, which initially conceived it as a fortified seaport. Anchorage had traditionally relied on port towns like Seward for shipping. Yet as World War II began, the military insisted on a closer and more secure port for its operations. In August of 1941, engineers began drilling a two-and-a-half-mile hole through the mountains to a narrow shelf of rock on the other side, which they called Whittier. The name came from the Quaker poet John Greenleaf Whittier, whose poems often described the rugged beauty of the seasons, including the awesome power of winter.

By 1954, roughly a thousand men were living in Whittier, mostly inside a giant six-story complex called the Buckner Building, which included a library, a hospital, a photographer's darkroom, a hobby store, a post office, a barbershop, a jail, a 350-seat movie theater, a four-lane bowling alley, and an indoor shooting range. In 1956 the military completed a second complex, a fourteen-story high-rise that qualified as the tallest building in Alaska. The Pentagon hoped Whittier would be not just a secure port but also a lookout onto the Soviet Union, which sat a few hundred miles to the west. But just a few short years later, the entire project was abandoned. In all likelihood, Whittier's strategic value was overestimated from the start, and the Pentagon was simply trying to clamp down on one of its many cold war spending sprees. In any case, by the early 1960s there were just thirty-two people living in Whittier, all of them civilians.[3]

In the ensuing years, officials across Alaska debated what to do with the former fortress in Whittier. There were a number of ideas proposed, from developing it into a resort to making it a prison. One of the most seriously considered plans was to turn Whittier into a giant mental institution. Yet according to a 1964 issue of *Time*, opponents to this plan successfully argued that "a psychiatric center in such forbidding surroundings would set mental health back 50 years."[4] Ultimately, Whittier was left to the handful of civilians who claimed it as home.

According to the 2000 census, precisely 182 people lived in the city of Whittier, and I wanted to know more about them. Naturally, I was curious about Whittier's avalanches and its harsh, wintry environs, but that was just part of it. Whittier promised to offer something new—not a story just of man versus the great outdoors, but also of man versus the great indoors. There was something both claustrophobic and otherworldly about Whittier, as if its residents were preparing for life in some distant space colony, and I wanted to know what kind of psyche it took to deal with these conditions—and, more importantly, want them.

After about seven minutes of subterranean driving, Kent navigated our taxi out of the tunnel and into a blinding flash of snow-reflected light. We emerged into the crook of a narrow valley with mountain walls rising straight up several thousand feet. In front of us lay Passage Canal, one of Prince William Sound's many handsome inlets, and its waters covered most of the valley floor except for a narrow stretch of ground where a road headed out along the inlet and around a bend. Kent pointed across the water to a little black spot. "Sea otter," he said with a smile. "Only one who can hunt that boy is a native." Kent sat upright in his seat, giving his large belly some clearance from the steering wheel. "It's beautiful out here, all right," he added.

"So what made you leave?" I asked finally.

Kent just laughed, then shook his head. "You ever hear of the experiments with all the white lab rats in the same box?"

"Don't think so," I said.

"Well they put all of them rats in one big box, and they got along okay for a bit, then just started killing one another."

Before I could respond, we pulled around a bend in the road and Whittier slid into full view. The whole town stood on a narrow shelf of rock that jutted off the canyon walls like a giant soap dish. First came the railroad yard, eight or nine tracks across, loaded with ice-covered boxcars stretching down a good mile or so to a loading dock, where a barge idled alongside chunks of floating snow. As we drove away from the water and inward along Whittier's rock shelf, we came upon a series of warehouses rising out of the snow in a dreary procession. They were easy prey for a tough winter. According to Kent, a few years back so much snow accumulated on one that its roof caved, blowing the front door across the street. Sprinkled between these structures was a wasteland of heavy equipment—radar dishes, front-enders, beached boats, giant spools of telephone wire, and a crane—all firmly entrenched in snow. At last came Whittier's fourteen-story high-rise, sitting flush against the canyon walls. It was a grim concrete slab, speckled with a few hundred small windows, the uppermost ones disappearing into a cloud of light snow. The whole scene had a definite sci-fi feel to it. With a few well-placed props, Whittier might easily have passed for a mining colony on Pluto. Kent jolted me back to reality with a heavy foot on the brake.

"This is it," he said as I hauled my backpack out of the taxi and into a gusting wind. I had sentenced myself to two weeks here, and suddenly my mind was swarming with second thoughts. Kent must have caught the look of apprehension on my face, because just before he motored away, he imparted some final bits of advice. Much of it was lost in the wind, but I heard the last few words crisply: "You'll want to find Babs Reynolds—she'll take care of you." Then with a sprightly honk of his horn, he was gone.

$$\sim$$

The first-floor hallway is the center of daily life in Whittier, the equivalent of Main Street in a normal town. Along this vast, windowless stretch I found a series of rooms containing the post office, the laundromat, the general store, the weather station, city hall, police headquarters, and a shop called Cabin Fever. At both ends of the building were elevators leading to the "residential" floors above. By the time I arrived, the first-floor hallway had pretty much shut down for the night and there wasn't a person in sight.

Eventually I wandered into Cabin Fever, which occupied a very cramped one-bedroom apartment at the far end of the hallway and functioned as the town's video store and tanning salon. It was here that I met Babs Reynolds. Babs was sitting in a walk-in closet outfitted with a small desk and a wraparound bookcase with several hundred movies, including a great many horror and action flicks. She was of medium height and buxom, a hearty woman in her early sixties, whose face was daubed with makeup and whose skin was deeply bronzed from the generous use of liquid tanner. Her clothes were all denim. Between her breasts rested a lone ornament: a small leather holster for her lighter, which hung as a necklace on a piece of rawhide. We exchanged pleasantries for a few minutes, during which time she used her necklace to light a long brown menthol cigarette resembling a small cigar. This was her brand of choice, she explained. They were tightly rolled smokes, the sort that put themselves out if you didn't really haul on them. Babs worked the cherry as we

*Babs Reynolds stands beside one of the many towering mountains that surround the city of Whittier.*

chatted, occasionally flicking off the ash or glancing around the corner for any would-be customers. "So what do you think of Whittier?" she asked me finally in a deep, throaty drawl.

"When I first came through that tunnel I was a little spooked out," I admitted.

"Yeah, well, who wouldn't be?" said Babs with a laugh. She reached into the desk drawer, pulled out a deck of cards, and began dealing herself a round of solitaire, which she played effortlessly, as if for the ten thousandth time. "When I first got here I couldn't believe it either," she said without looking up.

"Did you think of turning around?"

"Not for a moment," replied Babs. "I had an ex-husband on the other side who was trying to kill me." Neither of us spoke for a moment. Babs glanced up at a small TV that was hanging from the ceiling, and as she did I noticed several scars on her chin. Later she told me that these were the traces of reconstructive surgery. Before she came to Whittier her ex-husband used to beat her. On one occasion he broke her jaw, and the scars marked the places where a doctor had drilled several magnesium bolts into her mandible and connected them to a fiberglass brace.

"There's the ace of spades," said Babs. She flashed me a sweet, almost girlish smile, as if I'd brought her this luck, and then offered me a seat on a footstool in a corner of the closet. As I sat down, Babs began retelling the story of how she came to Whittier. "I started off in Maine, but I moved to Alaska in the late sixties, and I became the first legal girl bartender in Anchorage," said Babs, pausing for a drag on her menthol. "I was the hottest bartender in the state."

Babs continued to pluck cards out of the deck, all the while recounting the details of her years working the bars on Fourth Avenue in Anchorage, intoxicating and beguiling the city's toughest men, sweet-talking the cops and cabbies, brawling with the whores, and heaving in the tips. Those were the party years, Babs recalled. During this time she married her first husband on the top of a Ferris wheel at a carnival in the Sears parking lot. The judge, who was perched precariously in the car below, hollered them man and wife; the best man and lady, who sat in the car above, slid the rings down on a carefully rigged set of wires; meanwhile, Babs and her new husband teetered awkwardly in the wind, above an expanse of circus tents, bumper cars, and newspaper reporters.

"It was the third husband that nearly did me in," she explained. By then Babs was almost forty. She had been working on Fourth Avenue for more than a decade. The bar scene was losing its charm, and so was Anchorage, which was overrun with the business of the oil boom. Meanwhile, her third husband had begun to beat her. "He broke my jaw, hit me with a baseball bat, then he ran over me with the truck and broke my shoulder, so it was just a matter of time before he finished me off," explained Babs. "That's when I decided to get out." What she really wanted, Babs recalled, was to vanish, to disappear, to hide away in some far-off nook. Then, as luck would have it, she heard about Whittier—nestled at the foot of a valley, protected by an immense tunnel, and in need of a bartender.

Upon arriving in Whittier in the summer of 1978, Babs showed a picture of her third husband to the train crew and explained that he was out to kill her. "Back then the train was the only way into Whittier, and that train crew controlled who got in and who got out," said Babs. "So I told them my situation, and they told me not to worry." In the coming years the crew made good on its promise, never letting Babs's third husband aboard an incoming train. Still, Babs worried. She heard rumors from mutual friends that her husband was trying to hike the tunnel into town, and at night she often found it difficult to sleep. For the first nine years in Whittier she slept with her clothes on, ready to bolt at a moment's notice, even though there was really nowhere to go. Gradually, however, Babs began to relax. She came to know her neighbors. She opened a business. "I even started wearing a nightgown to sleep," she told me.

I chatted with Babs until closing time, and as she locked up Cabin Fever for the night, I asked if I could help out with her newspaper route the following day. In addition to working the video store, the tanning salon, the weather station, and a small restaurant that she owned, Babs was also Whittier's papergirl. "Sure, that'd be nice," she said. "Be downstairs at nine o'clock tomorrow, and we'll head over to the tunnel to pick up the papers. And if you're lucky, I'll make you breakfast afterward."

As we parted, I couldn't help but marvel at the pure Tom Sawyer beauty of what had just happened. I was genuinely excited at the prospect of lugging newspapers for this woman. She seemed to be Whittier's de facto spokeswoman. During the whole road crisis, reporters invariably found their way to her. Babs's many jobs and outgoing demeanor gave her an almost ubiquitous presence in Whittier. What's more, she was one of the few residents who had lasted more than twenty years, an accomplishment that I found both remarkable and perplexing. Babs seemed to be part of the town's bedrock, and I felt drawn to her—much the way I'd felt drawn to Thad Knight.

From Cabin Fever I headed upstairs to the local B&B, where I'd made reservations (quite unnecessarily, as it turns out, for I was the only guest). I rode the elevator to the ninth floor, where I met Kathy Elliot, a timid, white-haired woman who helped run the B&B. "How's the weather outside?" she asked. Cold, I told her. "I'm sure it is," said Kathy, who went on to explain that she hadn't left the high-rise in weeks. "I like going outside, but it drains you," she explained. "When you come back indoors to a man-made situation, you have to acclimate. I guess it's something like what the astronauts go through."

"So you just stay inside for weeks at a time?" I asked.

"I've stayed inside for months at a time," explained Kathy. "In the wintertime I hibernate like an old bear."

I took my key and proceeded to the fourteenth floor, where the B&B was located. The elevator doors opened onto one of the building's many long, linoleum corridors. The inside of the high-rise was a hybrid of several institutional styles of architecture—part 1950s college dormitory, part aging mental institution, and part nuclear fallout shelter—the effect was immediately confining and at times creepy. The halls were built with heavy yellow cinder block that echoed my every footstep. Nothing seemed to stir. Then suddenly the wind came, gusting off a distant glacier, slamming into the back side of the high-rise, squeezing its way into the building, then whistling up the elevator chutes, through the utility shafts, and along the expansion joints. The tower has two major "joints" or "gaps" that allow the structure to flex properly in the event of an earthquake. The practical effect, however, was that of a massive wind vent, causing the entire building to creak and groan through the night. "Sometimes," one resident told me, "in the middle of the night, you'll sit right up in bed and ask yourself: *What do I hear?* And the answer is: *nothing*. The wind has finally stopped, and it's enough to wake you."

Luckily, my room was equipped with a great old sound system, complete with a turntable, radio, eight-track, and cassette player, all sleekly mounted along a six-foot wooden cabinet. It was the sort of gigolo accouterment you could imagine advertised in *Playboy* for a few grand in the early 1960s. The accompanying albums looked to be from the same era. I grabbed *Elvis' Christmas Album*, put it in the eight-track, and cranked up the volume to drown out the wind. The only real downside was the apartment's stale air. Like a jumbo jet, the high-rise recycled its air. This tended to spread an ailment known as the "Whittier Crud," which much of the high-rise's population came down with each winter. To get a fresh breeze I cracked open a window, but this created a series of crazy convection currents within the apartment that opened and closed doors randomly. For a light sleeper like me, it was hard to doze off, and at one point I became so frustrated that I got up and walked the high-rise's empty hallways, which were even creepier than usual in the dead of night.

Determined to better understand the intricacies of the building's airflow, I eventually paid a visit to Dennis Limpscomb, the high-rise's chief custodian. Dennis told me the biggest problem with the wind was when it caused a lock-in. "When the wind is really blowing," he explained, "you'll get this vacuum where you can't get out of your apartment because your door is sucking shut. So you either call a neighbor, or just keep pushing until you manage to get it open. Once the seal is broken the door swings open real gently, but as soon as you let go, that door slams shut so hard it could take your hand off." Dennis also told me about some of the high-rise's supernatural problems. "Some of the units are haunted," he explained. "Cam Bender up in apartment 607 said he saw someone in the apartment, and the girl who lived there before him, Angie, used to see somebody all the time too. The incidents where we have problems are usually where somebody has died in the unit." Talk of hauntings was common in the high-rise. I met one woman who referred to the building as the "Overlook Hotel," a reference to the snow-covered resort in Stephen King's novel *The Shining*, which eventually drives its overseer mad.

After a restless first night, I met Babs at nine A.M. the following morning to help out with the newspapers. She drove her weather-beaten pickup truck out toward the tunnel, and together we struggled to see through the steadily falling snow. As if we didn't already have challenges with visibility, the cab of the truck was soon filled with a thick cloud of cigarette smoke. "I've been smoking since I was fourteen," Babs told me. "I've done everything possible to abuse my body. By the age of twenty-two my hair was white and by twenty-four I was

almost bald. Yet people can't believe how old I am." She shrugged
her shoulders, as if the secret of her youth was a mystery even to her.

We continued along the narrow stretch of road that hugged the
mountain walls and led to the mouth of the tunnel. Finally we pulled
up to a red stoplight, indicating that traffic was on an incoming route.
Currently, however, there wasn't a car in sight. Together Babs and I
peered into the mouth of the tunnel, down its dark shaft. From our
vantage point, it was impossible to see the distant gleam of Bear Valley, the first of several passes that led the way back to Anchorage and
the world beyond.

"How's this road working out?" I asked finally.

"Well, it's here, so we use it," she said. "But right until that first car
came through, I had to believe it wasn't going to open. We fought it
hard—got thousands of petitions. The kids at the school were even
talking about blowing up the equipment and stuff, but I told them it
wouldn't do any good. I think they were disappointed, but I told them
that if they were really serious about it, I could get them the explosives." She gave me a deadpan look and then cackled. "And they wonder why all the kids come and talk with me."

Babs dug into the depths of her winter coat, pulled out her neck-
lace-lighter, and lit another of her menthols. "The day the road
opened it was raining like a whore," she continued. "They had to do
the whole ceremony inside the tunnel. They brought in all the digni-
taries. The governor shows up, drives in, says a word or two, makes a
U-turn on the tarmac, and drives right back out."

"Was it hard on you?"

Babs nodded. "You got to understand, I came here more than
twenty years ago, running for my life. Coming here I found safety and
some of the most beautiful country you'll ever see. And I wasn't the
only one. A lot of people came here running from something."

This is something I would hear again and again in Whittier. People came through the tunnel on the run from a whole gamut of troubles: ex-husbands, ex-wives, parents, jobs, warrants, child support, God, or perhaps just themselves. Alaska was as far away as they could go and still speak English, and Whittier was a good safe leap beyond that. For years before the road arrived, the town's mayor, Ben Butler, who was also the ticket-taker on the only train into town, regarded his title of mayor as something of a misnomer. "I was always, as far as I looked at it, the gatekeeper of Whittier," he later told me. "Before you could come into or leave town, you basically had to give me a ticket, so I pretty much had the ability to keep track of everybody who was in town. In fact, people would call me at home at all hours of the day or night and wonder if a certain person had left or come in." With Butler as the lookout man, no one got into town unnoticed, and if it looked like trouble was on its way, one of Whittier's three cops would be waiting on the other side.

Babs popped open the driver's side door and stepped out into a powdery patch of knee-deep snow. "I'm going to check to see if the tunnel crew already dropped off the papers," she told me. I followed her through the snow to a partially submerged phone booth. I helped her pry open the door, and inside we found several dozen copies of the *Anchorage Daily News*. We carried the newspapers back to Babs's truck. By now the wind was really howling, and both of us hurried into the front seat. "The way I see it, this road was done *to* us — not *for* us," concluded Babs. "They brought us the world. Hell, we could have had the world if we wanted it, but we didn't — that's why we all ended up here."

Babs spun her truck around, and as we drove back toward the highrise, she played a fast-paced country tune on the truck's stereo. It was her favorite rallying song, her morning pickup. When its refrain came on, she began singing along and cranked up the volume so loud that the CD player began to skip beats. At this point the two of us were both pretty pumped up, and Babs steered us off the road through a field of virgin snow alongside the rail yard. The truck's wheels threw off a huge spray of snow, the steering wheel slipped momentarily out of control, and Babs's eyes lit up with a rare look of unadulterated glee.

We motored past the high-rise and along a narrow road that I hadn't noticed before. It climbed a small bluff and skirted the dilapidated remains of the Buckner Building, which was the first structure built by the U.S. Army in the early 1950s — the one that was six stories high and had a four-lane bowling alley. The Buckner Building was abandoned in the 1960s. There had been some plans to turn it into a prison, and others to use it as a luxury resort, but none of them panned out. Now the windows were all broken, and the metal fixtures were caked with rust. Later in my stay, I ventured inside and discovered that after years of neglect the ceiling was actually hanging with stalactites. The old movie theater, a grand room where Rita Hayworth and Johnny Carson once supposedly entertained the troops, was now shrouded in ice and almost impossible to walk through. I didn't stay too long, and this was probably for the best, because several locals later told me that bears sometimes hibernated in the basement.

Babs navigated us past the Buckner Building, and a minute or so later we came upon a small, two-story apartment complex called Whittier Manor. Babs was one of the few Whittier residents who did *not* live in the high-rise. "I spent my first thirteen years living in the BTI," she explained while parking her truck. (BTI was short for Begich Tower Incorporated, the official name for the high-rise.) "The main problem was the lack of privacy," she told me. "Moving to Whittier Manor was one of the best decisions I ever made."

Babs led the way back to her one-bedroom apartment, which was cramped but cozy. The inside was decorated with the skin of a bear that she had killed, thirteen framed photographs of Willie Nelson, and a bed full of vintage Mickey Mouse dolls. "I've never seen a Mickey Mouse without a smile, have you?" she asked. "The Mickeys reinforce the positive, and you need that to keep you going. It just lightens the load. I started collecting them twenty-five years ago. My favorite is the oldest—it walks when you hold its hands and squeeze its palms, which have air pumps in them." Babs lifted her favorite Mickey off the bed and walked it across the room for me, squeezing its palms in a careful, steady rhythm.

Eventually Babs put away the doll and headed over to the kitchen to get breakfast started. As she fished for the correct frying pan, I walked over to her bay window and looked out at a panorama of mountains, glaciers, and the waters of Prince William Sound. It was an awesomely beautiful sight, but after a while the barrenness of it all became a little unnerving, and I returned to the kitchen for a cup of coffee. "The winters can be really tough here," Babs told me as she cooked up some eggs. "I believe in my heart that if you can make it through three winters in Whittier, you're tough, and people can't argue with you—you're just tough."

"Why *three* winters?" I asked.

"I'm not sure why that is—just is," said Babs. As I would later discover, the three-winter mark was a well-established endpoint in Whittier. According to the local phone company, the average stay in Whittier was just three years. Naturally there was some variation, but the general trend was clear: After a few short years, most people left, no matter what was waiting for them on the other side of the tunnel.

According to Babs, and most everyone I talked to in Whittier, the winter presented two basic challenges: wind and snow. Whittier gets an average of 250 inches (or twenty feet) of snow a year, burying much of the town for the entire season.[5] The two-story schoolhouse, which sits just a few hundred feet from the high-rise, often resembles a giant snowdrift. Most of the thirty or so students get to school via an underground tunnel. In a bad winter, the snow may rise well past the first two stories of the high-rise. In the early 1970s, kids allegedly drove their snowmobiles over the City Shop Building, which is more than forty feet high.

The real wickedness, however, is the wind. The mountain walls surrounding Whittier are so steep and narrow that they effectively create a giant wind tunnel, blasting gusts of air at fifty knots (almost sixty miles per hour) for weeks at a time. The moisture makes this air especially heavy and therefore more powerful. When the local phone company first tried to harness this power by installing a series of wind-powered generators, the result was disastrous. "The generators couldn't dissipate the energy fast enough," the owner of the phone company later told me. "When I took them apart and did a biopsy, just charcoal came out. It actually generated so much energy it just fried the insides."

When such winds blow over icy streets, walking outside can be treacherous. Jan Latta, the school administrator, later related this story to me: "I was walking to school one day, and the wind was blowing so hard that I was shoving my arms into the snowbanks to hold my position. I watched a neighbor's Labrador retriever blow down the road past me." This sort of wind also creates low visibility and instant snowdrifts. Sometimes cars have to drive directly behind giant snowplows, and if they fall too far behind they are immediately engulfed in snow. The combined effect of all of this is simple: People stay indoors, often for weeks at a time. The first year of dealing with these conditions doesn't seem to bother most people, but by the third year it often becomes unbearable.

"Did you ever consider leaving during the third winter?" I asked Babs.

"No," she replied. "I really didn't. There are different kinds of toughness. I wasn't tough enough to live in a city anymore, but I was tough enough to live out here."

After breakfast was finished, Babs fixed me another cup of coffee and led me out onto a small wooden deck off her living room. This deck was the real perk of living in Whittier Manor, she explained. It allowed her to step outside any time she wanted. "It's not bad out today," she said, as we stood in a biting wind, sipping coffee and staring blankly at the mountains. "Hey," she said suddenly, "let's feed the birds." Babs stepped back inside, then reemerged clutching a softball-size chunk of frozen chicken, still smoking from the frosty burn of the freezer. Without warning, Babs swung the chunk of chicken well above her head, and then launched it skyward with a soft grunt. Seconds later, the frozen scrap of poultry was spinning wildly against a spectacular backdrop of mountains and sea, until it hit the ground, bounced, and then headed skyward once again, this time in the talons of a bald eagle. "That a boy, Charlie!" Babs hollered from her terrace, eyeing the bird with wonder as he worked his massive six-foot wingspan and flew over a distant curtain of pine trees. "He'll be back," Babs assured me.

Over the years, Babs had grown quite fond of her "pet eagle," she explained. But when she first moved to Whittier, she was more leery of eagles in general. Back then, she had two Pekinese dogs, which, along with other small dogs in Whittier, are known as "eagle bait." In fact, the following morning, when I was having breakfast with Babs, the *Anchorage Daily News* ran a story that read in part: "A Sterling woman witnessed five bald eagles feeding on her twenty-pound poodle on Wednesday."[6]

As it turns out, Charlie was just one of Babs's many pets. On a regular basis she also fed a number of other wild animals, including a chipmunk that lived beneath her deck, several stray cats that somehow survived in the engine of an old school bus, and a sea otter named Oscar who lived in the sound. Babs's favorite, however, was her one domestic pet—a gigantic, 110-pound black dog named Jake, whom she referred to as "the horse I never had." This designation was rather fitting, because at one point she had actually planned to harness Jake to her "old lady's tricycle" to create a sort of dog chariot. She even jury-rigged a reindeer halter with a quick release system, but at the last minute Babs decided against it. "I'm getting too old for that kind of stuff," she told me.

As Babs scraped the leftovers from breakfast off her plate and into Jake's mouth, she stroked his fur and spoke to him softly. When all the scraps were eaten, she looked back up at me. "It's just nice," she said. "I come home, the dog bounds over, the cat snarls, the eagle eats—I feel like I'm wanted."

⚡

For the next two weeks, my days started like this: Babs and I picked up the newspapers at the tunnel, ate breakfast at her house, and then drove back to the high-rise to make our deliveries. Usually, I held the elevator at each floor while Babs flung out a few copies of the *Anchorage Daily News*.

During the afternoons I often paced the hallways of the high-rise, looking for people or a rare community event. Once I joined a group of ladies for bingo in a grim, concrete rec room. Another day, when the sound of organ music drew me into the hallway, I discovered the local church, which was situated in the apartment next to mine. After the service, I met the members of the small congregation and joined them for a potluck. Several times I visited Whittier's schoolhouse, a very modern and well-run facility, which has won both state and national recognition for its innovative teaching techniques. Because there are just thirty or so students, ranging in age from three to eighteen years old, the school designs a unique learning program for each child.[7] In many ways, this individualistic style of education seemed to suit Whittier.

For the most part, the town as a whole was not very community-oriented. Instead, people tended to congregate in small cliques—the barflies, the senior citizens, the school kids, the church crowd, the fishermen, the bingo players, and so on—and interaction between these groups seemed limited to forced hellos in the elevator. As far as I could tell, residents kept to themselves. Even Babs, as busy and outgoing as she was, rarely had people over to her apartment or spoke of having any real friends in Whittier. Many people simply stayed in their rooms all day long, content not to be bothered. "Whittier's not the sort of place where you want to know too much about your neighbors, because a lot of them are on the run from something," one woman told me. "And, well, you're better off not knowing why."

In the evenings I would help Babs run Cabin Fever, which involved sitting in the closet, listening to country music, and chatting about life in the town. Once every hour, Babs hustled down the hallway to do some readings at the weather station and left me to man the store. During these regular intervals I either played solitaire or perused the movies on the shelves. Sometimes customers came in. I would take their two bucks and write down their room number. Occasionally a tanner stopped by to spend some time in the booth. Once I tried it myself. I applied Babs's Ocean Potion: Australia's Extreme Tanning Intensifier, closed myself inside the long steel coffin, and let the heat work into my bones. As I did this, I was overcome with a deep sense of relaxation that I hadn't felt since arriving in Whittier.

Light, or the lack thereof, is a serious problem in Whittier. For several months during the winter, no direct sunlight makes it over the mountains. This often causes a funk, clinically known as SAD, or Seasonal Affective Disorder. According to Babs, however, SAD was just an excuse to get depressed.

"I don't really buy into that SAD stuff," she told me one evening as we sat in Cabin Fever. "At my apartment I have fluorescent lights for the plants that work on a timer. They come on at nine A.M. and they make a little sunshine." Babs shrugged. "I don't know. I worked in bars so long maybe I'm just used to the dim light. In any case, it does no good to blame the sun. The real problem is that people don't leave their rooms. That's why doing the newspapers and chatting with the train crew is so good for me. Same with the video store—it gets me talking to people. It's certainly not about making money. Last night I rented out one movie."

Babs turned up the volume on the store's small TV set, which was broadcasting the Grand Ol' Opry live from Nashville. A lone fiddle echoed across the walls of the closet in which we sat. Babs lit a cigarette and smiled contentedly. "Two thirds of life is mental," she said finally. "However you condition your head, says how you are going to make it or not, don't you think?"

I nodded my head vaguely. It wasn't that I disagreed with Babs. Her bullish optimism was obviously a key to how she'd lasted so long, but it was also making it difficult for me to understand just how brutal Whittier could be.

⚡

The Anchor is Whittier's only bar, not to mention the only restaurant open year-round with regular hours. It's located in a dingy three-story building that sits just a few hundred yards from the high-rise. A week into my stay, I stopped in for a beer.

Inside, the Anchor was furnished with truck-stop decor: red leatherette seats, mirrored paneling, and a handful of neon signs. In the center of the room was the "Liars' Table," a twelve-foot hulk of wooden tabletop around which a bunch of regulars would sit, chat, and recount the bar's greatest moments—like the time a fight broke out and a city councilman put a fire axe through their beloved table. On this day there were about half a dozen men in coveralls lounging about, and they heckled me with a number of perfunctory threats as we got to know one another.

"Hey, kid, you know what we do for reporters around here?" one of them asked me. "We give them free rides out into the harbor—one way!"

I considered explaining that I was actually a fact-checker, then thought better of it. I was already in a bad spot because of a magazine reporter who had been there a year earlier and taken special care to lampoon everyone in the bar. Now they all took turns threatening to thrash that son-of-a-bitch magazine reporter the next time he showed his face in town, and I joined in, sharing my contempt, as I was rather disgruntled at the prospect of taking a beating in his place.

"You've got balls coming in here alone," another member of the Table yelled as I sauntered over to the bar (you had to saunter in a place like this). Immediately there was talk of my buying everyone beers.

"Kid, you got an expense account?"

"Uh, no," I said.

"Somebody get the rope!" another yelled. As I fumbled for my steno pad to take a few notes, someone else shouted: "Hey, put that away!"

"Look," I said as I paused mid-saunter. "I don't want to make the same mistakes that magazine reporter made—so how am I supposed to get the story right if I don't write down what you say?"

An awkward moment of silence ensued. Finally, a veteran of the

Table spoke up: "Good for you, kid!" Someone nodded and another called for a toast. "To Whittier!" shouted a man at the far end of the Table. "Where the men are men, and the women are too!"

At the bar, a sturdy blond woman in her mid-thirties poured me a beer and introduced herself as Beverly Sue, the Anchor's official babysitter. "I take care of everybody, serve them, and drive them home in my little Subaru at the end of the night," she explained with a warm smile. Later in the evening, I found her comforting a white-haired man whose good friend had drunk himself to death not so long ago. Drinking was a full-time occupation for some people in Whittier. The few times I had breakfast at the Anchor I could usually find someone having a beer. In the days before the road arrived, some of these habitual barflies were referred to as POWs, or Prisoners of Whittier. As one regular at the bar explained to me, these were people who came to Whittier, ran out of money, and couldn't afford a train ticket out of town. So they worked at the Anchor, ate at the Anchor, drank at the Anchor, bought cigarettes at the Anchor, and at the end of each week they barely broke even. "People really got stuck here like that, for a year or two," he insisted.

As I sat at the bar, sipping my beer, I met a tall, thin woman dressed in all black and wearing a clunky amulet around her neck. She looked both stylish and mystical, and needless to say, completely out of place amid the other clientele. She introduced herself as Elena Meyers and extended a slender hand. We chatted for a while, and eventually I managed to ask her how she'd ended up in Whittier.

"I was running from a husband," she told me bluntly. By now I had gotten somewhat used to this explanation.

"And how long have you been here?" I asked.

"Oh, I don't live here," said Elena. "I'm just visiting."

"So you *used to* live here?"

"Yes, I used to work here at the Anchor," she said with a nervous laugh.

Elena explained that initially she was quite happy here, simply because her husband couldn't get in. "I knew all of the people who worked on the train, and I told them here's the deal, here's what he looks like, and I don't want him in. They said, 'No problem.'"

"So a number of people had this deal?"

"Yes," said Elena. "It was easy to block people out. It's like you're living in a dorm. You just go room to room, or floor to floor. The police lived down the hall and I just said, 'Could I borrow some sugar, and hey, don't let him on the train today because I have to work and I don't want to deal with him.' That's how easy it was."

"The problem is," she quickly added, "we have long winters. It's dark, we have hellacious winds, people are all in the same building, and everybody knows every little thing about you, and it builds until you just go over the edge. That's when people break—in the winter."

"How long did you last?"

"Three winters," she replied.

"Three winters?" I put down my beer. "What's the deal with three winters?"

Elena laughed. "The first year you like the seclusion," she explained. "The second year you are sort of in between. By the third year it just overwhelms you—suddenly the little peaceful town gets to be like a prison. You're either in your cell or you're in the community area, and that's all you see and all you do, and by the third year you can't deal with it anymore. You got to get out. I just had to move. I couldn't handle people knowing every single thing about me. I mean, they knew what kind of underwear I had on a particular day."

"How did they know that?" I asked.

"They would guess," she said exasperatedly. "The guys at the bar would have these little betting pools to see what color of underwear I was wearing on any particular day, because they had nothing else to do."

"How would they know?"

"They had their ways. I would usually wind up getting asked by somebody randomly whom I didn't suspect, or somehow they would catch a glimpse. Then you'd hear this roar: *I told you today was pink!*" Elena shook her head.

Over the course of my stay, a number of people complained to me about the lack of privacy. They claimed that Whittier was a place where your neighbors could drive you nuts—especially if you lived in the BTI, where Lisa lived. Eavesdropping was ubiquitous. At the post office word would get out about the letter you got from the IRS; at the medical clinic news would spread about your skin rash; or on the police scanner someone was bound to hear about any trouble you had with the law. Even the walls had ears, in the form of air vents, which carried a din of conversation from floor to floor. Smells also carried. "I always know when my neighbors are cooking fish," one resident told me. This also made it difficult for the occasional pot smoker. "Don't smoke any dope in your apartment," another resident warned me, "because the cops will smell it through the vents." Getting outdoors was no guarantee of privacy either. So many residents in the BTI used binoculars that the building was often jokingly referred to as the "Beady Eye." Basically, in the winter there was so little to do, and so few things to focus on, that any small piece of information was a treasure, even the color of a barmaid's underpants.

Elena finished her beer and set the empty glass firmly on the bar. "By the third year you can't deal with it anymore," she told me. "It was like I was living in this twilight zone and all of a sudden I couldn't get a paper, I couldn't get on the phone, I couldn't get out of town, I couldn't do anything I wanted to do, and all of that piled up to the point where I walked into the store, and I couldn't find any decaf coffee, and I'd already been through this like three or four times, and that's when I sort of lost it, started screaming. I just lost it, and then I moved."[8]

❧

A few days after I visited the Anchor, I accompanied Babs into Anchorage for her weekly supply run. It was a whirlwind tour. We visited several thrift shops, the grocery store, a hardware store, Sam's Club, a place called Jack Rippies that sold only lottery tickets, a watch store where we got a new battery for Babs's "Mexican Rolex," and, lastly, the home of Babs's bookkeeper, which was distinguished by a large sign emblazoned with a gun that read, FORGET THE DOG, BEWARE OF THE OWNER.

As we drove the sixty barren miles back to Whittier, Babs inquired about my visit to the Anchor, and I told her about my encounter with Elena Meyers. Babs said she didn't remember Elena Meyers per se, but she seemed familiar with details of Elena's breakdown. "We get a lot of cases like that," explained Babs. Working as a bartender in Whittier doesn't help matters either, she added, because you end up spending your time with the town's most depressed residents. Babs knew this firsthand, because when she first moved to Whittier in 1978, she also worked as a bartender—not at the Anchor—but at the Sportsman, which is now closed. Within two years, however, Babs had struck out on her own. In the summer of 1979, she opened a small seasonal restaurant called Hobo Bay Trading Company. "I needed a change," she recalled. "And I was tired of working for other people."

The following day, Babs drove me down to Whittier's small boat harbor to visit her restaurant. The harbor is protected by several man-made seawalls, which shelter a few hundred boats owned by fishermen, wealthy Anchorage residents, and charter captains who take tourists out into the sound. During the summer the harbor is often bustling with activity, but today there wasn't a person in sight, and the only sound was that of wind and the clang of steel rigging cables against metal boat masts.

Hobo Bay Trading Company occupied a tiny cabin at the edge of the harbor. In front was a very large, ornately carved wooden sign that read, CELEBRATING 20 YEARS IN WHITTIER, 10 HARBOR MASTERS, 12 CITY MANAGERS, 23 EVICTIONS, 42 CITY STUDIES, 11 INCHES OF RAIN IN 24 HOURS, 9 NEW HAR-BORS, 1 FISHING DERBY AND 11 MAYORS. Babs walked carefully around her restaurant, inspecting damage from the winter and knocking off a few large icicles that hung from the roof. "The restaurant is open from eleven A.M. to seven P.M., and is closed on Tuesday so I can get the groceries," she explained.

When Babs first decided to open Hobo Bay Trading Company, most people didn't think it would work, she told me. She had no experience running a restaurant, and at the time, there was almost no development along the waterfront—just the boat harbor, a small harbor office, and a long stretch of rocks visited by the occasional bear. The only structure that Babs could afford was a small cabin, mounted on a set of wheels. The building's I-beams came from the old fuel dock; its windows came from the old railroad terminal; the hood of its stove came from a beached ferry that was accessible at low tide; and its door, which was engraved with the word "Library," came from the abandoned Buckner Building. The man who actually built the cabin, Jerry Protzman, charged a mere three thousand dollars. According to Babs, this was one of the great things about Whittier—it cost almost nothing to start a business. Cabin Fever, which Babs also owned, came almost as cheaply, she told me.

The term *pioneer* is something of a cliché in the business world, but it applied quite literally to Babs in her early years at Hobo Bay

Trading Company. With a spatula and her trusty .38 snub-nosed police special in hand, she fed people and fended off the bears. One of her most memorable customers in those days was a man who crashed his plane in the mountains, slid into town bloodied and bruised, and wandered over to her stand for help. "I gave him some of the brandy I keep down in the shop for situations like that," Babs explained. "Then we got him medevaced out of here."

Ill conceived as the whole enterprise initially seemed, residents and visitors came to like the idea of eating by the water, and they showed up in droves to let her know. Now, after twenty years of flipping hamburgers, Babs's business was doing quite well — and so was Whittier's waterfront. In the time since Babs first opened, more than a dozen other shops had opened around the harbor. When I asked her whether the new road might help her business further, she just shrugged and changed the subject.

"You know what I call this whole area?" she asked.

"What?"

"The Great White Beach," she said with a smile.

"Why?"

"Well," said Babs, "we're sitting on a pile of rocks that slopes down to the ocean, right? So why is it the Great White Beach? *Because it is!* You don't think I want to work on a pile of rocks, do you?" When I asked Babs if she'd ever considered visiting a real great white beach, she told me that she had been down to Mexico several times, but just for a vacation.

A bitter blast of glacial wind blew across the sound and hurried the two of us back into Babs's pickup. Together we pressed our hands into the warm blow of the truck's heaters. Nothing was said for several minutes as we thawed. "Do you ever think about retiring?" I asked finally.

"I had thought about retiring at one point," she confessed as she lit a cigarette. "I thought I could sell the restaurant, maybe buy a fifth-wheeler and go to the lower forty-eight to a lot of places I haven't seen. I could stay at those camper parks. They all need help—they need somebody to work the front desk, or sell groceries, or pump gas, or whatever. In the wintertime, I could go down on the southern border, and then when it got warmer, go into Michigan and Utah—places where I've never been. I thought that would be kind of neat, but then I thought, boy, I don't know any of those people down there."

❦

Two others reasons for Babs not to go anywhere were her younger sisters, Brenda and Carolyn, both of whom had followed her to Whittier. Carolyn Raye Casebeer, the middle sister, was a lifelong wanderer who rarely stayed anywhere for more than a year at a time. She had moved to Whittier five different times, and was currently living in an apartment on the tenth floor of the high-rise, which was furnished with a few spartan items, including a wooden box with an open plane ticket in it. Brenda Tolman, the youngest sister, arrived in 1982 and had been in Whittier ever since. Brenda was a professional artist. She had a studio on the first floor of the high-rise, but she lived in Whittier Manor, just a few doors down from Babs.

During the second week of my stay in Whittier, I spent a fair amount of time with both of Babs's sisters. I got to know Brenda first. We chatted several times at the weather station, and eventually she invited me back to her apartment. She told me that she rarely had anyone over to her place, so I should excuse the mess.

Brenda's apartment was teeming with plants. They hung from every conceivable nook, soaking in the colored light that poured through the apartment's many stained-glass windows. The reverse image of this scene appeared across the surface of Brenda's indoor fishpond.

Much of the apartment's floor space was taken up by a giant indoor fountain that pumped 350 gallons an hour and was inhabited by six giant Koi carp. These fish—along with two dogs, a cat, a ferret, and a handful of reindeer—served as Brenda's pets.

Brenda and I sat along the wooden casing of her fountain, where we chatted and watched the fish. Brenda was a pretty woman in her early fifties, with long, braided blond hair that came down over the shoulders of her Mickey Mouse winter jacket. "When I first came to Whittier I couldn't believe this place," she told me. "Babs took me for a drive around town and she pointed out this old dilapidated building

*Brenda Tolman with two of her pet reindeer. So far Brenda has had no major problems with her pets, except the time that an antler poked through the white of her eye and slammed into her skull.*

that had water running down the sides. She told me this was the local phone company. I started laughing. There was absolutely *nothing* here. And then it came to me: What a land of opportunity!"

Despite Brenda's enthusiasm, Whittier did not strike me as an obvious artist's retreat. There was plenty of beauty around, but almost none of it was man-made. "With a few sticks of dynamite Whittier would be a beautiful place," one local cop had told me. It was an old saying in town, and for the most part I agreed. Very few of the town's buildings had any aesthetic value, with two notable exceptions: a gorgeous Nordic chalet with a great sloping roof and overhanging eaves, built down by the water; and an ornately carved Hansel-and-Gretel-style barn, which sat at the foot of the high-rise. As it turns out, both were designed and built by Brenda Tolman.

The Nordic chalet was Brenda's gift shop, where she sold the artwork that she made each winter. Her most popular work were her wildflowers, which she carved on the soft bark of cottonwood trees and then painted in delicate detail. She carved dozens of pieces each winter. "The winters here help me create at my max," Brenda told me. "For some people it might be a nightmare, but it's just what I need to stay focused. I was just one of those people who were lucky enough to find a place where they actually belong." In addition to carving cottonwood, Brenda also painted with watercolors, shot her own postcards, wrote in calligraphy, engraved wooden signs, created her own jewelry (including porcupine quill earrings), sculpted and fired porcelain Christmas ornaments, and offered a full line of handmade leather products.

When Brenda became bored with the gift shop, she decided to build the barn, where she did most of her woodwork, stored her power tools, and kept her reindeer. The reindeer proved useful with the tourists and were also a natural fit amid her burgeoning wildlife collection. They were, however, wild animals, and they could be extremely dangerous. Occasionally they made charges. So far there had been no serious mishaps, explained Brenda, except the time that an antler jabbed through the white of her eye and slammed into her skull. "Luckily I didn't lose the eye," Brenda told me.

Later on, when Brenda took me down to the barn to photograph the reindeer, one of them managed to sneak out of the pen, and we spent the better part of two hours trudging through Whittier's massive snowbanks, trying to recapture the animal. Eventually Babs showed up in her pickup truck. Immediately Brenda rolled her eyes. "Here comes Babs to save the day," she said under her breath.

Although Brenda and Babs lived next door to each other and relied on each other to do everything from running the weather station to lassoing runaway reindeer, they did not seem to get along particularly well. Once they went for two years without talking, Babs told me. "We used to pass in the hallway or ride the same elevator without even looking up," she explained. "It was like we didn't exist for each other." In addition to being somewhat standoffish to each other, the two were also highly competitive, not just for my attention, but for that of the entire town, it seemed. Carolyn, the middle sister, explained this best.

"My sisters are like celebrities around here," she told me when I visited her tenth-floor apartment toward the end of my stay. "I mean, sometimes you'd think they'd stopped world hunger or something," she added with a laugh. "But they are really both remarkable women, and of course that creates some competition."

Carolyn was a very thin, almost nymphlike woman in her late fifties who fidgeted and chain-smoked through most of our interview. When I asked her how she fit into the Whittier scene, she told me that she didn't. "I'm just passing through," she said. "I could never live here permanently."

"Why not?"

"I never live anywhere permanently," she told me. Carolyn explained that her favorite places were Lake Tahoe, Las Vegas, Hawaii, and Alaska—each of which she had lived in at least four times. "Sometimes people ask me what I am running from," remarked Carolyn. "They ask me why I don't want security. But I tell them: Security comes from the inside."

"How much longer are you going to be in Whittier?" I asked her.

"I have absolutely no idea," she told me.

Before leaving Carolyn's apartment, I made a point to ask her why she thought her sisters were so attached to Whittier. Carolyn didn't answer me immediately. Instead she sat silently for almost a minute, smoking her cigarette, as if I weren't even there. "You can get a bit institutionalized here," she said finally. "Everything here is so simple and secure. When I've left in the past, I've thought, *Oh, shit, what have I done?* Suddenly I have to start carrying a wallet again. I have to worry about rent, utilities, jobs, everything. For me, that's the real world. I need that. But what do I know? Maybe this is really paradise and I am just too much of a damn fool to see it."

After meeting Carolyn, I returned to the vacant living room of my B&B, made myself some coffee, and listened to *Elvis' Christmas Album* for the seventh or eighth time. Eventually I found a deck of cards and dealt myself a round of solitaire. As I played, I thought again of Carolyn and her endless migration between Alaska, Vegas, Tahoe, and Hawaii. In many ways I admired her lifestyle, but I wondered if she found it exhausting—hopping from place to place, freefalling through her life. Later in the evening at Cabin Fever, when I asked Babs about this, she nodded her head knowingly. "Carolyn has never been connected to anything," she told me. "And never will be."

On one of my last nights in Whittier, Babs invited me over to her place to watch the Oscars. She said she would make some chili, and I said I'd bring her up to speed on the nominees. "You must be the only person I know who has actually seen any of these movies!" she told me over the phone.

Before I headed over to watch the awards, I met up with Brenda, who had prepared something of a goodbye salute. Earlier in the week, when I visited the barn to help her feed the reindeer, I noticed a large piece of PVC pipe that was hooked up to an air compressor. "What's that?" I'd asked.

"It's a potato gun," she told me. "You can shoot a potato from here all the way over to that building," she said, pointing to a distant warehouse. Firing off potatoes, she told me, was one of her favorite forms of entertainment. Today, quite graciously, she had taken time to set up the gun. Brenda crammed a good-size potato down the five-foot shaft of the gun, popped on the air compressor, and told me to squeeze in some air. Suddenly the butt of the gun slammed back against my ribs and the potato blasted outward, hurtling into the sky until I could no longer see it. "Yaaa-fucking-hoooooo!" yelled Brenda.

"Got any more?" I asked. We shot off a few more rounds, and Brenda broke out some M&M's that she'd brought along for the occasion. When we'd sufficiently shelled the town of Whittier, we set down the gun and grinned at each other like two adolescents who'd just broken the rules. "Thanks a lot," I told her. "It's a great gun."

"I think I have a spare one I can send you," she said. "They ought to like that back in Boston."

Later in the night while Babs and I sat in front of the TV, I told her about the movie *Erin Brokovich* and we discussed at length whether or not Julia Roberts had already prepared an acceptance speech for her role in the film. "Oh, you'll know when the time comes," said Babs. "Because sometimes they get up there and they don't have anything to say, and they're so happy they're just slobbering." So we kept watching until Julia Roberts won the Oscar for best actress and sniffled her way through a very impromptu speech.

Afterward we stepped out onto Babs's deck under the murky light of a crescent moon, which illuminated the glassy waters of the sound and the deep blue arctic ice along its edges. After a while I posed a question that I had been wondering about for the better part of a week, namely, whether she ever worried about her third husband anymore.

"No, no," she said with a laugh. "He's been dead for over ten years."

This came as a surprise. Until now, I had assumed that he was still lurking somewhere on the other side of the tunnel. I had assumed that, on some level, it was this threat that kept Babs in Whittier.

"Babs, do you think you'll ever leave here?" I asked.

Babs shrugged. She thought for a moment, then explained, "The best thing that could happen is that I would just die down there one day when I'm cooking hamburgers. I'd just drop dead, and they could just throw me on the grill and cremate me." She laughed. "I guess that's kind of sick, but you know, what else am I going to do?" Babs smiled, fumbled for another cigarette, and then headed back inside.

⚡

On the morning of my departure Babs offered to drive me to the airport. "You really want to haul me all the way to Anchorage?" I asked her.

"No," she replied. "But I've enjoyed having you here and somebody has got to drive you, so hurry up before I change my mind."

Around ten A.M. Babs and I set out in her pickup truck, driving south along the snow-covered bends of Portage Valley, through a forest of trees with branches that were hung with long, delicate icicles that fell and shattered like champagne glasses whenever the wind blew. We took the Seward Highway into Anchorage and, just to kill a bit of time, drove down Fourth Avenue past the honky-tonks where Babs had once tended bar. "Not much left here," she muttered as we sped down the avenue so quickly that it was impossible for me to see much of anything.

About half an hour later we pulled into the airport. "I'm not big on goodbyes," said Babs, "but you know where to find me if you ever want to come back." Babs slammed on the brakes, stopping just long enough for me to plant both feet on the curb, and then she was gone.

# The Lava-Side Inn

## Royal Gardens Subdivision, Hawaii

UNLIKE EVERYONE ELSE waiting to board Flight 276 to Honolulu, I was in the unique situation of not knowing whether my final destination still existed. Unfortunately, there was nothing I could do. On this particular trip I was dealing with something that was by definition unpredictable: a volcano.

Of all people, it was my eighty-two-year-old Grandma Norma who put me on to this story. A few years back, Norma visited Hawaii and took a helicopter ride over Kilauea, one of the world's most active volcanoes. From her view in the sky, she could see how rivers of lava had oozed down the mountainside and taken out entire neighborhoods. "What's really amazing are the houses that are still standing," Norma told me. "They're just sitting on these little lava-encircled islands."

I was intrigued. Eventually I contacted the Hawaiian Volcano Observatory and spoke with a staff geologist who told me that one of these "islands" was inhabited by a man named Jack Thompson, who'd been cut off by lava for almost fifteen years. "He now operates his house as a bed and breakfast," the geologist told me, "though I'm not sure how many guests he gets." In theory, Jack's B&B sat on the eastern flank of Kilauea, right in the heart of the lava's flow. I say "in theory" because no one seemed to know for sure whether his house was still standing.

Jack's cell phone did not take long distance calls, and his PR man, John Pillsbury, wasn't returning my messages. When I finally reached Pillsbury after several weeks of trying, he had little to tell me other than that he no longer worked for Jack. "I guess I wasn't able to bring in enough customers for him," lamented Pillsbury bitterly. "It's a hard sell—people are just scared of volcanoes."

From what I could gather, Jack Thompson wasn't scared of much. Before leaving for Hawaii, I called a number of local officials (volcanologists, civil defense coordinators, community association reps, and so on), and all of them described Jack in similar terms: stubborn, solitary, and fearlessly devoted to his home. Legends of Jack were ubiquitous. He allegedly ignored roadblocks, rode his motorcycle across molten lava, fended off hoards of wild pigs, and even kept the looters at bay. "I don't know him personally," the chief scientist at the Hawaiian Volcano Observatory told me, "but Jack is very well respected around here."

The most current information that I was able to find on Jack's house came from the observatory's Web site, which put out daily "eruption updates." I never found any direct mentions of Jack, but occasionally there were references to Royal Gardens—the abandoned, lava-encircled housing development in which he lived. I tried to visit this Web site or call the observatory every few weeks. This was one of the first things I did upon returning from Whittier, and what I learned convinced me to head directly for Hawaii. Apparently, the lava was now closer to Jack's corner of Royal Gardens than it had been in a decade.

All of this was very much on my mind as I waited for the last ticketed passengers to board Flight 276. "You've got to get me on this flight," I told the clerk behind the check-in counter. She nodded but didn't look up. At last, with her eyes still fixed on the computer screen, she pursed her lips and asked me that most welcome of questions: "Mr. Halpern, what do you want: window or aisle?"

❧

I was headed for the island of Hawaii, also known as the "Big Island." The five major Hawaiian Islands—Hawaii, Oahu, Molokai, Maui, and Kauai—are essentially the tops of gigantic volcanic mountains that have formed gradually over the course of several million years. The formation has occurred as magma from the earth's liquid core oozed upward through cracks in the ocean floor. The magma, which is known as lava once it breaks the surface, immediately hardens and over time accumulates. The Hawaiian Islands are just a few of the several hundred volcanoes that have built up on the ocean floor along a ridge that stretches north all the way to the Aleutians. The Hawaiians are simply among the tallest of these volcanoes—some of them tower more than 30,000 feet above the ocean floor—and together they break through the crashing waves and form what Mark Twain called "the loveliest fleet of islands that lies anchored in any ocean."[1]

Hawaii is the largest of the five major islands, and it's getting larger by the day. This rapid growth is the work of Kilauea, which produces the equivalent of 40,000 dump trucks full of lava each day.[2] Unlike the legendary Mount St. Helens, which went off in one violent blast in 1980, Kilauea has vented gradually over the course of many years.[3] Its most recent eruption began in the winter of 1983, and almost two decades later, it was still going strong. The steadiness of Kilauea's flow is due to the highly fluid and runny form of its lava, which allows it to move freely both beneath the surface and upon eruption. Some scientists call volcanoes like Kilauea benign, which they pretty much are, unless you insist on living downslope of their lava flow, which is exactly what Jack Thompson was doing.[4]

Contacting Jack by telephone was an exercise in precise timing. The morning after I arrived in Hawaii, I awoke shortly after dawn and began dialing his number. From my brief chat with John Pillsbury, I knew I had to call the B&B at exactly 6:30 A.M. This was the time each morning when Jack turned on his phone and called Blue Hawaiian Helicopters to give his daily lava/weather report. Apparently, Jack had an informal deal with the company's pilots: He told them where to find the best lava for the tourists, and in return, they provided him with an industrial-strength mobile phone to use whenever he wanted. According to Pillsbury, however, electricity and privacy were two of Jack's most valued commodities on the volcano, and consequently, the phone was rarely turned on.

Just shy of 6:40, I reached Jack. It was a moment of great relief, and after explaining at length who I was and how glad I was to hear his voice, I finally let him get a word in edgewise.

"How long do you want to stay for?" he asked with a bit of a southern drawl. He sounded skeptical.

"I don't know," I said. "A week . . . maybe two."

"Do you have a sleeping bag?" asked Jack. "I mean, do you mind sleeping on the floor?" This struck me as an odd request coming from a man who ran a bed and breakfast, but I didn't press the point. In the end, this arrangement worked out because Jack offered me a special "floor rate," which spared me from paying his usual hundred-dollar-per-person nightly "bedroom rate." In any case, the floor sounded much better than camping outside near the lava.

"No problem," I told him. "I love the floor."

"Well . . ." There was a long pause. "All right, then."

Jack and I arranged to meet the following morning in Hilo, a port town not too far from the slopes of Kilauea. In the meantime, I had the day to myself, so I decided to visit the Hawaii Volcano Observatory. I rented a compact car and ascended the eastern flank of Kilauea until I reached a large flattened area that appeared to be the summit. Unlike the perfectly conical volcanoes in the movies, Kilauea is flat-topped. Its cone collapsed long ago, and now all that remains is a plateau with a giant "caldera" or crater in the center. The observatory is dramatically perched on the brink of this caldera, but when I peered over the edge I was disappointed to find not a single trace of fiery red. As far as I could tell, the observatory was not positioned to observe much of anything.

When I finally ventured into the observatory, I learned that all of the action was taking place down slope, at a "vent" known as Pu'u 'O'o. Every so often the giant reservoir of magma beneath Kilauea shifted its flow and surfaced from a different vent. Most recently it was Pu'u 'O'o that was getting all of the flow. Meanwhile, the caldera and all other potential vents were getting bypassed, which meant that the observatory was up too high and over too far to see any real volcanic activity. Jack, however, was in the thick of it. After the lava gushed out of the Pu'u 'O'o vent, it rolled downhill directly past his place. "He's got the best seat in the house," one staff member told me quietly. "But I don't know how much longer he'll be around—his house has been condemned by the volcano."

After this visit to the observatory I still had some time to kill, so I drove to a nearby airport, where I bought a ticket for a helicopter tour. I chose Blue Hawaiian's "Ring of Fire" tour because it went directly over Jack's house. According to Blue Hawaiian's ground crew, pilots used his house as a landmark (as in, "I just passed Jack's place, over and out"), while tourists used it as a photo op (as in, "Wow, some nut actually lives down there"—*snap, flash*). So I loaded into a helicopter with a bunch of tourists from the *Rhapsody*, a five-star cruise ship, and darted off toward the lava.

After twenty minutes in the air, we reached the Pu'u 'O'o vent. Here at last was the classic cone of volcanic rock, roughly six hundred feet tall and puffing out a giant plume of white smoke. My first impression was that it seemed conspicuously misplaced. Instead of being on the summit, where I still felt certain it belonged, it was nestled on a nondescript eastern flank of the mountain. Although the vent was smoking, it was not visibly spewing any lava. Instead, the lava was rising from the earth's fiery depths and being channeled into a series of tubes that lay buried just beneath the surface, like a network of giant water pipes. These tubes insulated the lava, keeping it warm and allowing it to flow much farther before it cooled and then hardened. As the lava made its journey downhill, it often broke out of its tubes and flowed freely along the surface, meandered down the face of the mountain, taking out anything in its path. This was exactly the sort of renegade stream that was now drawing dangerously close to Jack's house.

From the Pu'u 'O'o vent, we flew downhill, across a sprawling path of destruction that the lava had created. Over the years, various surface flows had wiped out almost all of the vegetation and houses that once covered this side of the mountain. Now all that remained were endless fields of hardened lava.* Its charred, black crust covered the landscape like a blanket, sprawling in every direction as far as the eye could see, and was broken only by the occasional glimmer of red where a new flow was oozing out.

As our helicopter crested the final bluff that led down to the sea, an unexpected clump of trees came into view. This is what the Hawaiians called a "kipuka," an isolated piece of land that the volcano has spared. Basically it's an oasis of greenery, surrounded on all sides by miles and miles of smoldering lava. We passed over a number of these

---

* Hardened lava is not necessarily cold or inactive. Because molten lava cools so rapidly, its surface often forms a thin crust, like the skim on a bowl of chocolate pudding. Beneath this thin crust of rock there are often massive rivers of hot, flowing lava.

kipukas on the way, but this one looked different. It was larger, much larger, encompassing several hundred acres. Eventually I realized that this had to be Royal Gardens, the abandoned suburban development in which Jack lived. Royal Gardens had been cut off from the world since the late 1980s, and it showed—streets were overgrown with vegetation, buildings were falling apart, and absolutely nothing was stirring.

A moment later, our helicopter angled downward and we were hovering over the bright red roof of a perfectly intact house. Our pilot turned on his microphone and told us that this house belonged to a man named Jack Thompson. He then gave a brief spiel on the volcano's legendary hermit. At last, in a perfectly choreographed maneuver, our pilot's monologue gave way to the helicopter's sound system, which was playing Jimmy Buffet's famous volcano ditty: "I don't know where I'm a-gonna go when the volcano blows!" The schmaltz was flowing faster than the lava, creating a decidedly Epcot Center–like effect, only there was the added rush of reality. Despite all the gimmicky hoopla, there was actually a man down there. Exactly who he was and how he got there was unclear, but, quite certainly, he was making a rather extraordinary stand.

For a minute our helicopter hovered over Jack's place. All of us wanted to have a good, long look. The woman in the seat next to me leaned across my lap in order to get a better view out the window. Eventually she glanced back at me with her eyebrows raised and her mouth hanging open. Of course, I recognized the look on her face— that curious, baffled, utterly confused stare. Even if briefly, she and all the other passengers in my helicopter were contemplating the same question that I did almost every day.

Jack Thompson looked nothing like I'd imagined. He had no gnarled walking staff or Rip Van Winkle beard, no Mad Max motorcycle gear or lava-scorched boots, no zipperless Amish-style clothing or partially melted glass eye. Jack was a handsome man with a rugged, freckled face, long blond hair pulled back in a ponytail, and a lean but powerful build. He was at once the image of a stoic: modestly dressed, efficient in his movements, and deeply contemplative. He was also immaculately clean — his T-shirt looked ironed, his face was meticulously shaven, and his skin seemed to glisten. At the age of fifty he was the personification of good health. And as I stood next to him, with scruffy hair and a wrinkled shirt, a passerby could easily have mistaken me for the hermit and him for the travel writer.

More than anything else, however, Jack struck me as grouchy. Unlike the other home-keepers I'd met thus far, he was hardly welcoming. As planned, we met up the following morning at ten A.M. sharp, and from the start he seemed to be in a foul mood. As he drove me around Hilo in his 1985 Toyota Tercel, I tried to keep conversation light. I started with the golden safety net for grown men with almost nothing in common — I asked him if he followed sports. "If any kind of game comes on the TV or radio, it comes off immediately," he replied. "You see all these people jumping up and down for a ball-game, but they wouldn't lift a finger to save a tree, or a bird, or an animal species!" Unfortunately, every question I asked seemed to elicit a similar response. "Yeah, I was married," he told me, none too enthused about this brief mistake. As for kids: "Kids? No thanks. Then you're a family man, driving down the freeway, stuck in traffic . . . and they only end up hating you when they grow up." Over lunch he told me, "In my fifty years of living I can count on one hand the people who have treated me fairly." When I later asked him who those five people were, he replied, "Five was being generous."

As the day progressed, Jack's many misgivings seemed to form a decidedly apocalyptic vision for the future, where overpopulation, hoof-and-mouth disease, deadly grain-eating molds, fish-depleted oceans, and air-polluting SUVs had ruined the earth. Much of what Jack said was well reasoned and quite true, but there was something aggressively misanthropic about his manner, and I began to wonder whether it was really such a good idea to follow him home to such an extremely isolated area.

My saving grace was Don Bartel, one of Jack's best friends from high school. As chance would have it, Don was flying in from Los Angeles that very afternoon to spend a few days of "rest and relaxation" up on the volcano. We picked Don up at the Hilo airport early in the evening. Don struck me as a quintessential Californian: well tanned, smiling, friendly, and imbued with a commanding sense of leisure. He wore surfer's shades and a sun-bleached baseball cap, which masked his soft, almost boyish features. Like Jack, he was a young fifty, yet there was something decidedly paternal about Don. I would later learn that he had two adolescent children who lived with his ex-wife in Oregon, as well as a grown daughter from a previous marriage. Currently Don was on marriage number three. Overall, his life seemed to be full of exactly the sort of messy familial entanglements that seemed to scare the hell out of Jack. Nonetheless, the two men appeared to be good friends, and Don's arrival definitely lifted Jack's spirits.

From the airport, the three of us drove to the outskirts of Hilo and pulled into the driveway of Jack's one-bedroom city house. It was a simple prefab, a bachelor's pad with wall-to-wall carpeting, a handful of drying dishes in the sink, and your basic TV/VCR centerpiece. Jack bought this place to avoid a daily commute across the lava. As he explained, "I built this house so I could go to work." In the early years of the eruption, Jack's commute was manageable. He simply drove around the lava on a series of back roads that led to Hilo, where he worked as an air-conditioning/refrigeration technician. By the late 1980s, however, he was surrounded by lava on all sides. "When the lava cut us off, my neighbors really started to leave," explained Jack. By 1991, he was the last resident left in Royal Gardens. Even still, he tried to make his arrangement work. For a while he hiked to a nearby lot where he kept his car, but as the lava flows widened, this became increasingly difficult. "I had to hike one mile, then two miles, then it just became too much," said Jack. By the mid-1990s, Jack had no choice but to build a house on the outside. For a while he spent his weekdays in Hilo and his weekends up on the volcano, but this proved exhausting. Finally, in 1998, he opted for early retirement. He quit his job, opened a B&B, and moved back to the volcano full-time. Now, despite the fact that Jack rarely had any paying guests, he spent most of his time manning his B&B.

After showing us around his place, Jack invited us to sit on the couches that surrounded his TV, and before long, he and Don were reminiscing about Bakersfield, California, their hometown. "Bakersfield is just an old oil refinery town," Jack explained to me. "It's not California the way most people think of it." According to Jack, his home life offered little reprieve from the bleak, industrial surroundings of Bakersfield. Both his father and his older brother bullied him, he recalled, and by the age of ten he was already dreaming of a life somewhere else—he would travel westward, leaping across the Pacific to a place where things would almost certainly be better. "Or that's what I thought," said Jack with a wry smile. "I never imagined I was going to end up like this—I mean, living on an erupting volcano."

"But you're one in a million," added Don. "No one gets to see what you see. No one has what you have up there."

"It's true," said Jack with a nod of his head. "You're right."

As the evening progressed, the prospect of our imminent return to the volcano seemed to infuse Jack with a rousing sense of purpose, and around dinnertime he explained the plan. We would spend the night here at his city house and then wake up early the next morning and set out for the volcano. Ideally, if money weren't a factor, we'd just fly in by helicopter; in fact, this was how many of Jack's wealthier guests often arrived. There was a cheaper path, however, a sort of "economy route" that fit my budget and Jack's sense of adventure. In short, we'd be trekking across the active lava. It would be a strenuous journey, explained Jack, and we needed all the rest we could get.

Before going to sleep, Jack told us about a TV show called *Living on the Edge* on the Home & Garden Television channel. Each week, the show featured a different location where people were living in extreme circumstances. "Pretty soon," explained Jack, "my house is going to be on the show." At this point I noticed a look on Jack's face that I hadn't seen before: He seemed pleased.

Moments later Jack popped a tape into the VCR. The people at *Living on the Edge* had sent him a recording of some past shows. Together we huddled around the TV. From the start it was clear Jack had watched the tape before, perhaps several times, and before long he was providing a line of running commentary. One episode featured an extremely obese woman living in a yurt (a circular, domed tent traditionally used by the Mongols). The woman's foremost complaint was fueling her stove, which required her to chop wood. "Oh no," said Jack dramatically, with a quick roll of his eyes. "She has to chop her own *wooooood!*" Not long after this, the show's narrator revealed that the woman had only recently moved into her yurt. Don and I both shook our heads. I think both of us felt a brief, vicarious swell of pride: Our man Jack had lasted twenty years.

Another episode featured a family living in an old powerhouse situated at the edge of a cliff in Telluride, Colorado. Midway through the show, there was footage of a wobbly, open-air cable car that the family used to get down from the cliff. Jack conceded that this was pretty amazing. "I would consider doing a house swap with them," he told us later. "But just for a few months."

Near midnight, as Don and I bedded down to sleep on the floor of Jack's living room, we got a chance to chat briefly about the purpose of *his* visit. Don told me that this was his third time vacationing on the volcano. "If it weren't for the fact that my lifelong buddy was living here I probably wouldn't be doing this," he told me.

"So what's it like on the volcano?" I asked him finally.

"It's just like another world," replied Don.

⚡

The next morning Don and I sat braced in the back bay of a dusty pickup truck, bouncing up and down like kids on a carnival ride as we made our way across a field of hardened lava. It was the very first leg of our journey onto the volcano. Our driver was a frail man with a hearing aid and a long braid of white hair. His name was Olympus Israel, and he used to be a neighbor of Jack's back before the lava came and took his house. Today he had agreed to take us as far as his truck would go.

As Jack and Olympus chatted in the front seat, swapping opinions on the latest lava flows, Don and I sat in back and gaped at the landscape. All around us the lava had hardened in wild, surging patterns. In some places it was draped in folds like a wet blanket; in others, it formed long doodles, as if squeezed from a giant tube of toothpaste; and still elsewhere it cast one dome after another, unfolding like the rooftops of some Byzantine city. The rocks were a lustrous black, and they shone with a metallic gleam in the morning sun. None of this hardened lava seemed even remotely hot, which meant we still had a very long way to go.

We were driving along a makeshift access road that cut its way through the rippling rock flows around us. I later learned that the road was made with a lone bulldozer, which used its front blade to break apart the brittle rocks and then clear the way. The project was financed by the Royal Gardens' Community Association. Despite the fact that most of Royal Gardens no longer existed—and that its official population was down to approximately one—the association still collected dues. The thinking was that someday the volcano would stop erupting and people would return home, even if home was just a pile of black rocks. In the meantime, the association occasionally used the dues to rebulldoze the road when it disappeared. The disappearances occurred when a tube burst and the surface was flooded with molten lava. Apparently this was happening a lot lately. Several miles of road were lost within the last three months alone.*

Roughly twenty minutes later our truck rolled to a halt. Several meters ahead of us, the road tapered into a much rougher stretch of rocks that appeared to be still smoldering. All around us the horizon line was warped by massive heat waves shimmying off the rocks. Ahead of us was a sprawling flatland, roughly two miles wide and ten miles long. To the right of these flats were the first slopes of Kilauea, rising up toward Jack's house and to the Pu'u 'O'o vent beyond; to the left was the Pacific Ocean, deeply blue and rippled, stretching southward all the way to Antarctica. Along the coastline I could see a massive mushroom cloud of steam where the molten lava was pouring into the ocean and boiling the water. Off to the side of us I now noticed a wooden sign posted by the park services. It stood precariously close to the active lava, and I had to assume it wouldn't be around long. It read:

---

* I eventually contacted Robert Stearns, vice president of the Royal Gardens' Community Association. Stearns told me that as of 2002, the association was no longer maintaining the access road or even collecting dues. "The situation is just too grim," he told me. "People don't want to put money into a place that's just going to be covered by lava anyway."

# DANGER

- AVOID FUMES: Lava entering the ocean creates a toxic cloud that contains hydrochloric acid, superheated steam, and volcanic glass.
- Do not approach areas where lava enters the ocean. . . . Steam explosions hurl hot lava rocks inland.
- Be aware of getting trapped by lava. Never enter areas where molten lava may cut off an escape route. Keep a safe distance from fresh lava, which is about 2000°.

Rather uneasily, I thumbed through my copy of the Hawaii *Moon Handbook*, which is generally considered one of the best references

*Jack Thompson pauses for a breather as he crosses the miles of lava that surround his house. For the most part, the volcanic crust here is stable, but there is always the possibility of taking a bad step and falling downward into an active lava tube.*

on the island. The author, Robert Nilsen, included a brief passage on the area we were about to enter. In addition to listing many of the same risks that the park services' sign mentioned, he also had this to say: "For those of you who are still intrigued, realize that you are standing on the most unstable piece of real estate on the face of the earth. For those maniacs, fools, adventurers, and thrill-seekers who just can't stay away, give yourself up for dead and proceed."[5]

Jack stepped out of the driver's seat and raised his eyebrows. "Ready?" he asked. Moments later the wind shifted and we were hit with a gust of hot dry air, the sort that blasts out of the oven when you open the door to check on dinner. I nodded my head vaguely.

"If you have to evacuate you can stay at my place, and pitch some tents in the back yard," said Olympus with a shrug. "But don't worry," he added. "I think this one is going to miss you."

"Me, worry?" said Jack, with a slight chuckle. In the days to come I would recognize this as Jack's lava-laugh. Whenever things got a bit touchy on the volcano, I came to expect this dry laughter and the cathartic effect that it seemed to have on all of us.

We set out along the sprawling flatlands, packs strapped to our backs and brittle lava rock crunching underfoot. I could soon feel the rocks heating up beneath me, warming my feet, softening the worn-out soles of my running sneakers until it seemed that I would soon be barefoot. A short while later, the ground began to split along a series of small crevices, through which we could see a bright red glow. We were now treading across an active flow. The rocks beneath us were just a thin crust, floating atop a large river of molten lava. Jack paused for a moment to admire a crevice with me. "My neighbors used to cook potatoes in cracks like those," he told me. "It's a nice little oven." Gingerly, we stepped our way across a lattice-work of these crevices. I couldn't help but remember doing the same thing as a child, tiptoeing across the splintered sidewalk in front of our house, joking about not falling into a sea of make-believe lava. As I recalled, the game usually ended with my tumbling head over foot into an imaginary cauldron of fiery red. "Remember now," said Jack, perhaps sensing my uncertainty. "Falling is not an option."

Any passage across the flats poses a number of dangers. For the most part, the surface crust is relatively stable, but there is always the possibility of taking a bad step and falling downward into an active lava tube. A far more common problem, however, is the arrival of rain. When raindrops hit hot lava, they produce steam, which can create instant whiteout conditions. Later in my stay I would see a heavy rain roll in off the Pacific, causing most of the flats to disappear in a giant steam cloud. Other concerns on the flats include the mini-cyclones or dust devils that occasionally sweep through. These swirling air movements pick up not just dust but copious chards of volcanic glass as well. Jack witnessed a dust devil of this sort just once, and luckily it never got close enough to spray him with any volcanic shrapnel. In all likelihood, Jack Thompson had seen just about every danger the flats have to offer. Yet the greatest danger of all was still in the making. Eventually the flats themselves—which are forever extending further seaward as new lava accumulates—will simply extend too far and break off into the Pacific Ocean. This would most likely trigger a tsunami, which would blitz across the Pacific Ocean at the speed of a jumbo jet. "We're hoping that doesn't happen any time soon," explained Jack.

We continued hiking along a stretch of smoldering rocks until we came to our first stream of lava. The lava was oozing from a gash in the rocks and beginning to snake toward us, inch by inch, at a slow pace. Luckily, it was a newly hatched flow, and it wasn't big enough to cut us off or pose any real dangers. We set our packs down and played with it a little, tossing in pennies and watching them shrivel and squirm into blackened rivulets.

"I'd usually ride my motorcycle right over a flow like this," Jack told us. "The tires move so quickly they won't burn or anything."

"You ride your bike over *lava like this?*" I asked incredulously.

"Sure," replied Jack. "And I've ridden over much worse. That's how I get my supplies into the kipuka. What, did you think I took a chopper?"

"What if your bike gets stuck in the lava?" asked Don.

"Once it did," said Jack. "My back wheel broke through the crust and sunk into the red. Just as I feel that tire sink in, the engine stalls. So I just hit the starter, the engine comes back on, and I was out of there."

"What if the starter hadn't worked?" I asked.

"Well," said Jack. "I probably would have set the bike down and run like hell, just in case it blew up or something."

"So when you get home, you just pour water on your tires to cool them off?" I asked.

"That's a new one," said Jack. "Who told you that?"

"My helicopter pilot," I explained. "He gave a whole monologue on you as we passed over your house."

"Really?" said Jack.

As it turns out, most of what the pilot had told me was bunk—including his opening story on Jack's first encounter with lava. According to my pilot, Jack was hammering the last nail into his roof when the lava first appeared on the horizon in 1983. In truth, Jack was urinating when he first saw the eruption—he had woken up early to relieve himself. "Guess you heard the romanticized version," said Jack.

For the most part, Jack didn't seem to mind the many myths and half-truths that circulated about him. Yet nothing irked him more than being compared to Harry R. Truman, another highly mythologized volcano dweller. Truman was a hard-nosed, craggy-faced eighty-four-year-old man who defied the authorities and kept his home on Mount St. Helens until the volcano blew in 1980, burying him beneath three hundred feet of rubble. "Truman didn't think the volcano would hurt him," Jack told me as we continued our hike. "He was out of touch—he took the science and the danger of it too lightly—and that was what killed him."

⚡

We knew we were getting close to Jack's kipuka when we came upon our first tree hole, which was basically a deep round shaft that had formed in the hardened lava. At one time, a tree trunk inhabited this space, then a flow of molten lava rolled in, cooled itself off, and hardened around its base. The tree itself didn't last long. It quickly burst into flames and burned down to nothing, leaving just an empty cavity in its place. This particular tree hole went down roughly two yards to the earth below. Here there was actual soil, and from its fertile base, a new tree was now growing upward.

The next tree hole we encountered was only knee deep, and the one after that was shallower yet. Slowly the lava was thinning out, and before long it receded completely into a field of grass. After treading across several miles of smoldering lava, we had finally reached the edge of Jack's kipuka.

In front of us, almost out of nowhere, a road emerged and sloped its way upward into an expanse of dense, tropical vegetation. Its pavement quickly narrowed to the width of a bike path. Years of abandonment had allowed weeds and shrubbery to cover much of the pavement. Off to the side, in the thick roadside grass, were two rusty traces of civilization: a faded street sign and the corroded wreck of a car.

We set our packs down on what was once probably a busy suburban intersection, and Jack quickly slipped off into the woods. Moments later he returned with two coconuts. Together we hacked open their thick shells, then passed them around like flasks, sipping the cool watery milk inside. For a second course, Jack rustled up an armful of wild guavas. "Eat up," said Jack encouragingly. "There are plenty more." When we'd eaten all the wild fruit that we could stomach, we hoisted on our packs and continued along this road. It climbed steeply in an almost vertical, San Francisco fashion, cresting the bluff above us and disappearing into the depths of the kipuka.

Jack's kipuka was even larger than I had imagined. It sprawled for some six hundred acres and was lined with almost thirteen miles of road. Through the extremely dense roadside vegetation it was still possible to see the crumbling remains of Royal Gardens. Often, not much was left—a cement foundation, a broken-down doorway, and perhaps a few steps—all shrouded in a frenzy of dark jungle vines.

*An overgrown intersection near Jack's house, where a sun-bleached road sign still stands—a last relic of the Royal Gardens subdivision, which has been cut off by lava since the late 1980s.*

Now and then the façade of a dank corroding house showed itself, revealing a darkened window or two. They were the sort of gaping sockets that invited the imagination to play tricks, and perhaps flicker for an instant with the image of a face that once belonged. It was no wonder that Jack nurtured so many apocalyptic fantasies, for he was living amid a landscape of ruins, in a spooky cobwebbed world that still seemed to be reeling from some Armageddon. As if on cue, we soon encountered a wild boar trotting across the road in front of us. Apparently the kipuka's fragile ecosystem was overrun with these animals. Together with the rats, they had the run of the place.

The absence of other people in Royal Gardens did not seem to depress Jack in the least. His take was that the lava had "cleaned up the neighborhood." Apparently Royal Gardens was once filled with squatters—nomadic surfers living in little sheds nestled back in the woods. Jack didn't mind them at first, but they quickly proved to be terrible neighbors who blasted their music at night and left their garbage everywhere. Jack recalled how the squatters directly behind him treated their pets: "Their dog had puppies and they let them wander back into the woods behind my house, where they yapped and yapped while a mongoose ate them alive."

As I would later learn, Royal Gardens had never been a particularly well planned or managed development. Technically it was a subdivision, a cross between suburbia and the frontier, a vast tract of mountainside that was divided into one-acre parcels and bisected with a handful of paved roads. There were no power lines, water mains, or public sewers, but the price for a lot (as low as a hundred dollars cash down in the 1960s) couldn't be beat. According to George Cooper and Gavan Daws, who wrote a detailed history of Royal Gardens in their book *Land and Power in Hawaii,* the subdivision's developers advertised far and wide. In brochures and in promotional videos they billed Royal Gardens as a suburban paradise. In

1961, one plot was even given away as a prize on ABC's hit TV show *Queen for a Day*. Most of the lots in the subdivision were sold sight unseen, and ultimately the subdivision's building codes—which forbid temporary structures, dirt driveways, or the use of second-hand lumber—were ignored. Some areas looked like shantytowns, Jack told me. The other major problem with Royal Gardens was its location. One promotional brochure touted the subdivision as being located "directly adjacent to Hawaii Volcano National Park with its spectacular attractions," but as Cooper and Daws point out, one of these spectacular attractions was an active volcano.[6]

We continued walking upward through the heart of the kipuka until we came to Plumeria, the street on which Jack lived. We turned onto Plumeria, but almost immediately it was cut off by a massive finger of hardened lava, roughly fifty yards across. This was the "Warrior Flow," a monumental vein of lava that had infiltrated the kipuka a decade ago. Apparently, it was just one of Jack's many close calls. "The lava has been within a block of my house four or five times," Jack told us as we paused to catch our breath. "I just hope it's not coming again."

We hiked across the Warrior Flow and continued along the other side of Plumeria. Right away, however, I noticed something peculiar about the street. Its pavement was sleek, and its shoulders were carefully trimmed. Someone had been maintaining the road. Then, at the far end of the block, I saw a modern two-story house with an unmistakable bright red roof.

The front end of the house was propped up on stilts, allowing it to soar off the hillside and offer a commanding view—down the mountain, across the flats, and far out over the Pacific Ocean. A wooden deck wrapped around the house on all sides, and the front section was furnished with a dining area and a swinging loveseat. The best view, however, appeared to be from the second floor; this was Jack's

room, a small crow's nest with windows on all sides. Beneath the house were two Machu Picchu–style stone terraces, each overflowing with yellow orchids. A small gravel path led the way upward, along the edge of a palm tree–lined garden and over to a narrow set of steps that ascended to the front deck.

As the three of us strolled down the remainder of the street, Jack explained that the house practically took care of itself. The roof was outfitted with solar panels, which provided him with all the electricity he needed. His drinking water was gathered by a "catch system," which drained rainwater from his upper roof into a large, elevated basin beside his house. This water was filtered and then channeled downward into the house's pipes. Water was always on tap, and, as I would soon learn, even the shower pressure was good.

Food was just as plentiful, Jack explained, as he took us behind the house to visit his two-tiered garden. The upper tier was lined with palm trees and giant red hibiscus flowers, but the real stunner was the lower tier, which Jack referred to as his "Hobbit Land Garden." A secret wooded path led down into a miniature valley buttressed by a number of sturdy mountain rocks and concealed overhead by a canopy of trees. The entrance path was booby trapped with a number of "pig snares," which kept the fruit safe from the hoards of roaming pigs. The fruits were plentiful, including papayas, bananas, poha berries, and ava (a cure-all herbal medicine, according to Jack). The walls of the Hobbit Land Garden were lined with thumbilina vines, which grew delicate white flowers known to glow radiantly in the light of a full moon.

Together with the upper tier, Jack's garden grew an astounding range of produce, including four different types of avocados, seven different types of mangos, an abundance of cherries, bread fruit, mandarin oranges, tangerines, Key limes, star fruit, white pineapples (some as big as twelve pounds), string beans, tomatoes, zucchinis, and occasionally eggplants. To spice things up, he also had a steady crop of black pepper, cilantro, and basil.

As Jack gave us the quick tour around his garden, he identified various flowers, offered samples of fruit from each tree, and promised to make fresh guacamole for dinner.

"This place is beautiful," I told him at one point.

Jack nodded his head in agreement. "And I know it's beautiful out there too," he said, gesturing back toward the direction from which we came. "I can just appreciate it more in here."

❧

After touring the garden, we climbed the front steps up to Jack's house and sat for a moment on his deck, taking in the sweeping views of the Pacific. Yet our attention soon shifted to some thin wisps of black smoke rising in the distance. "Shit," said Jack. "Looks like some trees are on fire."

"How close?" asked Don.

"Don't know," replied Jack, "but it looks like it's somewhere in the kipuka."

Earlier in the day Jack had expressed his concerns that lava was on the verge of infiltrating the kipuka once again. Jack's house was positioned on the western edge of the kipuka, roughly a quarter of a mile from where the trees stopped and lava began to flow. The lava here was no small trickle. As Jack explained, it was one of the main channels flowing directly downward from the Pu'u 'O'o vent. Here, at this most important juncture between jungle and fire, stood Jack's saving grace: a massive rock wall that stretched all the way down the mountainside, keeping the lava at bay. This wall formed in the mid-1980s when a large finger of lava worked its way down the mountainside, grazing the side of the kipuka. Much like a rivulet of wax running down the side of a candle, this rivulet hardened and left a decisive trail—only it was made of solid stone and stood at least twenty feet high. The other factor working in Jack's favor was that the ground on the far side of the wall was sunken, creating a kind of chute that guided the lava downward. Crucial as these natural fortifications were, Jack hardly ever saw them because the trees around his house were too thick and too high. Consequently, if and when his protective wall was ever breached, Jack would know only because of indirect warning signs, much like the black smoke that was currently billowing in the distance.

"Do your hear that?" Jack asked. As the three of us stood in silence, we began to hear a faint popping noise in the distance. Gradually the popping got louder, and after two or three minutes we heard the sound of several small explosions. "Definitely trees on fire," said Jack. "Those are methane explosions."

The floor of the jungle is actually filled with pockets of methane gas, which are created by tree roots. When these pockets explode it's a sure sign that trees are burning. I gave Don a mild look of concern, but he just nodded his head as if everything were normal, as if this is the way his volcano vacations always began.

Moments later, as we were entering the house, Jack discovered a small note tucked into the front door. The note was scrawled hastily across the face of a business card from a local helicopter pilot named Richard Gruno. It read: "Jack, stopped by to talk to you about lava. Call me, Richard."

Jack shook his head, chuckled, and then pondered aloud, "Why didn't he just say, 'Run like hell'?"

The inside of Jack's house centered around his living room, a large, airy space with vaulted cathedral ceilings and an abundance of windows looking out in all directions. The room was furnished with several couches, a hand-woven rug emblazoned with the Hawaii state emblem, and a television set that no longer received much of a signal from its vine-entangled satellite dish. Off the living room were two guest bedrooms, a bathroom, and a modern kitchen (furnished with a refrigerator that Jack left unplugged and used as a giant Tupperware container). At the far end of the living room was a narrow stairway leading to the crow's nest above, where Jack's bedroom was located. The entire place was immaculately clean, with every last item placed just so, as if arranged for a photo shoot.

"The place looks great," said Don. In the background the methane explosions were still very much audible.

"Thanks," said Jack. "What I'd really like to do is put on a new roof, but with the lava just over there, I can't really justify doing that right now." In the coming days Jack named a number of home improvement projects that were currently on hold until the situation with the lava improved. "Otherwise," he explained, "I'm just rearranging the deck chairs on the *Titanic*."

As we settled down and unpacked our bags, I asked Jack if his house had sustained any serious damage since the eruption began in 1983. "You know," he replied, "it was actually an earthquake that got me the worst." Jack went on to explain that one morning, several years ago, he was working in his garden when a ten-foot "land wave" rolled down the mountain, through the woods, and across his back yard.* It popped his house up in the air like a toy, he recalled, and plunked it down on the roof of his Toyota. This was a good thing, in-

---

* In addition to spewing lava, volcanoes are often known to cause earthquakes, which commonly roll down the mountain like giant waves. These quakes are triggered as magma fills the chambers beneath the volcano. As the volcano swells, the strain on the chamber walls can create many small "volcanic earthquakes." Hawaii experiences thousands of these each year. For the most part they are quite small and harmless, though occasionally they can grow to significant size.

sisted Jack. If it weren't for the Toyota, which was quickly crushed under the front end of the house, the whole structure might have hit the ground much harder or simply toppled forward down the hill.

In the weeks after the quake Jack lived in a veritable funhouse, with the floors slanting at wild angles and the staircase running nearly flat. In order to sleep properly, Jack recalled, he placed wooden blocks under his bed to stop himself from rolling onto the floor. Eventually he went to Western Auto, bought two twenty-ton hydraulic jacks, and proceeded to crank his house back up to its proper height. The only problem was that he applied too much pressure on one small point, creating such torque that the window above him started to crack. Eventually Jack decided to crank his house upward very slowly, two inches at a time, along forty different posts. When his house was at its proper height once again, Jack set to work on his Toyota. He used a sledgehammer to pound the roof back into shape, got back into his car, and started the engine. "It still drove quite well," Jack recalled.

Later in the afternoon, as Jack and I ventured into his garden to pick avocados for dinner, I asked him about the current situation with the lava. "The lava is always on my mind," he said as we both eyed the black smoke in the distance, "but I can't jump out of my skin every time I get a warning."

In Jack's two decades on the volcano he had received dozens of warnings like Richard Gruno's, he explained. They came from the police, the civil defense, his former neighbors, helicopter pilots, and countless others. He didn't ignore these tips or doubt their veracity. Somewhere in the back of his head he took note, put himself on alert, and in his own quiet way readied himself to walk away from it all. If and when the time came, there would be no need to run, explained Jack, because new lava creeps through the jungle very slowly.

"But isn't the lava closer now than it has been in ten years?" I asked.

"No," replied Jack. "The lava is closer now than it has been in about twelve years."

"So doesn't that make you nervous?"

"Sure it does," said Jack. "But that's just part of the deal here. And besides, I can deal with Mother Nature. It's people I can't handle, especially mean people who want to take advantage of you. Dealing with the volcano, she lets you know she's there, but she isn't malicious like some of the bosses I've had. The volcano is just nature stirring—it is not somebody that is deliberately abusing you or deriving some perverse pleasure from it. You know what I mean?"

Actually, Jack's preference for isolation made me think of the other home-keepers I'd met—like Thad Knight, who preferred the company of "bygones" in the Princeville cemetery, and Babs Reynolds, who opted for the solitude of a gated mountain hideaway. The drawbacks to all of these places were obvious, perhaps even overwhelming, but the payoff was the absence of society and all of its hassles. Nobody wanted to live on an erupting volcano, and this (among other things) made it the perfect place for Jack. Of course, there were undeniable downsides to his arrangement, but Jack had come to terms with them. As he put it: "For me, the lava is just the price of paradise."

Together, Jack and I picked almost a dozen perfect jade-green avocados. We then returned to the kitchen, where Jack proceeded to mash them up and mix in tomatoes, onions, and lime juice. Around twilight we all sat down for dinner on the front porch. Don grilled a chicken that he'd carried in, Jack presented his guacamole, and I uncorked a bottle of red wine that I had schlepped across the lava. As night rolled in from the east and the last hues of orange and violet sank into the sea, darkness arrived and the lava began to gleam. Beneath us on the flats, all the cracks and crevices, all the trickles and streams, every last trace of lava that had barely been discernable in the glare of the noonday sun, now exuded a deep, fiery glow. A vast network of flickering veins stretched across the flats for miles, as if the earth itself were coming apart at the seams. Occasionally, one of these veins overflowed, and within minutes a small pond of lava accumulated. These outbreaks were especially beautiful, and we took turns admiring them with Jack's binoculars.

"You'll never meet another guy like Lava Jack," said Don after a while. "My wife thinks he's crazy. 'Why in God's name is he out there?' she asks me. Any other place I go, she wants to go with me. 'Why can't I come?' she says. But not here. She won't come here."

Throughout the day Jack had quipped that Don came to the volcano to take a "mind shit"—to clear his head of all his worldly troubles. This was Don's third vacation on the volcano, and once again he seemed to be enjoying himself. "It is such a fantastic show," concluded Don. "When this thing is all lit up and the lava is flowing, you just can't experience that anywhere else."

"Yeah," said Jack finally. "I feel kind of privileged that I've been able to witness this."

After dinner, Jack turned off all the lights and appliances in order to conserve electricity. We bussed our dishes and then returned to the darkened comfort of the front deck to continue our volcano gazing. Far off in the distance, we could still hear the methane explosions, and off to the side of the house, above the curtain of trees, the sky was now glowing red.

⚡

The following morning I awoke to a chorus of songbirds, which sounded much better than the methane explosions I had fallen asleep to. It was seven A.M. and Jack was already up. When he saw me stirring, he brewed us a pot of coffee and poured it into two large mugs. We carried our mugs onto the front deck, leaned up against the wooden rail, and listened sleepily to the buzz and hum of the jungle.

"When I first moved up here I thought my ears were ringing," said Jack. "Then I realized it was just the sound of the insects." Over the years Jack had grown accustomed to these sounds and the deep, familiar solitude that they invited. "People rarely spend an hour alone—I've spent years alone," he told me. "When you're by yourself, it's just your own movie spinning through your head. You're dealing with your own problems. Once I nearly forgot how to talk. I opened my mouth and just a bunch of babble came out." Jack smiled as he took another sip of his coffee. He seemed quite content, and it was almost impossible to believe that this was the same man I'd met just the day before.

For breakfast Jack prepared some delicious french toast and another round of coffee. By then Don was awake, and the three of us sat together in the kitchen, chatting and eating. "It's kind of nice having people up here," said Jack as chewed his eggy bread and stared dreamily out the window toward the Pacific Ocean.

"Sure," said Don, "but we don't want to get in the way of you doing whatever it is that you do up here."

"This *is* what I do up here," replied Jack as he continued to stare at the Pacific.

For the next several days our mornings began exactly in this manner—a cup of coffee on the deck, a leisurely breakfast of french toast in the kitchen, and then a few good hours of reading, walking, or simply staring out over the lava and into the sea. At one point, several days into our visit, Don asked what the date was. It took the three of us a minute or so to come up with an answer. Afterward, I asked Jack if the days often blend together on the volcano.

"The days? Hell, the months blend together," he replied. "Sometimes I don't know what month it is. I open the calendar and I don't know where to look." This was a good thing, according to Jack, for he'd already wasted too much of life being a slave to the clock.

Over the course of my stay, Jack recalled a number of his less-than-memorable job experiences. As a boy he had worked at a chinchilla farm, cleaning up sawdust in one musty cage after the next. The females would sometimes stand on their hind legs and fire out a spray of urine. "And they were deadly accurate," added Jack. When he was still living in Bakersfield, he became a sheet metal apprentice, where he worked in a poorly ventilated attic that cooked him in 125-degree heat. After coming to Hawaii, things didn't improve much when he took a job working on the air-conditioning system at Hilo International Airport. "I had dirt on me from all over the world," he remembered. Perhaps his worst job of all was working under the pier in Hilo, reinforcing its underside with gunite, a concrete mixture that is pumped through a hose and sprayed from a special gun. Jack worked all day in the dark, firing out tons and tons of gunite from the discomfort of a small raft. At the end of his shift he emerged with hardened concrete strewn across his cheeks and hair, as if his weary looks were forever to be etched in stone.

In 1998, Jack finally devised a way to end his occupational drudgery: He would open a bed and breakfast. Initially, the idea made perfect sense: Jack was a homebody living in an incredible natural setting who wanted to make some extra cash without having to leave the kipuka. However, a few problems soon cropped up. To begin with, as John Pillsbury explained to me, most people were scared of volcanoes. But even if Pillsbury had managed to lure in a great many guests, there was the added problem that Jack was—by his own admission—not a people person. He was ill at ease with strangers, let alone strangers living in his house. What's more, Jack loathed self-promotion. As I would find out months later, when the TV crew from *Living on the Edge* finally visited, Jack didn't plug his B&B, he refused to do anything too stagy, and he didn't really encourage the crew to stay for the night (when the lava is at its best). All in all, this did not make for good business. Since the grand opening, Jack's B&B had hosted a few memorable guests, including William Shatner and a high-level Russian dignitary, but nothing resembling a steady flow of customers. Of course, Jack was disappointed by this, but I also got the sense that he was somewhat relieved.

When it came to paying the bills, Jack didn't seem overly worried. He had no mortgage, utility bills, or homeowner's insurance.* His property taxes were negligible. Shortly after the lava cut him off, his house was appraised at two hundred dollars, dropping his yearly taxes to a very affordable twenty-five dollars a year. In general, Jack was extremely frugal, and with the help of his garden and an occasional guest he felt confident that he could last until Social Security kicked in. In the meantime, his only remaining connection to the financial world was a lone savings account, which he drew on as infrequently as possible.

According to Jack, the more time that he spent on the volcano, the better he felt about his decision to live there full-time. As his memories of the workplace drifted away, so did many of his daily complaints. "It took me a year after working to learn to digest properly and enjoy a meal," he explained. Now he claimed that everything tasted better. Jack was very keen on the "fresh twang" of his own tap water, which he called the "champagne of drinking water," fresh from the clouds above. Occasionally, he powered up the icebox and cooled off a glass for himself. "I like to get it teeth-hurtingly cold," he told me.

Besides eating better, Jack had also learned to rest properly. Before retiring to the volcano, he rarely slept well. "I was constantly thinking of work," he explained. "I would wake up in the middle of the night, my eyes would slam wide open, and I would think: Shit, did I tighten that valve or fix that wire?" Nowadays, despite his room being occa-

---

* Jack's insurance company refused to renew his policy shortly after the eruption in 1983.

sionally illuminated by the demonic red glow of the volcano, he claimed to sleep better.

Much of Jack's day was now spent in the garden—watering the plants, pruning the trees, and picking the fruit. When he wasn't gardening, he was reading, or listening to the radio, or keeping an eye on the lava. He had only one real obligation: Once a day, at six-thirty A.M., he telephoned the helicopter company to give them a lava/weather report. These were the staples of his life, though he was quick to admit, "The whole thing is a big experiment."

Jack's use of the word "experiment" made me think of another famous American hermit who also referred to his life as an experiment—Henry David Thoreau. In 1845, Thoreau took to the woods and built a crude hut along the edge of Walden Pond in Concord, Massachusetts. "I would rather sit on a pumpkin and have it all to myself than be crowded on a velvet cushion," Thoreau wrote in *Walden*. He found his new life of isolation to be quite pleasing. "I have, as it were, my own sun and moon and stars, and a little world all to myself," he wrote. Thoreau soon came to enjoy the silence, broken only by the sound of the birds—"those thrilling songsters of the forest which never, or rarely, serenade a villager." His days soon blended together, no longer "minced into hours and fretted by the ticking of the clock."[7]

Jack seemed to share Thoreau's rugged individualism, his self-reliance, his pride of home, his respect for nature, and his desire to be free from both government and society. In truth, so did Thad and Babs. Yet, perhaps needless to say, all of their situations were far more precarious and challenging than Thoreau's. For them, the personal freedom of isolation came at a cost. This was particularly true with Jack. On any given day the lava stood to devour everything that he had built, and, on some very fundamental level, this had to undermine his peace of mind.

Despite all of his nonchalance, Jack did show signs of stress. In our first few days on the volcano, we were plagued by helicopters sweeping directly over his house. In addition to causing a terrible racket, these flybys were a sure sign that the lava was near. In the weeks leading up to my arrival, Jack's house had become a main attraction for the many tourists constantly hovering overhead. At one point, Jack's favorite radio station even announced that the lava was getting dangerously close to the "house with the red roof."

Finally, on our third day on the volcano, Jack took me on a lava-scouting mission. We hopped on his Kawasaki motorcycle and set out for the uppermost point on the kipuka. It was a harrowing ride. We sped along several overgrown roads, ducking under tree branches, dodging shrubs, blowing through old stop signs, and watching for pigs that occasionally lurched out of the jungle. We continued upward until the road disappeared into a mound of volcanic rock. Jack parked his bike and the two of us climbed over the rocks for ten minutes until we had a pretty good view of the kipuka below. We could see several places where smoke was billowing, but with the wind and the uneven terrain, it was almost impossible to determine its origin. Eventually, after another hour of unsuccessful scouting, we returned to Jack's house, where we sat on his front deck, ate lunch, and watched the helicopters overhead. By this point, the constant clatter of the mechanical blades was getting to all of us.

"Man," said Jack finally. "It's like I'm living at a damn airport."

⚡

After four days on the volcano it was time for Don to leave. He was scheduled to meet his wife on the island of Molokai, roughly 150 miles to the northwest. Jack agreed to walk his friend back to civilization, but first we all spent one last morning hanging out.

In the preceding days, Don had talked at length about how much he enjoyed visiting the volcano. He was taken with the lava, particularly the "magical" views that it created each and every night. Yet Don was also interested in the verdant undergrowth and animal life of the kipuka. Don's job, as a "vegetation/pest management consultant," made him well situated to consider many of Jack's predicaments. Periodically the two of them discussed road maintenance, the overpopulation of pigs, and the cultivation of various garden plants. Above all, however, Don was impressed with the life that Jack had created—a life that seemed to be devoid of "real-world worries."

"I want this life," Don said at one point.

"You can have it," replied Jack. "You just have to give up everything you've got."

"I know," said Don, "and there are really just a few things holding me back—like seeing my kids through college, and being there to help my mother."

Jack continued to encourage his friend to act on his impulses, but cautioned that it would come at a sacrifice. To his credit, Jack was always very realistic about both the advantages and disadvantages of his life. "Sometimes I have to wonder whether I am blessed or cursed," he remarked at one point.

On that final morning together, the subject of Don's appreciation for life on the kipuka came up once more. "So why not buy a house in here?" asked Jack finally. "It wouldn't cost much, and we could be neighbors."

"Yeah," said Don, very quietly, as if to himself. He smiled and then looked away. There was nothing more to say. At least for the time being, this was not a valid option. Unlike Jack, he had obligations to keep—kids, a job, a wife, an aging mother—a life on the outside. After a long and somewhat awkward pause in which nothing was said, I finally glanced back at Jack and noticed a rather curious look on his face. I struggled for a moment to place it, and then I knew: It was pity. "I don't know how he does it," Jack told me later. "I really don't."

⚡

As Don was preparing to leave, I asked Jack if he minded my sticking around for a few more days. I felt as if I was just getting into life on the volcano, and besides, I wanted to see how things developed with the lava. I was a bit uneasy about infringing on Jack's privacy, but when I finally summoned the nerve to broach the subject, Jack didn't bat an eye. "Sure," he said, "you're welcome to stay for a while longer." So while Jack escorted Don back across the flats, I stayed on the kipuka.

After Jack's return, with just two of us in the house, life grew decidedly quieter and I began to get a better sense of Jack's daily routine — the early-morning radio dispatches to the helicopter company, the midday hours of reading biographies and other nonfiction, the afternoons spent working in the garden or mowing the grass, the dinners on the front deck, and the evenings of watching the lava and listening to blues songs like "Nagging Woman," "A Hard Night on the Planet," and "I'm Going to Kill My Buddy."

One evening, as we sat on the porch, the subject of Jack's ex-girlfriend came up. Her name was Patty and she had lived with Jack for almost ten years. Initially the volcano wasn't a problem in their relationship, insisted Jack. Both of them enjoyed the isolation that it created. "Patty used to spend hours on her shortwave radio, talking to people in Australia and Brazil," he recalled. "And we also worked on things together, like growing coffee beans and sending them out as Christmas presents." Yet according to Jack, the isolation ultimately made Patty unhappy. "She missed being able to visit her friends, or the beach, or the local store," he explained. "She wasn't enjoying herself anymore, and I can't blame her."

"When exactly did she leave?" I asked.

"In 1991, shortly after the earthquake," said Jack. "That whole earthquake episode was really hard on her. She felt like her home was violated. It was never the same for us after that." Jack paused to look out at the lava, which was forming a sizable pool on the flats below. "But what can I do?" he asked finally. "It's all a tradeoff, and I chose to live up here."

"Was it hard after she left?"

"Sure," said Jack. "She left her shortwave radio here and I had to put the thing away in the desk drawer. Suddenly she was gone. A woman's touch was just gone. Yeah, the first few months were pretty hard to take."

"Do you ever think about calling her?" I asked.

"No," he said quietly. "Not anymore."

"What about you?" asked Jack. "Do you have a girlfriend back in Boston?"

"Yes," I told him.

"That's good," he replied. "Living alone can get tiresome."

⚡

I spent another three or four days on the volcano with Jack. Peaceful though much of this time was, the sounds of helicopters and methane explosions were pretty constant. Periodically we experienced a few hours of complete quiet, but without fail the clamor eventually resumed. "It hasn't been like this in years," Jack told me. "All the red flags are starting to go up."

By my last evening, things had really heated up. As the methane explosions grew louder and louder, Jack and I discussed whether they sounded more like propane tanks exploding or howitzers going off. By late evening we were both pining for a little white noise—anything to get our minds off the explosions. We flicked on the radio and tuned in to Art Bell, a late-night talk show host who covers a range of paranormal subjects ranging from vampire monkeys to UFOs. To my surprise, I found the show immensely comforting, and I was lulled to sleep with the rather cozy feeling that the entire world was as spooky as Jack's lava-side B&B.

Around midnight Jack woke me. "Listen," he said in a dramatic whisper. I heard nothing for a moment, and then a loud explosion. "Come on," he said. "Check it out." Groggily, I followed him upstairs to his bedroom and pressed my face against the picture window that faced westward, toward the hidden wall of stone that kept the kipuka safe. Above the silhouettes of the treetops I could see a large, flickering red glow. Without question, a forest fire was blazing.

"Wouldn't it be something if this place went down after all these years?" said Jack. "I mean, I can't visualize it, but I realize it's a possibility." Jack shook his head. "This has been going on for eighteen years, and sometimes it's just fucking torture." There was another explosion. "At what point do you walk away from your life's dream?" asked Jack, as if to himself.

"If you had to leave tonight, what would you take?" I asked him.

"I'm not sure," he replied. "You can't exactly run away with the icebox." He grew silent, but eventually he came up with an answer. He'd grab the rug that he'd woven. It had taken him three years to weave, and he said he rather liked it. This sounded like a good choice, I told him. Then Jack looked over at me, bunched up his lips, and smiled. There was nothing sardonic about it. Just a sweet, rather sad smile—a rare offering of friendship on his part—and I returned it through the darkness.

"I guess if this place goes, a certain burden would be gone," Jack admitted finally.

"What would you do then?" I asked.

"I'm not sure," said Jack. "I haven't thought that far ahead."

*After bushwhacking through the jungle on a narrow pig trail, Jack leans on his machete and gazes out across the giant stone wall that steers the lava away from his house.*

The following morning I awoke at six-thirty to the sound of Jack calling the helicopter company on his telephone. "Hello from Royal Gardens," he said. "We're still here. We've got a few clouds but it looks like a nice day on the mountain."

After breakfast we decided to hike westward through the jungle toward the area that seemed to be on fire the night before. We set out on a well-trodden pig path, but it soon got so tight in places that we had to duck though narrow tunnels that were sheathed in vines and giant gauzy spider webs. Eventually, after some bushwhacking with a machete, we emerged from the jungle and came upon the giant stone rise that safeguarded the kipuka. It was roughly twenty feet tall and as solid as a seawall—though at this point, it gave me about as much confidence as the dike in Princeville.

Together, we scrambled up to the top and peered over. The stone rise descended into a small field of gravel about a hundred yards across. There, on the far side, we saw it: a river of lava oozing its way down the mountain. In the middle of this river was an island of trees, mostly burned but still crackling with flames. This is what we had heard the night before. The wall had not been breached. The kipuka was not on fire.

"I'll sleep a lot better tonight," Jack told me.

In the distance we could hear the clatter of helicopter blades, and moments later a tourist helicopter swooped down and began hovering just a few hundred feet overhead. Jack waved at the passengers happily. "Hey, I can see them waving back!" he said. Jack set down his machete and waved with both hands.

"I'm feeling really good," said Jack. "And everybody is having a good time, so no worries—right?"

Later that morning, when we made it back to the house, I began to get my things in order. When my bags were packed, Jack and I exchanged addresses. "Do me one favor," he said. "Sign my guest book." Jack then produced a slender bound volume with a number of written entries from the guests who had stayed at his B&B. Several of the entries belonged to Don, who signed in every time he visited. I grabbed a pen and wrote a few lines, thanking Jack once again for the incredible time that he had shown me.

An hour or so later, I left the kipuka on my own. Initially, I was reluctant to do this, but Jack insisted I could handle it. "You know how to walk across the lava now," he told me proudly. "Besides, this way you can come and visit me whenever you want."

Very cautiously I made my way across the several miles of semisolid ground that separated Jack from the outside world. Eventually I came upon two volcano-gazing honeymooners whose jaws dropped when they saw me emerge from the smoldering fields of lava. When I asked them if they might give me a lift back to Hilo, the couple exchanged nervous looks and reluctantly agreed.

Upon leaving the kipuka I felt something resembling withdrawal. This feeling was only compounded when I was soon stranded at Honolulu International Airport, waiting to be bumped onto a flight back to the mainland. As I tried to sleep on the airport's cheaply carpeted floors, receiving occasional visits from Gator and Agent 99, the airport's two beagle drug dogs, I thought of Jack's place. I already missed the long mornings spent on his deck, chatting and taking in the views; the lush green of the jungle; the blue sprawl of the Pacific; and the constant stirrings of the volcano. By comparison, the outside world seemed so thoroughly drab and uneventful, and now I understood why Don Bartel had such misgivings about returning to the "real world."

As I continued my wait at the airport, mingling with the crowds of newly arrived mainlanders—pale-skinned, adorned with leis, and utterly ecstatic to be in paradise—I thought again of Jack. Earlier in the day, as we said our goodbyes, I asked him if he was going to be all right. It was a stupid question, and we both laughed as soon as I asked it. "It was good having you," said Jack finally with a clap on the shoulder. And like two grown men with nothing in common, except perhaps an awkward feeling of mutual goodwill, we shook hands and parted ways.

# Canyon of the Firefighting Hillbillies
## Malibu, California

I'LL BE THE FIRST to admit, Malibu seems like an odd choice. What could be so dangerous in the land of movie stars, millionaires, and scantily clad hangers-on? The answer is simple: wildfires.

Malibu is situated on a rugged stretch of coastline so arid and combustible that it is known as the wildfire capital of North America. Roughly once every two and a half years, Malibu is hit with a blaze that wipes out a thousand acres or more, and at least once a decade things get wildly out of control, as miles of property and hundreds of homes are reduced to ash. Since 1970, these infernos have claimed more than a thousand luxury homes and caused more than $1 billion in property damage. And yet, as everybody knows, Malibu is not a ghost town. Far from it: Malibu's property values are higher than ever, and its beachfront palaces—some of which have burned down and been rebuilt several times—are more beautiful than ever.[1]

Malibu first appeared on my radar when a friend from college encouraged me to read a book called *Ecology of Fear* by Mike Davis. The book offers a detailed history of natural disasters in the Los Angeles area, including a feverish account of the wildfire that hit Malibu in 1993. According to Davis, during the height of the fire, Malibu was a "surreal borderland between carnival and catastrophe" in which celebrities such as Sean Penn and Ali MacGraw watched their homes burn as the sky above swarmed with television news helicopters. Traffic on the Pacific Coast Highway came to a standstill as incoming fire trucks encountered an onslaught of fleeing Bentleys, Porsches, and Jeep Cherokees. Meanwhile, two housewives from the Big Rock neighborhood loaded their dogs and jewels into kayaks and paddled out to sea, leaving their beachfront mansions and bewildered maids to face the flames. Davis observes, "The chaotic exodus was oddly equalizing: panicky movie stars, clutching their Oscars, mingled with frantic commoners."[2]

Not surprisingly, a common feature of the fires in Malibu is that almost everybody runs from them. Despite considerable research, I found almost no mention of any Malibu residents standing their ground. Both the *Malibu Times* and the *Los Angeles Times* highlighted only one such story from the 1993 fire—that of the British screenwriter Duncan Gibbins, who attempted to defend his house with a garden hose. It was an ill-fated stand. In a moment of panic, Gibbins scurried back to save his Siamese cat and ran into a wall of fire that charred 90 percent of his body. Paramedics later found him barely conscious, floating in his swimming pool. "I don't want to die," he kept repeating in a lung-scorched squeal, as smoke poured from his mouth. Gibbins, whose film credits seemed to foreshadow his demise—with titles like *Eve of Destruction, Fire with Fire,* and *Third Degree Burn*—died several days later in an area hospital.[3]

After reading about Gibbins's stand, I had to admit that fleeing seemed quite sensible. And yet, I also had to wonder: Didn't anyone know how to deal with these monster blazes? Surely there had to be someone who had a better grasp on the situation. In an attempt to find just such a person I called practically every major establishment in Malibu—City Hall, the Chamber of Commerce, the *Malibu*

*Times*, Pepperdine University. "I'm not sure who you're looking for," one receptionist told me. "Neither am I," I replied.

Then it happened. I got a call back from a woman named Nancy Steiner who worked as an administrator for the City of Malibu. I told her I was looking for a veteran of Malibu, an intrepid home-keeper, someone who knew something about fires. "How about old Millie Decker?" she asked me. "She's the last of the Malibu hillbillies."

"Hillbillies?"

"Yeah, the Deckers have been around for a *long* time." Nancy paused to flip through some papers. "I don't have Millie's number, but her daughter Bonnie works over at Malibu Seafood—why don't you call over there?"

Like so many great leads, this one was born out of pure coincidence. In the early 1990s, Nancy Steiner had also worked at Malibu Seafood, preparing salmon filets alongside Bonnie Decker. Bonnie was a stout, ruddy-faced woman who talked mainly of horses and knew a thing or two about dynamite. In Malibu, she was the type of coworker you didn't forget.

Later that afternoon, I made a call over to Malibu Seafood and got ahold of Bonnie Decker. It was a fast-paced conversation, conducted over a steady din of clinking plates and whirling cash registers, during which Bonnie mentioned that the Deckers had been in Malibu since the 1880s, raising cattle and horses. As far as Bonnie knew, no one in her family had ever left a house to burn.

"What does your family do when the fires come?" I asked her.

"Well," she replied, as if the answer were perfectly obvious, "we stay and fight."

⚡

My choice to visit Malibu next was ultimately seasonally driven. By the time I left Hawaii, made it back to Boston, and got my notes in order, August had arrived. In many ways, this is my favorite time of year. The initial thrill of summer is gone, the days seem to grow long and sleepy, the crickets find their way into the city parks, and on clear nights you can almost smell the promise of a New England fall. In southern California, however, August marks the early days of fire season. It's a dry, arid time when deadwood readies to burn. And as the last days of summer grew hotter and hotter, my thoughts inevitably drifted west toward Malibu and the Deckers.

What intrigued me most about the Deckers was Millie, who at the age of eighty-one was the family's most seasoned firefighter. "She's been dealing with wildfires ever since the Pacific Coast Highway was just a wagon trail," Bonnie had told me in a subsequent phone conversation. In fact, we chatted several times over the course of that

*At age eighty-one, Millie Decker can still lasso. Here Millie is trying to teach me how to rope cattle.*

summer, and the more I learned about the Deckers, the more curious I became. According to Bonnie, her mother was well known for
riding bulls as a girl and for jockeying racehorses professionally as a
young woman. "Mom is a real mountain woman," insisted Bonnie. "I
guess you'll just have to come out and meet her for yourself."

I arrived in California in mid-August, exactly as fire season was
heating up. By then, much of the West was already aglow with wildfires. More than three hundred separate blazes were ravaging parts of
California, Idaho, Washington, Oregon, and Nevada. In California,
they were limited to the north, where seven blazes had already
charred nearly 80,000 acres and forced the closure of a major stretch
of Interstate 80.[4] In southern California all was still quiet, but people
had to be getting nervous. My timing was good, in a terrible sort of
way. By now I was starting to imagine myself as a harbinger of natural disaster—a precursor to floods, snow, lava, and wildfires—a sort
of loosely affiliated member of the Four Horsemen, only without a
horse or even a return ticket.

As if the many blazes already raging weren't enough, the Santa
Ana winds were soon due. At the end of each summer, these so-
called Devil Winds come from the northeast, gusting low and hard
across the Mojave Desert, cresting the Santa Monica Mountains,
and then sweeping down the many coastal canyons that lead to the
sea. Their timing is erratic, but once they arrive there is no mistak-
ing them. You can feel their parched breath on your cheeks and in
your lungs. It's a hot, steady, skin-crackling gust of heat. The effect is
unnerving. The mystery writer Raymond Chandler opens his short
story "Red Wind" with a description of the sense of doom that these
winds bring:

> There was a desert wind blowing that night. It was one of those hot
> dry Santa Anas that come down through the mountain passes and

curl your hair and make your nerves jump and your skin itch. On nights like that every booze party ends in a fight. Meek little wives feel the edge of the carving knife and study their husbands' necks. Anything can happen.[5]

There may be truth in what Chandler writes. According to some reports, LA's homicide rate increases dramatically on bad Santa Ana days.[6] Yet the real concern is always the brushfires. Fire stations go on alert, community groups like Arson Watch call out their volunteers, and nervous homeowners keep a steady eye on the horizon. Nowhere is this truer than Malibu, where the many canyons funnel these winds in a particularly deadly fashion.

On the evening that I arrived in Los Angeles there was a slight breeze coming off the mountains, and I followed it westward in my rental car—toward Decker Canyon at the edge of Malibu. My route took me along the Pacific Coast Highway, a spectacular seaside road that follows the cliff-hung coast of California all the way north to San Francisco and beyond. I had to take it for only about twenty-five miles to Malibu, and along the way I got my first glimpse at the legendary "burning coast."

The shores of southern California have been catching fire for thousands of years. Long before man arrived, wildfires were started by lightning or perhaps even by friction, as seasonal winds caused dry stems and branches to rub together. Fire is an irrepressible aspect of the region's ecosystem, and every wave of human settlement has had to deal with it in one fashion or another.

The Chumash Indians, who were the first known inhabitants of the Malibu area, set brushfires to feed themselves. They used the flames to clear fields for cultivation and possibly to drive out game when hunting. These fires were so prevalent that when the explorer Juan Rodríguez Cabrillo first visited the region in 1542, he dubbed it

the "Bay of Smoke." Eventually, in 1793, the Spanish governor en-
acted the first fire-control regulations in California history. Even so,
the wildfires were so prevalent that in 1841 a visiting French traveler
wrote: "Occasionally the traveler is amazed to observe the sky covered with black and copper colored clouds, to experience a stifling
heat, and to see a fine cloud of ashes fall." These burns "seriously
handicap travelers," he concluded.[7]

Malibu's narrow coastal meadows were first developed by ranch-
ers in 1800. The land was known as Rancho Malibu, and over the
next century it was owned by a succession of prominent families.
None of them, however, laid claim to many of the steep canyons
that buttressed the ranch's meadows. Finally, around the 1880s, the
first homesteaders began arriving, among them Marion Decker, the
first of the Decker family.[8] The homesteaders were a lean, tough,
and hungry sort. They were war veterans, tenant farmers, and disgruntled midwesterners looking for a better life and a bit of free
land. Under the Homestead Laws, they were entitled to as much as
160 free acres, and they found this land in the dusty canyons above
Rancho Malibu. Yet these canyons had one major drawback: They
were deadly firetraps. Surviving them took daring and know-how,
and the homesteaders became adept at it.

The glamour of modern-day Malibu arrived in 1892, with a mil-
lionaire from Massachusetts by the name of Frederick Hastings
Rindge. That year Rindge bought Rancho Malibu, all 13,000 acres
of it. He envisioned Malibu as an "American Riviera," and this is exactly what it would become, though Rindge would never live to see
it. In 1903 his ranch burned to the ground, and just two years later
Rindge himself died. Rindge's glitzy vision for Malibu was realized
only when his cash-poor family leased some beachfront property to a
budding movie colony in 1928. Quite fittingly, the colony's house-
warming was a raging wildfire that destroyed thirteen new homes

the following year. It would be the first of many such disasters, but modern-day Malibu had officially taken hold.[9]

Driving into Malibu, I passed a long procession of seafront mansions and a wide beach where a number of muscled surfers and bikini-clad knockouts were frolicking in the waves. Eventually I found some free parking at a Starbucks. I stopped in for a coffee, and as I waited for my order, I chatted with a refreshingly unattractive girl behind the counter. Somewhat grudgingly, she agreed to name a few of her more famous customers. "We get Mel Gibson, Dustin Hoffman, Martin Sheen, Emilio Estevez, Pierce Brosnan . . ." She cut herself off as she finished filling my cup. "I can't remember them all, but they come in here enough that it isn't a shock." I nodded. "It's not like we stop pouring the coffee when they walk in," she added. I soon learned that this was the unspoken rule of Malibu: You leave the celebrities alone. It was more than just a courtesy—it seemed to be the esprit de corps of the town. As one proud resident later explained to me: "This is probably one of the few places in the world that someone like Mel Gibson could a live a normal life."

After finishing my coffee, I hopped back into my car and continued up the Pacific Coast Highway. Within a mile or two the houses thinned out to a lonely rural sprawl. At last I had an unobstructed view of the sea to my left and the canyons to my right. It was a stunning, roughhewn, bipolar view. Then, before I knew it, I hit a steep little turnoff with a sign that said DECKER CANYON ROAD. As I would later learn, this canyon was once inhabited almost entirely by members of the Decker family. The children attended the Decker Schoolhouse, where they all allegedly referred to one another as "cousin." No one spoke of "Decker Canyon," or "Decker Road," just "Decker." Like the Scottish clans of old, the Deckers melded family and place until both had just one name. Yet as the rich and famous began migrating to Malibu in increasing numbers, property taxes went through the roof and slowly the Deckers moved away. Today all that remained was one last family and a lonely road sign that bore its name.

As I turned up Decker, right away I noticed the warning signs. DANGER: EXTREME FIRE HAZARD AREA, read one. NO FIRE-WORKS: FINES & JAIL SENTENCES MAY BE IMPOSED, read another. Beyond this, there was a gradual rise for about two hundred yards. Then, without wasting any more ground, Decker Canyon Road shot upward faster than the Roman candles it forbade.

⚡

The road cut itself into the canyon walls and snaked upward along a series of switchbacks and blind turns—the kind that send curbside pebbles flying off the edge to fall seemingly forever. As I continued upward, I caught a glimpse up a long, winding driveway that led to several southwestern-style mansions and oversize ranch houses. They were the types of homes that tried to blend in discreetly but were far too big to do so. One had an indoor pool. Another had several Mercedes cars parked in front. It was unclear who exactly lived here, but these were the Deckers' neighbors.

After driving roughly two miles, I came upon a sheer gravel driveway with a mailbox labeled "M. Decker." I pulled off the road. My tires struggled for traction, and then crunched their way upward through a curious vertical landscape. To my right was a steep orchard where the tree trunks formed acute angles with the ground. To my left was a narrow shelf of flat ground where somebody had carved away enough rock to create a small horse corral. I continued to the top of the driveway and parked between a vintage powder blue pickup truck and a dilapidated garage strewn with rusting tools and dozens of dusty deer antlers. Here I found Millie Decker, on her way over to the chicken coop to collect some eggs.

"Hello there," said Millie as I got out of my car. She was a slight woman, not much more than five feet tall, with a full head of curled white hair and two fierce blue eyes. From the hesitation in her every movement I guessed that her eyesight was very poor. Millie gave me a close look, nodded her head as if confirming a suspicion, and then took a step back. She was wearing a pair of reddish cowboy boots, green denim work pants, and a turquoise shirt with a wide butterfly collar. These were just her work clothes, she would later tell me. At her feet were several sheepdogs dashing about frantically, guarding her every step and barking at me in unison. Without saying a word, Millie reached down and began to stroke the largest of the dogs, patting his head and rubbing his fur. Gradually all of the dogs quieted down.

"Bonnie told me that you'd be dropping by," said Millie as she brushed a lock of white hair away from her eyes. "I thought I would show you my chickens. Would you like that? They're so pretty, when the sun shines on them they're green."

"Green?" I asked.

"Green," said Millie.

"All right," I said. "And by the way . . . I'm Jake."

"Very glad to meet you," she replied. "I'm Millie."

Together we followed a small dirt road that ran above the dug-out horse corral that I had passed on my way in. The road itself cut deep into the mountainside. In fact, almost every single swath of flat ground on Millie Decker's eighteen-acre ranch was scraped out in this fashion. It was a near vertical piece of property. The Deckers had carved a multitiered horse ranch into the steep walls of Decker Canyon. The first tier contained a horse corral, a barn, and a riding ring. A little ways up was the second tier, which included Millie's house, a garage, a few trailers, and the chicken coop. The third tier belonged to Millie's son, Chip, the fourth to her daughter, Bonnie, and the fifth to a renter named Dave. They all lived on the same ranch, but most of the time you would hardly know it, for the rise was so steep that no matter where you were it was almost impossible to see the tier above or below you. The landscaping seemed to exemplify the old homesteader spirit, making something out of nothing. The problem for Millie was the possibility of falling, a concern that she raised as she walked cautiously toward the chicken coop. "I'm getting old," said Millie with a smile. "I'm eighty-one years old, and I don't see too well, but I can still work a horse."

As we walked Millie explained that she was a Decker only by marriage. Her husband, Jimmy, was the last of the bloodline Deckers to live in the canyon, and he had died in 1991. In truth, Millie had only a tenuous claim to the Decker legacy, and yet she seemed to be a worthy heir. Her father, Perc Meek, was a renowned mountain lion hunter who once ran a small ranch near the top of Decker Canyon. As a young girl, Millie attended the Decker Schoolhouse. She first met Jimmy at the age of five when her father saved his dog from a hungry mountain lion. After that they became friends, yet they didn't actually marry until their forties. By then Millie had two young children from a previous marriage (Bonnie and Chip). Jimmy Decker never had children himself, but he treated Millie's like his own. Bonnie even changed her last name to Decker.

"We're horse people," explained Millie. "I've been riding since I was one year old. My father just set me down on a horse and went about his business, so I guess you could say that horse was my babysitter."

"At what point did you start riding in the rodeo?" I asked.

"When I was twelve," replied Millie. "My daddy ran a series of horse shows throughout the area, and I used to ride the bulls for him." According to Millie, her bull riding was often the opening act. To give the spectacle a little extra oomph, her father would usually tie a "bucking strap" around the flank of the bull to really make it mad. For eight long seconds Millie would hold on for dear life, until her father rode up beside her and whisked her away. By the age of sixteen, explained Millie, she was racing horses at fairs throughout southern California. It took an enormous amount of wrist strength to work the reins of a racehorse, and Millie conditioned herself by milking the cows as much as she could. Within a few years she was jockeying professionally, riding against men who jealously guarded the sport as a bastion of masculinity. "Once they tried to run me through a fence," Millie recalled. "That was one time I swore."

When we reached the chicken coop, Millie paused for a moment at the door. "Now, where did you say you were from, honey?" she asked.

"Boston," I told her.

"And you came all this way to see me?" Millie shot me a girlish smile, but before I could reply, she slid into the chicken coop and began talking to her hens. "There's no eggs under you, so you shouldn't be so mean," she told one of them in a scolding voice. Slowly she made her way around the coop, chatting as she went. I had to admit, the hens did have a bit of a green sheen, but none of them appeared to be laying any eggs. Eventually, Millie emerged empty-handed but none too worried. Gently she closed the door to the coop. "How about a glass of water?" she asked me. "Would you like one?"

Millie led me back past my car and up an old stone walkway that cut through an overgrown garden adorned with a broken fountain, a few old wagon wheels, and two rusting metal elephants. We emerged onto a stone patio with a nice view of the apricot and plum orchard down below. Millie proceeded directly into her parlor, which was decorated with some forty mounted deer heads. It wasn't a big room, and the heads were packed in so tight I could barely see a trace of wood paneling. What struck me most were the eyes — dozens of them, watching my every move—lifeless but eerily alert. If these heads still had bodies, I realized, I'd be standing thick in a herd of deer.

"The deer were my husband Jimmy's," said a voice from the kitchen. Millie emerged with a tall glass of ice water and continued: "You either loved Jimmy or you hated him, and he was enemy number one of the hunters around here."

"Why's that?" I asked.

"You're only allowed to shoot two deer a year and sometimes Jimmy shot a hundred," said Millie.

When Jimmy Decker wasn't hunting he was usually blowing things up, explained Millie. By trade, he was a dynamiter. Many people knew him simply as "Dynamite Jimmy." There was an art to dynamiting, and Jimmy was often called on to do the most difficult jobs in

*The Deckers' living room bears the heads of more than forty deer, which were shot by Millie and her husband, Jimmy.*

Malibu—blasting a hole for a pool without breaking a giant picture window, or splitting a massive boulder that was on the verge of crushing a mansion. According to Millie, Jimmy was an imposing figure— more than two hundred pounds and "solid as a rock." In his youth he ran a gym and trained with Johnny Weissmuller, the muscleman who starred in the original Tarzan movies. Jimmy's strength was legendary. Sometimes, said Millie, he would hold up the back end of a car when a tire needed changing. When people gathered to play "donkey softball"—a raucous game in which players rode donkeys around the bases—Jimmy was famous for opting to carry the donkey instead, running full speed about the field with the bewildered beast in his arms. Over time, Jimmy became something of a folk hero in Malibu. Both Millie and Bonnie told me about the movie stars who came to visit: Rock Hudson, Cary Grant, Clark Gable, Orson Welles, and many more. They came to hunt, and camp, and be one of the boys, but most of all to spend time with Jimmy. Rough as he was, Jimmy was the real thing, and in a town dominated by the movies, inhabited by pretend heroes and would-be gunslingers, there was something very alluring about Jimmy's real-life virility.

"Of course, I knew plenty of stars when I was a girl," boasted Millie as she made her way across the parlor to the couch where I was sitting. She handed me my drink and then plopped down on the cushion next to me. A sudden explosion of dust and lint burst upward, then glittered in a thick shaft of light that was angled down to the floor. Even more noticeable than the dust were the cobwebs, which seemed to connect every single antler in the room, forming a veritable superhighway for the local spider population.

"A lot of the Western stars used to come to my daddy's horse shows," said Millie. Many of those early Westerns were shot in the Santa Monica Mountains not far from Decker Canyon, she explained. Over the years Millie and her father, Perc, came to know

Buck Jones, Leo Carrillo, Roy Rogers, Dale Evans, and John Wayne. Bill Boyd, the actor who played Hopalong Cassidy, lived just across the canyon from them and became a good family friend.

It struck me as odd that mountain people like Perc, Millie, and Jimmy got tossed into the Hollywood coterie—but during the 1930s and 1940s Malibu itself was at a strange crossroads. The movie colony had not yet fully taken hold, nor had all of the old homesteaders yet moved away. It's hard to imagine many other communities in American history shared by such radically different contingents, yet still linked. Here was a last pocket of wildest America neighboring a colony of wealthy actors who often played their part on the big screen. These were dimly mirrored worlds, both in love with a vanishing way of life and linked by a mutual curiosity of how the other lived it. And it wasn't just the movie stars who crossed over. Millie worked with horses in a number of movies, including *Reds* and *Bounty Hunter*, and Jimmy even did a few explosions for television, including an entire jumbo jet for the show *Emergency*. It seems fitting, however, that Jimmy's and Millie's involvement was limited to those tasks that were too challenging or downright dangerous for an imposter to pull off. I think a disappointing truth of Hollywood has always been that so many of its heroes lack the nerve and the know-how that they so gracefully seem to exude on the screen. After all, they are actors, not fighters, and in Malibu nothing makes this plainer to see than the fires that chase them away.

❧

"So I guess you want to talk about fires," said Millie finally as she settled back onto the dusty pillows of her couch.

"Yeah," I said. "I understand you've seen quite a few."

"Certainly have," replied Millie. She paused to stroke her favorite sheepdog, Concho, who was still chomping on a handful of garlic vitamin pills that Millie had just tossed him. "My first fire was in 1928," she began. Millie was just eight years old at the time, but she claimed to remember the scene well: standing with her two sisters in the blazing heat, watching her mother and father beat the ground furiously with wet gunnysacks in an attempt to smother the flames. "I was scared and I'm pretty sure I was crying as the fire circled the ranch," recalled Millie. "I was too young to help, but my older sister was wetting the gunnysacks and taking them to Mom and Dad."

This was just the first of Millie's many fire memories. Years later she was ushered into the principal's office at her high school to receive some dreadful news: Another wildfire had swept through the canyon where she lived, and both of her parents were dead. Grief-stricken, Millie and her sister left the school and began sobbing by the side of the road. Then, quite miraculously, her two parents drove around the bend in their automobile, alive and well. The reports had been wrong. Somehow the Meeks had managed to survive.

The key to fighting wildfires was preparation, insisted Millie. This was something she had learned from a very early age, as she watched her parents clear all the flammable plant life from around their house. As a girl, Millie had her own firefighting chores, like keeping all of the ranch's water barrels full. They were big vats, up to one hundred gallons in capacity, and there were roughly twenty of them set around her parents' property. Filling them was no easy task, and Millie was constantly making trips to a nearby creek or spring. She was also charged with checking on the gunnysacks, making sure they were all carefully stowed away. If and when a fire came, everyone on the ranch would grab their gunnysacks, dip them into the barrels of water, and start beating the ground furiously in order to smother the flames.

Improvised as this "sack and barrel" technique may sound, I later learned that it was once widely used on the Great Plains. Millie's father probably learned it in Iowa, Oklahoma, or Missouri—the places where he grew up. In that part of the world, they used gunnysacks to fight prairie fires. In fact, Laura Ingalls Wilder describes such a scene in *Little House on the Prairie*. She writes of a wildfire that races toward her farm "faster than a horse can run." Immediately her father takes charge: "'Prairie fire!' shouted Pa. 'Get the tub full of water! Put sacks in it!'" The true originators of this technique in North America were likely the Plains Indians. Their use of wet blankets was documented by a number of American travelers, including the painter Alfred Jacob Miller. His 1836 painting *Prairie on Fire* depicts a scene in which an Indian village confronts an approaching wildfire with a frenzy of blanket beating. This was just one of the many techniques that the Plains Indians may have handed down to American settlers.* The Plains Indians also cleared vegetation as a form of fire prevention. Additionally, they set "backfires"—another technique also used by the Deckers—in which a smaller, controlled fire is used to burn off a designated area and cut off the path of an advancing wildfire. The Plains Indians had a rich firefighting tradition, and to some extent the Malibu homesteaders were likely the beneficiaries of this knowledge.[10]

"We never had much water up here in the canyons," continued Millie. "Even now, we don't have metered water like the people on the coast. We rely on spring water. And we still fight fires with the gunnysacks and barrels." Apparently, this technique had served the Deckers well. According to Millie, the house we were now sitting in had been through half a dozen or so major blazes since it was built in the early 1940s, and not once had it burned. "To tell you the

---

*Many American settlers may have already known how to "beat out" a fire. This concept is somewhat universal. As far back as the Middle Ages, there are accounts of Europeans using brooms or swatting devices to squelch fires.

truth," said Millie, "I've been very fortunate—no house of mine has ever burned down."

As Millie and I continued to chat in the parlor, I heard the sound of another car crunching up the steep gravel driveway. A minute or so later, Bonnie Decker appeared. She was a sturdy woman: busty, frizzy haired, and youthful-looking. She wore an oversize Hawaiian shirt, blue jeans, and a pair of black leather moccasins. "I've never been into fancy clothing," she later told me. For this and other reasons her classmates at Malibu Junior High often called her a "hill-billy." This was actually a point of pride, claimed Bonnie, in part because her cousin (Donna Douglas) played the role of Elly May Clampett on the TV show *The Beverly Hillbillies*. Still, there were awkward moments, like the time a truckload of hunters, toting rifles and a few bloody deer, swung by school and whisked her away. A concerned parent called the police to say that Bonnie had been abducted, but it was just Jimmy picking her up from school.

"Hey," said Bonnie, as she paused to catch her breath. "Is Mom telling you everything you need to know about the fires?"

"He didn't know what a gunnysack was," interjected Millie.

"It's true," I admitted.

"Well, we wouldn't trade you," Millie told me consolingly.

Bonnie, perhaps sensing the crowdedness of the room, with its now forty-plus heads, ushered us out onto the back patio where we took seats and gazed down the sloping orchard that led to the road below. We sat there for a long while, chatting, flipping through old photographs, and sipping ice water. "Are you hungry?" asked Millie finally. "I can fix a good sandwich. No, wait, how about a barbecue? I'll fix us some steaks."

As preparations for dinner began, Bonnie gave me a tour of the lower ranch. She led the way down through the orchard, stopping here and there to pick wild plums and tell stories. Almost every structure on the ranch seemed to have an accompanying anecdote. "That barn over there was built by a one-armed cowboy by the name of Tex," explained Bonnie. "And he was probably eighty when he built it."

Bonnie soon returned to the topic of firefighting, emphasizing the same prairie-tested techniques that her mother had. "Brush clearance is your best protection against wildfires," she explained. Each spring the ranch assembled a small workforce to clear vast amounts of brush so that every structure was surrounded by at least two hundred feet of cleared or carefully trimmed ground. This created a natural shield, so when a wildfire swept through, it would simply burn around a house. Then, if any flames breached the shield, they could be beaten out with the gunnysacks. "We have to be very careful around here because the plant life is extremely flammable," explained Bonnie. "Especially the chaparrals."

As I would later learn, the region's many species of chaparral plants (including sugar bush, chemise, scrub oak, and California lilac) survive the heat by growing stiff, oily leaves. The oil on the leaves works as a kind of seal. Just as the ancient Egyptians used perfumed oils to keep their skin supple in the dry heat of the desert, these plants coat their leaves in oil to retain what little moisture they can. The downside is the fire hazard. These leaves are highly flammable and their plant stems are exceedingly dry. Together these elements create a deadly fuel for wildfires—which, once ignited, must be fought boldly and strategically.[11]

According to Bonnie, the Deckers' firefighting strategy hinged on water. "You need a reliable delivery system," she explained. The ranch's system began with a small pump house on the first tier. Here water was drawn from a natural spring and pumped upward to the very top of the ranch, where it was stored in two giant 12,500-gallon tanks. These twin reservoirs ensured a steady and reliable supply of water. From here, the water could flow downward via gravity to any of the various tiers. (When a fire came, the power lines usually burned, so it was crucial that the water could flow without the use of an electric pump). All across the ranch, a network of water pipes spread out to some fifty hose faucets. This way, no matter where fire threatened, water was sure to be nearby and could then be sprayed onto a house or put into barrels for gunnysack dipping. "Sometimes you're fighting the fire with the hose and watering yourself down at the same time," added Bonnie. "You'll get yourself soaking wet and within three minutes you'll be bone dry—that's how hot it gets."

"Hey," said Bonnie rather suddenly, "did Mom show you the magazines where Jimmy kept his dynamite?"

"No," I replied.

"Well, that'll be fun!" she said. So Bonnie led me back up the orchard and out along the second tier. Just before the chicken coop, she guided me around a large pile of rusting junk, until we found ourselves standing flush against the canyon wall. I glanced around for a moment, and then I saw it: a small cave burrowed into the cliff face. Bonnie scampered about the mouth of the cave for a moment, making enough noise to alert any lurking rattlesnakes. There was no reply, no rattling or even a rustle. Gingerly we crept into the darkness, inching our way toward the back of the cave. Here a lone ray of light gave color to a rusting red door and shape to three small words: EXPLOSIVES A — DANGEROUS. This was Jimmy's magazine. It was the same type of sturdy steel container that the military used to store ammunition. It was the ultimate fireproof box. No matter how bad things got, even if the whole ranch burned to the ground, this small space would be safe.

Impressive as all of this was, I still had to wonder why anyone would want to store large quantities of dynamite in the heart of a fire corridor. Apparently, however, Jimmy had complete confidence not only in his dynamite cave, but in his dynamite truck as well. He had a pickup that was specially outfitted with two magazines in back. During wildfires, he was known to run roadblocks in this truck. As Bonnie and I made our way out of the cave, she recalled one such story from the 1978 fire: "The police were blocking people from getting into the canyons, and Jimmy just looked at them and said: 'You either let me through or I'm running the block.'" Apparently the police were concerned, not only because Jimmy was in a dynamite truck, but because in that particular fire the flames were leaping over the top of the road, creating what the locals call a "fire tunnel." By most accounts this looks like a passageway straight through hell, but Jimmy was dead-set on driving through it. "Well, the police didn't want him hanging around the roadblock," continued Bonnie. "They said, 'If you want to drive through a fire with a bunch of dynamite, that's up to you!'"

Jimmy, like all of the Deckers, felt that the Malibu Fire Department could *not* be counted on. They could barely save the mansions on the coast, let alone smaller houses in remote canyons like Decker. Consequently, the Deckers always stayed to fight the flames and protect their horses. They had an old family saying—*If you leave, you lose*—and they had no intentions of losing. At some point their toilsome and preventative strategy clearly gave way to something far less controlled, and Bonnie spoke of this as we stood by the mouth of the cave. "Your adrenaline is running so fast during a fire," she explained. "You don't feel the temperature, you don't feel anything. Only when it's over, and your adrenaline has calmed down a bit, do you start getting your wits about you. *Then* you start feeling the burns that you've got, and checking out the damage that's been done."

Bonnie laughed again. It was a tough, humorless laugh that

seemed to say, *You can't possibly know what I am talking about.* Then she guided us back around the pile of junk. "Come on," she said sweetly. "Let's see about dinner."

As we waited for the steaks to finish cooking, I sat by myself for a few minutes at the edge of the orchard, looking out over the expanse of the canyon and thinking some more about the Deckers. In many ways they seemed out of place in Malibu, and yet it was becoming increasingly clear to me that they were probably among the few who actually belonged. For them Malibu was more than just a posh address—more than just a scenic vista on which a mansion could be placed—it was a demanding physical reality to which they had adapted. Contrary to what the U.S. Census Bureau reports, the Deckers would *not* move twelve times over the course of their lives. They were deeply connected to the land, and like the Plains Indians they knew almost by birthright the tricks to surviving the dangers of home. For them, wildfires were a natural part of life, something to be expected, something to be lived with, and in this way the Deckers would always belong in this canyon.

That evening we ate on the back patio, watching twilight repaint the landscape a hundred different times. The dim light of dusk coaxed out an astounding number of colors. Earlier in the day everything had seemed washed out, like an overexposed photograph. But now the land looked lush—the leafy orchard, the blush red dirt, and the sapphire sky.

As we ate, Millie and Bonnie conjured one memory after another. My favorite involved Miner and Kitty, the ranch's two pet mountain lions. They were big animals, 125 pounds each, and Millie used to keep them in a double-gated cage. "The male I didn't trust," said Millie, "but the female used to sit on my lap and suck my thumb." During one of the ranch's many fires, the Deckers were forced to evacuate the two cats by walking them out on lead ropes. At some point, a nervous neighbor spotted the lions and called the authorities. Not long after, Miner and Kitty were confiscated. This upset Millie greatly. "We should've had proper permits for those lions," she lamented. Bonnie just shook her head. There was nothing they could have done, she insisted. Malibu was just changing.

As dinner drew to a close, Millie broached the subject that I had been forestalling for some time. "Where are you staying tonight?" she asked.

"Well," I replied, "I was kind of hoping to pitch a tent . . ."

"Why don't you just sleep in the trailer," interjected Millie. "We got a nice feather bed in there."

Later that night, as I nestled down to sleep in Millie's trailer, I listened to a cacophony of howls. The ranch's dogs were having their nightly standoff with the coyotes over in the orchard. It was a slightly unnerving chorus, but also comforting in a way, for I knew that all in Decker was not yet tame.

❧

For the next two weeks my mornings on the ranch began with my knocking on Millie's bedroom door and asking permission to take a shower. "Come on in, honey!" she would yell. That was my cue to hustle past her bed and into the only real bathroom on the second tier. Afterward, I would sit in the parlor with the deer and read while Millie showered and got dressed. When she finally emerged I would marvel at her clothing, which became increasingly showy: bright floral shirts, silver string ties, saucer-size belt buckles, red cowboy boots, and quite often a skin-tight pair of riding pants. "I like your outfit," I'd tell her. She would smile bashfully and shrug her shoulders, as if to say, *What, this old thing?* Then it was time for breakfast. That first morning Millie made me an omelet with jalapeño cheese and bacon. She fussed over her creation even as I ate it. Millie was also very proud that she could eat as much as I could. One morning she made herself four large pieces of french toast. "Are you going to eat all of that?" I asked skeptically. Sure enough, she cleaned her plate and then needled me for doubting her. In the evenings I tried to reciprocate by making her dinner, but this was never easy. "If you bang that can of pasta sauce on my table again I'll have to hang you!" she would holler playfully.

Millie led a decidedly upbeat life, though occasionally she did worry, and on that first morning, as the jalapeno omelets sizzled in the skillet, Millie voiced some concerns about the future of her ranch. "It costs so much just to keep this place up," she told me. Millie shook her head as she related two of her most recent expenses: four thousand dollars for brush clearance and five thousand to fix the pump on the well. "And I already owe the bank tens of thousands of dollars," she added, "mostly from Jimmy's medical bills." Jimmy had died of cancer, and the debt that his illness had created now sadly seemed to be imperiling his ranch as well.

As bad as all of this was, Millie was not without options. Every few months the postman delivered a form letter that proposed a simple, one-step solution: Sell the ranch. The letters came from a variety of local realtors who wanted to broker the deal. Sometimes they even offered a free appraisal. Millie already knew that her five-tier ranch was worth a total of about $2 million, but she had no interest in cashing it in. "I won't sell," she vowed. Still, the letters came. During my stay she received one from Coldwell Banker. "It seems like I've gotten a lot more of these since Jimmy died," she told me as she threw the offer into the trash. "Maybe they figure it's too much for me to handle." And it *was* a lot to handle, but the Decker family had been turning down offers like these for more than a century. Ever since the mid-1890s, the Rindge family had been trying to buy out the old homesteaders. May Rindge, the ambitious widow of Frederick Rindge, was especially determined to clear out her neighbors. For the most part she was successful. Survey maps from the teens and twenties show the Rindge estate steadily expanding into the canyons. Quite fittingly, however, the Deckers were never consumed. On map after map the Decker plots remained intact. "There was a lot of tension between the Decker family and the Rindge family," I was later told by Glen Howell, a local historian and a docent at the Adamson House Museum. "But to their credit, the Deckers were one family that refused to sell."

After eating breakfast together, Millie and I usually retired to the parlor, where we sipped ice water and continued to chat about the various challenges that she faced on the ranch. It soon became clear to me that Millie was battling not just the constant threat of wildfires but also the steady encroachment of modern-day Malibu. "I remember when Malibu was just empty beach and mesa," she told me. In the intervening years, Millie witnessed enormous changes: Roads were paved, fields were fenced in, taxes were raised, hunting was restricted, and everywhere massive homes were built. This was the force that had rid the canyon of Deckers—not the wildfires—and it weighed on Millie.

In the evenings Millie and I had root beer floats and watched the Western Channel on her television, via a Direct TV satellite connection. I'd never realized that there were actually enough Westerns to supply an entire channel, but apparently there were, and they played twenty-four hours a day in an endless marathon of saloon brawls, Indian powwows, and stagecoach romances. For Millie, Direct TV was more than just television; it was a direct connection to the past. Not only did she recognize most of the actors in these Westerns, she often knew them personally and remembered exactly where they lived. "Oh, that's Dale Robinson," she would say. "He lives over in Hidden Hills." A few minutes later she would recognize someone else:

"That's Buddy Ebsen. He lives over in Agurra, right next to the old Bob Hope ranch." Millie always spoke of these actors as if they still lived in these places, even though usually they had long since died or moved away.

Millie's sense of place was defined by memories. This was particularly apparent when she took me on a walk through Nicholas Flats Park, the site of her girlhood home. The parks department had bulldozed all of the ranch's old buildings and had even redone the landscaping so as to erase any remaining structural traces. "When I first came and saw it like this I sat and bawled for hours," she told me. Yet even now she could find hidden traces of the past—a nearby cave where forty Chinese laborers once slept, a rock with three smooth dimples that the Chumash Indians used as bowls, and a tree with an oddly bent branch that marked the site where a treasure was once buried.

One place in the canyon that still heartened Millie was Dale Rickard's ranch. Dale was an old friend of Millie's, a former mounted police officer who left the force to wrangle horses for the TV show *Little House on the Prairie*. Eventually, Dale saved enough money to fulfill a lifelong dream, and now at the age of eighty he ran his own movie prop business. Dale's niche, not surprisingly, was Westerns. He had transformed his property into a fake Western town, complete with a saloon, a feed store, a jail, a blacksmith's shop, a general store, and a number of other ramshackle structures. A few days after my arrival, Millie and I paid him a visit.

Main Street on Dale's ranch was a dusty boulevard strewn with steers' heads, wagon wheels, cowbells, horse troughs, a cannon, and a few signs with sayings like "Trouble rides a fast horse" and "Ten miles to water, Twelve miles to Hell." Millie and I found Dale inspecting one of his many horse-drawn wagons. Dale was a tall man with a big cowboy hat, false teeth, and a cigarette bobbing from the corner of his mouth. Apparently he was expecting us, for he broke immediately into a tour. "This here was an army wagon built in 1873," Dale told us. "So it could have fought Indians."

As we walked the streets of Dale's small town, learning more about medicine show wagons and cowboy bathtubs, Millie pulled me aside for a moment. "Isn't this place something?" she asked. "It just takes you back in time."

❧

Not long after my arrival in Malibu, a brushfire swept through the nearby resort town of San Clemente and destroyed several condominiums. A photograph of the burnt-out remains made the front page of the local news section in the *Los Angeles Times*. Millie and I both studied the article and the photograph. The brush around this building wasn't properly cleared, concluded Millie. What's more, the condos had cedar shake siding, making them very flammable. "My house has stucco on the outside," explained Millie. "It's not too pretty but it's fire resistant."

"What would you do if your house did burn?" I asked.

"I don't know," she told me. "It would be tough, because we don't have fire insurance." When I asked her why not, she said it was too expensive. When I asked her how much it cost, she told me that her son, Chip, was the best person for me to ask about this. Nowadays, he handled most of the ranch's fire preparation. "You'll like Chip," insisted Millie. "He's wonderful with horses."

I was already quite intrigued by Chip. Both Millie and Bonnie had described him as a kind of horse whisperer. People came from all over, asking him to break their horses. No was his standard reply. Chip never broke animals—he *worked with* them.

The following evening I made arrangements to visit Chip. Around nine P.M. I borrowed a flashlight from Millie and headed up a narrow footpath that led to the third tier. Along the way I passed a makeshift sweathouse. Basically, it was an old water tank with a hole for an entranceway and a drop cloth for a door. The heat came from a wood-burning furnace that boiled water and cranked out steam. I continued on the footpath, up through a large screened-in garden with swinging doors at both ends. From here the path hooked around a house and dropped me off at Chip's front porch.

A lean, handsome man with deep blue eyes came to the door. He wore a dusty pair of blue jeans and no shirt. "Glad you came," he told me coolly. "I'm Chip." He then led me into a tastefully furnished dining room and introduced me to Claire, his wife. Claire was a tall blond woman from New Hampshire who had graduated from Dartmouth and eventually landed a job teaching Shakespearean literature at UCLA. In her spare time she rode horses, which eventually led her to Chip. "Chip and I are fundamentally different people," Claire later told me. "Yet I think there is something classically American about our meeting. You know, Eastern schoolmarm comes west and marries a cowboy."

The three of us sat down at the dining room table and Chip told me a bit more about his career. "I started working other people's problem horses when I was about nine years old," he explained. "My grandfather would bring me these ponies that were really rank or tough. I would work with them, and in a couple of days they would be following me all over the place." As Chip got older, he developed a reputation as an excellent horseman. Often it was the riders who needed his help most. Many of them were poor communicators who gave their horses mixed signals—like goading them to gallop while fearfully tugging on the reins or doing any number of things that subtly begged the horse to slow down. By the time Chip intervened, many of these horses had lost their trust and were wildly standoffish. Fixing this took time.

"Basically," explained Chip, "I communicate with the horses by recognizing their intelligence and using that intelligence to create a language."

I nodded vaguely. Perhaps sensing my skepticism, Claire threw herself into the conversation. "Chip really knows what the horse is thinking," she affirmed. "It's not ESP—it's more like reading body language or something."

Later in the week I would see this for myself on a visit to Chip's stables. Using hand signals and an occasional cluck of the tongue, he had a "troubled" horse walk, trot, gallop, turn, and stop as if via remote control. Often Chip's signals were too subtle for me to notice. The horse would simply change direction, and it was clear from Chip's unblinking response that this is what he'd intended.

On our first evening together, Chip also talked about his equally unusual relationship with fire, particularly his instincts for early detection. "I can smell smoke normally before I see any," he told me. "I know that there's a fire and I know what kind of fire it is, whether it's a brushfire or it's some kind of domestic smoke." Yet sometimes, Chip asserted, even before the scent arrived, he could "sense" a fire.

"What do you mean by 'sense'?" I asked him.

"I think you just have a knowing," answered Chip. "I think there is an inter-spirit that is constantly talking to us if we are listening. I think anytime you are sensing you are just aware of things that are going on."

The room fell silent for a moment. I looked over to Claire, but she had nothing to add.

"It's like rattlesnakes," continued Chip calmly. "I know if there is a rattlesnake around and usually where it is before I've heard it or seen it. And I can usually walk right up to where they are, without having heard them, just because I feel them. And it's the same thing with a fire."

Chip insisted that his abilities were not extrasensory, but simply a heightened awareness of nature. Still I pressed him. Who raised him to think in this way? Where exactly did that awareness come from? "Memories," he answered finally. According to Chip, his awareness was rooted in something deeper than his own experiences. It reached downward into a bedrock of family memories. "I am tied into these people that are of homestead clans," explained Chip. "I am tied into people that were raised in these mountains and literally had to eat off of what they were able to harvest, whether it was deer or rabbit or quail or fish. They lived off the land. By being raised with those people, I was raised on the stories, raised on their memories."

Toward the end of the evening, I finally got around to asking Chip about the issue of fire insurance, and why the ranch didn't have any.

"But we do have fire insurance," insisted Chip. He then reminded me that the brush was well cleared, the water and gunnysacks were always ready, and the ranch was occupied by people who knew how to fight fires. "That's your best insurance," he told me, "not the monthly check that you send to some company."

❧

The following day, I had plans to visit Malibu proper. As I got into my car, I bumped into Carl, a youngish-looking man in his forties who was staying in the trailer next to mine. He was a friend of Millie's who had moved onto the ranch after his marriage went bad. Officially Carl worked for the Universal Studios theme park, where he monitored such rides as Back to the Future, Jurassic Park, and Terminator II. In his spare time he worked as Millie's ranch hand, helping her with her daily chores and learning as much as he could about horses. I had seen him around several times, but this was our first real meeting. "I'm in love with this old way of life," he told me as we chatted in Millie's driveway. Is it weird, I asked him, when you drive down

Decker Canyon Road into the bustle of Malibu? "You mean going through the wormhole?" he asked. "Yeah, it's weird, all right."

I said goodbye to Carl and drove through the "wormhole," following the PCH all the way to Las Flores Canyon, where I turned left and parked at the offices of the *Malibu Times*. Here I had an appointment with Arnold York, the newspaper's editor and owner. Roughly ten years ago, York's life was forever changed when a wildfire destroyed his Malibu home. He was one of roughly 350 homeowners who got burned out in the 1993 blaze. In the wake of that disaster, York distinguished himself as a champion of the rebuilding effort. His story of flight, survival, and refinancing was a modern-day classic in Malibu. Or so I gathered from chatting with Nancy Steiner, the PR woman who first put me in touch with the Deckers.

York was a short, distinguished-looking man in his mid-sixties, a former lawyer who now tinkered with journalism and wore golf shirts to work. I caught him on a busy day, but he agreed to squeeze me in for a quick meeting. "Come on in," he said in a faded New York accent. Like so many Malibu residents, York was a transplant, a graduate of Brooklyn College who came to UCLA for law school and then moved to Malibu in the 1970s, back before real estate had jumped from pricey to prohibitive. Today he was a member of Malibu's middle class, which encompassed a mishmash of highly successful professionals who in any other community would be the upper crust. York led the way into a large air-conditioned room with a wraparound desk. "So what's the story?" he asked me as we took our seats. "I'm interested in how Malibu copes with wildfires," I explained. York nodded and began to recollect the events of the 1993 fire.

On the afternoon of November 2, as a massive wall of fire moved toward Malibu's La Costa neighborhood, Arnold York hopped in his truck and drove homeward to save a few irreplaceable family possessions. By the time he arrived, the police had already cleared out the neighborhood. "It was like a ghost town," York remembered. Hurriedly he entered his house and began gathering what valuables he could find, including a few paintings, some Persian carpets, and his dog. "By this time," recalled York, "The fire was sort of moving in our direction, very slowly, kind of at the speed at which a man walks, and my dog was beginning to bounce off the walls and essentially say, *Let's get out of here.* So I threw the last of the things I could grab into a truck and we started down the hill."

The next time York returned home, he found his neighborhood charred to the ground. Nothing was left but smoldering ruins and a procession of freestanding chimneys, which stood like tombstones marking the plots where homes once stood. Slowly, as the shock wore off, Arnold York struggled to get his life in order. "Your immediate priority is just finding a clean set of underwear and some clothes to change into because you don't have anything," he recalled. His next concern was housing. Here he got lucky and managed to find a small rental property in Malibu. With shelter and clothing accounted for, York began to organize. He and his wife formed a grassroots organization called Operation Recovery and publicized a series of meetings in their newspaper.

"The weekly meetings were part informational, and part group therapy," explained York. "A number of the older folks nearly had breakdowns, so we became sort of a support group." As Operation Recovery became more coherent, its focus shifted from comforting to collecting. The group facilitated a series of meetings with all the major insurance carriers. Some of these exchanges got "really heated," explained York, because the insurers didn't want to pay. To deal with this, the group came up with a winning strategy that tapped into the town's inherent resources. "We said we would make commercials," explained York. "One of the things about Malibu—you have a lot of people in the TV business. We said we would make commercials and we would go on, first-person, and for those insurers who treated us decently we would say: You're in good hands. And those who didn't, we would relate our personal experiences and make sure they ran as public service announcements. Needless to say, that changed the equation significantly."

By all measures, Operation Recovery was a success. It strong-armed the insurance carriers, won over the local politicians, and helped victims get back on their feet. The Los Angeles Times heralded the group as a "political force" that overcame "what seemed an endless parade of insurmountable problems."[12] Except for a handful of elderly residents who didn't have the wherewithal to start anew, almost every member managed to rebuild. York and his wife were now living in a new house. Overall he seemed quite pleased with how things worked out, though he made it clear that he had no desire to go through it again. "So why did you rebuild?" I asked. York offered several reasons, including his genuine devotion to the community, though ultimately his decision came down to simple economics: His land was worth a lot more money with a house on it. This was another of Malibu's unspoken rules: After a fire you always rebuild, and because the city usually relaxes its building codes, you rebuild BIG. "You don't rebuild a small house," explained York. "It's not economical to do it anymore. You don't under-build on what the land is worth—the land is the major asset—so it almost forces you to maximize what you can build on it." It came down to resale value, concluded York: "You've got to figure that somewhere down the line you're probably going to sell, and you want to maximize the investment."

As our interview drew to a close, I told York about my stay with the Deckers. While he didn't know the family personally, he said he was familiar with their firefighting motto: *If you leave, you lose.* This was conventional wisdom in Malibu, according to York, and while everyone knew it to be true, hardly anyone had the nerve to practice it: "When you've got a firestorm coming toward you, and the wind is howling and swirling and it starts turning dark, you got to weigh saving your house with spending nine months in a burn ward, and my feeling was, *The hell with this, I'm out of here.* I can rebuild my house; I can't rebuild my skin. So maybe that's not the courageous thing to do, but I sure wasn't going to hang around to test the theory."

The County of Los Angeles Fire Department agreed. "We don't recommend staying during a fire," affirmed Captain Jim Jordan of the Fire Prevention Division. I visited Jordan later in the day, and he was very blunt with his reasoning. "We'd rather come back to a burned house than a dead person." When I told him about the Deckers, he didn't seem too surprised. "There are a very few who stay," he conceded. Jordan also confirmed that the Deckers' firefighting techniques were sound—particularly when it came to brush clearance, which was required by law—yet he stopped short of endorsing their cause. Instead, he stressed just how dangerous it was to confront a fire. "Most people have no idea that you can get flames that are a hundred and fifty feet high," said Jordan. He then explained what to do when a wall of fire is barreling toward you: Go in the house, close all the windows, make sure to pull back the curtains so they won't burn if the glass gets blown out, wait for an interminable five to ten minutes while the fire passes over you like a wave, and then go back outside and carry on with your firefighting. "When you decide to save your house," he said finally, "my question to you is this: How brave are you?" Jordan gave me a long, hard look and then chuckled to himself, as if I were a fool for taking him seriously. "Truth is," said Jordan, "there isn't a home in the world worth dying for."

As I drove around Malibu for the remainder of the day, Jordan's last line remained in my thoughts. The core of its logic struck me as wise: Wasn't it better to be homeless than dead? This seemed especially relevant for someone like Arnold York. He knew very little about firefighting, and besides, his house was fully insured. But what about the Deckers? Clearly their house was more than a mere asset, just as the act of defending it was more than a desire to preserve material goods. Theirs was a different sort of home—one that encompassed an entire way of life, deeply rooted in a family history and a connectedness to the land. What's more, the Deckers had proven themselves time and again to be skillful firefighters. Certainly there were risks involved, but these were risks that the Deckers had long since measured and accepted.

Later that evening I met Bonnie Decker for a drink at the Dume Room. This was a bar situated on Point Dume, a narrow stretch of land that juts out into the Pacific and offers a handsome view of both Malibu and LA. From outside, the place didn't look like much, just another suburban pub built into a strip mall, sandwiched between a dry cleaner and a pizzeria. Inside, however, the place had the look of an old-style Western saloon, with weathered wood paneling, swinging doors, and a large oak barrel clock. The crowd wasn't made up of the usual Malibu beachgoers, more a mix of rodeo and truck stop patrons. The bartender was a small, tough-looking man named Blake who served me a Coors Light and gave me a brief history of the pub. "We used to have hitching posts outside in the late seventies and early eighties, and everybody would ride here on horseback," he explained. "A few times we even had a horse in the bar."

As Blake continued reminiscing, Bonnie showed up. "Hey," said Blake to Bonnie, "was it Gina's horse that used to come into the bar?"

"Yes," replied Bonnie. "His name was Dar."

"That's right," said Blake. "That horse loved peppermint schnapps."

Bonnie ordered a beer for herself and then pointed out a framed black-and-white photograph beside the bar. It was one of many such photos, but this particular shot included a surly-looking woman holding a shotgun. "That's my mother," said Bonnie. I looked at it closely, and sure enough it was Millie.

"Who are the people in the rest of these photos?" I asked.

"Old-timers from the mountains," said Bonnie. She then pointed to another set of photos on a nearby wall. It was a large display, containing roughly thirty shots of various wildfires that had ravaged Malibu. Most of them were taken directly from the Dume Room's parking lot. According to Bonnie, these smoke-filled photos brought back memories for her and a core of the bar's other longtime patrons. They were among the very few who still fought wildfires themselves. Like the Deckers, they tended to be canyon-dwellers who knew full well that the fire department wouldn't necessarily save them. They operated like a band of vigilantes, and in a pinch they always helped one another out. The day before, Chip had described this to me as a "rotating volunteer system" in which you helped a neighbor and then he or she helped you. This was an old practice that went back to California's ranching days, when even distant neighbors came to help battle a blaze. It was never anything official, just a loose network of people united by mutual self-interest and an underlying belief that fires could be fought. A number of the Deckers' friends fell into this framework, including their eighty-nine-year-old neighbor Ralph Neubert, who owned the Dume Room. Annie Ellis, a famous Hollywood stuntwoman and a close friend of Bonnie's, was another who sometimes pitched in. In the 1978 fire, one old friend of Millie's named Larry Houston drove thirty miles back to Decker Canyon. He took the back roads, circumventing the roadblocks, and then helped Bonnie evacuate the horses through a fire tunnel. Houston was sixty-one years old at the time.

"Blake has helped me evacuate the horses during a fire," said Bonnie. Blake smiled modestly. "I can always call the Dume Room for help," continued Bonnie. "And if the phone lines are working and the police blockade isn't too tight, people come and help."

"During a fire this place is like a crisis center," explained Blake. "Someone will call down here to say they need help, and ten or fifteen guys will get up and go."

As Blake poured us another round of beers, people along the bar began interjecting with their own fire stories. A sound engineer who'd worked for Britney Spears and Fleetwood Mac recounted the time that Fleetwood threw all his antique British silver into his swimming pool to save it from an oncoming fire. The bar's ancient proprietor, Ralph Neubert, showed up with a woman a quarter of his age and proceeded to tell me that he had "built a positively fireproof home" with a brick exterior and a sunken roof that he could fill with water "just like a lake."

"What's the mood like in here after a fire?" I asked finally.

"The drinks are definitely flowing," said Bonnie. "The stress is just so built up that you just need a release. After a disaster we just come down and unite. It's pretty much, *Well, we've survived*, and, yeah, I'd say we're partying hardy, because we've got a lot of cleanup afterward."

In Malibu, the aftermath of a fire is sometimes worse than the fire itself. Almost as soon as fire season ends, the winter rains arrive, and with them come the mudslides. When the rain pummels down on Malibu's burnt slopes, the rate of erosion typically increases anywhere from two to thirty-five times. The result is massive mudslides in which topsoil, ashes, charred tree stumps, and rolling boulders crash down on houses, wrecking property and sometimes smothering people in their sleep.[13] Then come the burned animals—rats, rabbits, ground squirrels, and coyotes—often crawling under people's houses and porches to die quietly in the shade. Bonnie remembered this quite vividly after the 1978 fire. "They were burned and infected and rotting and they smelled putrid," she later recalled. "I just shot them to put them out of their misery."

"Have the fires ever made you think about moving?" I asked her.

"No," replied Bonnie, unblinking. "This is my home. I don't rent. I didn't move here just to get the Malibu address and the 90265 zip code. Of course, after the major fires you see more houses for sale, but not mine."

⚡

When I returned to the Decker Ranch late that evening, I found Millie in the parlor watching a John Wayne movie. "I thought I would ride my horse tomorrow," she told me as I sat down beside her. Little did I realize that the preparation for this ride would take up much of the following day.

The next morning we set to work. First we had to wash the horse, let it dry, and groom it. Then we had to polish Millie's show saddle—an intricately engraved, custom-made leather seat with a sterling silver nameplate on back that read "Millie." Next we selected and polished an accompanying set of bridle and reins. Finally came Millie's personal preparations. I watched her try on roughly half a dozen outfits as she searched for the perfect combination of boots, pants, shirt, cowboy hat, and hairdo. When everything was ready, we walked down to the corral and Millie cantered around the ring on her horse, Skipper. "He's a palomino," yelled Millie as she whizzed past me. "Like the one that Roy Rogers rode!"

As late afternoon eased into evening, Millie suggested that we visit the gravesite of Jimmy Decker, which was something she'd been meaning to do for some time. In keeping with Jimmy's own requests, he was buried on a jagged cliff amid a den of rattlesnakes. Even in death, Jimmy Decker seemed capable of great bravado and bombast, yet few had the patience or nerve to visit his grave. "It isn't the easiest place to find," Millie told me, "but I think I could take you there." I shot her an uneasy look. "Don't worry, we'll take Carl, and he'll take his gun," she told me.

So just before twilight, Millie, Carl, and I set out in search of Jimmy Decker's grave. Carl led the way, with a loaded pistol tucked under his arm. Millie followed closely behind, stumbling over rocks she could barely see, calling out a steady sequence of directions, many of which were contradictory: "Over this way—no, that way . . . Down that way, but up first . . . This looks good, at least I thought it did." After a great deal of bushwhacking and a few rattlesnake scares, we emerged onto a narrow outcropping of rocks.

"I think this is it!" said Millie, catching her breath.

Carl and I exchanged skeptical looks. There were no markers of any kind. Unfazed, Millie paraded across the rocks until she came to a seemingly random spot. Here she stopped and bid me to dig up some dirt. Reluctantly, I agreed. I dug through a thin layer of topsoil until I came upon a dusty rock that was engraved with a crescent moon about two inches in diameter. I dusted it off some more and realized that this small carving was actually a perfect circle. "That's it!" shouted Millie excitedly. Then she explained how this could be: Before Jimmy died, he asked a friend to drill a hole in this rock so that his cremated remains could be deposited within. This was actually quite a fitting end for a dynamiter, explained Millie, for the hole was made with a dynamite drill and the ashes were poured in like ammonium nitrate (i.e., dynamite powder). Afterward, the top of the hole was sealed off with a narrow plug of concrete. "I told you I could find it," said Mille.

Together Millie, Carl, and I sat beside Jimmy Decker's elongated grave for about half an hour. "In the wintertime I come here to sit and pull a few weeds," explained Millie. "It's just nice and peaceful up here, don't you think?"

Later that evening, as Millie and I sat in the comfort of her parlor, she talked about her last days with Jimmy. "He died on the eighth of April," she told me. "A bunch of us were gathered around his bed when he went. The next day Neptune came and picked him up—that's the cremation people," she explained. "Those Neptune people are constantly sending me advertisements," she lamented. "It's not that I mind that my time is coming—it's just that I don't like being pressured."

❧

On one of our last days together Millie and I drove her powder blue 1969 pickup truck to the local pet store to buy feed for her chickens. Given Millie's poor eyesight, I was a little nervous with her behind the wheel, but she drove surprisingly well. On the way home we were chatting pleasantly when we came across what appeared to be smoke clouds. "Damn!" said Millie. This was the worst language I'd ever heard from her. Together we peered through the truck's grimy windshield, straining our eyes for any signs of fire. After a few tense minutes, we gave up. It was just a case of the jitters and a bit of LA smog. "I guess we've been talking too much fire," said Millie.

As we drove back through Decker Canyon, gingerly navigating the road's many hairpin turns, I asked Millie what she would do when the next big fire came. "I'm sure if we had another fire Bonnie and Chip wouldn't want me to be here," she told me. "But every little bit helps. I might not be able to help on the hill because I don't have the footing or the eyes. If nothing else, I could take drinking water to people. I could wet the sacks. There are any number of things that might save them a few steps. I know they wouldn't want me around, but I know if I left it would make me feel worse."

Millie slowed the truck down to a crawl as we pulled into the Decker driveway. "The thing is," she said, "I've never left the ranch during a fire."

⚡

After spending two weeks in Decker Canyon, I booked a standby ticket back to Boston, refilled my rental car with gas, and prepared for one last journey through the wormhole.

On the morning of my departure, I hiked to the upper ranch to have one last look around. Several of the friendlier sheepdogs followed me, scurrying underfoot, yelping playfully, and then dashing ahead to lead the way. Eventually I found a perch just above Chip's house, where I sat with the dogs and tossed pebbles down the slope. It was a cool, quiet morning. The sun hadn't yet cleared the mountains and much of the canyon was still blanketed with shadows.

The night before, Millie had asked me if I was ready to go home. Somehow this seemed like a loaded question. I *was* ready to go home, and yet I couldn't help but feel what a pitifully tenuous word that was for me. Up until now this had never seemed to bother me. In fact, it was a point of pride. I had wanderlust! But as now, as I surveyed the Decker Ranch, I had to suppress a slight twinge of envy. Why didn't my family have a home like this, with history and traditions and an almost organic sense of permanence? At what point had we opted for a life of transience—a life of following job opportunities, bigger yards, and better school districts? For months I had been assessing the costs of staying at home, but rarely had I considered the costs of moving, continually—twelve times in a lifetime and probably more—until home was nothing but a quaint thought smudged across a doormat. The simple truth of the matter was, I had never been connected to a place like this, and so of course the notion of braving home seemed both curious and perverse.

Later that morning, I cooked (though I should say burned) some french toast for Millie and me. "This is just great," said Millie appreciatively. "You'll have to cook it again on your next visit." I nodded my head, rather embarrassedly, and kept chewing. "Maybe you'll bring your riding boots and we can saddle up together," continued Millie. I told her this sounded like fun, but that I didn't own cowboy boots. Millie shot me a quizzical look, as if this were inconceivable.

After breakfast I thanked Millie for taking me in, feeding me, and sharing her stories with me. "I'm going to miss you," I told her finally.

"You big prevaricator," she replied. "Just give me a call once in a while. I can't hear the phone ring, but the dog will bark when he hears it, and I'll pick up eventually."

Hours later, as my plane cleared the runway at LAX, I looked out my window to take in one last glance at the Pacific Ocean and the Santa Monica Mountains in the distance. For a moment I thought I could make out Point Dume and the last stretch of the PCH that leads to Decker Canyon. Then we broke through the clouds and everything went white.

# Island of the Storm Riders

Grand Isle, Louisiana

"You're going to *Grand Isle?*" said the rent-a-car woman skeptically, drawing out every last syllable in a thick New Orleans drawl that seemed to give me just enough time to reconsider my intentions. "You going to the edge of the world—you know that?"

"Uh-huh," I said.

"I mean, that's the *end* of the line," she added, as she dangled my car keys over the counter, still unwilling to hand them over.

"I hear you," I replied. In fact, that's what I had been hearing for quite some time, almost verbatim, from a number of people, including the FEMA agent who had put me onto this story. A few months earlier I'd talked to a man named David Passey—one of many, many FEMA people I called during my location-scouting quest—and he convinced me rather quickly that Grand Isle was not to be missed. "Basically," said Passey, "you take this two-lane road down the bayou, way out into the marsh, until you hit a bridge that takes you to this little island that sticks out into the Gulf of Mexico. That's Grand Isle, and it gets pretty roughed up by hurricanes."

This was an understatement. In 1893, and again in 1965, Grand Isle was destroyed by direct hits. Then, of course, there were the near misses, the many hurricanes that just passed through the region but still managed to sink the island. Yes, *sink* it.

This is the principal problem with Grand Isle: Cartographers may call it an island, but it more closely resembles an oversize sandbar composed of silt from the Mississippi River. When hurricanes of even a small magnitude draw near, they tend to create tidal surges that wash over the top. In the hours after a storm, often there is no visible land, just a handful of houses and trees poking out of the water. Grand Isle sits at the very edge of terra firma, a boundary between land and sea that itself is really neither. Technically it is a "barrier island," a giant seawall for the continent at its back. Ask anyone in New Orleans and they'll tell you that Grand Isle is their rampart, their outermost line of defense against the Gulf. It's the only inhabited barrier island in the state, and to mainlanders, it's the end of the world.

"Insurance?" asked the car rental woman.

"The full package," I told her. Then, at long last, she relinquished the keys.

An hour or so later I was on my way, following David Passey's lead down the bayou and on toward the Gulf of Mexico. In this part of the world it is commonly said that there are only two directions—up the bayou and down the bayou. Strictly speaking, a bayou is a sluggish stream that meanders through a marsh or plantation. The bayou I was now driving alongside, known as Bayou Lafourche, was actually quite large because it was once a major distributary of the Mississippi River. At one time, the mouth of the Mississippi had dozens of distributaries, which branched out in a triangular fashion before dumping their waters into the Gulf of Mexico. At this broad interface, between the river and sea, a wide, silt-rich delta accumulated. Historically, this posed a major problem for the people of New Orleans. It made the mouth of the Mississippi virtually unnavigable. To solve this problem, the city built a series of levees that narrowed the river and channeled it far out into the depths of the Gulf. As a result, the many distributaries of the Mississippi turned into sluggish waterways—much like Bayou Lafourche—meandering their way across a great marsh before easing into the Gulf.

I was heading southward, or "down the bayou," along a small road that followed Bayou Lafourche to the Gulf. Gradually all traces of solid land disappeared, giving way to a vast marshland. The road continued onward along a narrow runway of rocks that tapered off into the distance. I found the never-ending flatness of the marsh to be oddly dreamlike—its reeds and water lilies extended as far as the eye could see, as if a giant Monet had been unfurled to the edge of the horizon. And through it all, almost nothing stirred. I drove for miles at a time without seeing another car. Occasionally I came upon a small house on stilts with a rickety gangplank that stretched down to the road. Once I passed through a small town that centered around a lonesome filling station and a Piggly Wiggly grocery store with a billboard that read, TRUST IN GOD WILL DRIVE AWAY FEAR. JESUS IS LORD. On the outskirts of this town were a handful of small shrimping boats anchored along the bayou, several of which had tattered Confederate flags fluttering in the wind. Two sunburned shrimpers looked up as my engine called to them, and they gave me hard blank stares as I sped past.

Fishing remains one of the most dependable ways to make a living along the bayou. Despite the landscape's vacant appearance, the entire region is actually teeming with shrimp, crabs, oysters, and fish. "Anyone who is hungry here is just too lazy to step outside and get something to eat," one fisherman later told me. The region's bird life is also abundant. Bird watchers estimate that three quarters of all the known birds in North America have been spotted in the Grand Isle area—from common fowl like black duck and snow geese to rare gems like the Eurasian collard dove and the magnificent frigatebird.[1]

At one time, there was an equally impressive range of larger animals. Early European settlers came upon bears, panthers, wolves, and bison. In 1858, a New Orleans newspaper reported that one marsh inhabitant managed to kill four hundred alligators in just three months.[2] The skins brought seventy-five cents apiece (a nice price back then), and before long the marsh was filled with hunters and trappers seeking their fortunes. A number of these hardy out-doorsmen chose to live on the sandy ridges that separated the marsh from the Gulf of Mexico. Among these ridges, two in particular stood out: a narrow peninsula that jutted out into the Gulf, known as Cheniere Caminada, and an island just a few hundred yards off its tip called Grand Isle. Both were remarkable because they had thick groves of oak trees with soil-gripping roots and protective branches that created a beautiful and apparently safe place to live. Word spread of this sanctuary at the foot of the Gulf, and by the end of the 1800s Grand Isle and Cheniere Caminada were occupied not just by trappers, fishermen, and farmers, but also by several luxury hotels.

Then, in early October of 1893, a massive hurricane swept in from the Gulf and devastated the two communities, killing roughly 850 people.[3] Afterward, the peninsula of Cheniere Caminada was al-most entirely abandoned, and it never regained its stature as a town. Grand Isle, on the other hand, survived. Although the luxury hotels closed for good, a number of the island's fishermen and trappers stayed. Several decades later, in 1965, they paid the price once more. In the late summer of that year, Hurricane Betsy plowed through the island, damaging or destroying almost every standing structure. Af-terward, as looters sifted through the rubble, even they must have been surprised at how little was left. Hurricane Betsy was so destruc-tive that the National Hurricane Center retired its name, as is cus-tomary with particularly bad storms.

As I drove onward, hurricanes were very much on my mind. The road down the bayou offered constant reminders in the form of small blue warning signs reading, HURRICANE EVACUATION

ROUTE: FOR INFO TUNE TO 870 AM, 101.9 FM. Grand Isle is particularly prone to evacuations. When the town's current mayor, David Camardelle, was first elected in 1997, he ordered mandatory evacuations on four weekends in a row. Evacuations like these are often a frantic race against time, or, more specifically, against one grim certainty: If a hurricane draws near, the tide will rise and large sections of the road to New Orleans will disappear beneath a swell of salt water. Needless to say, no one wants to be stuck halfway down the bayou when this happens. The options are either to leave early, which almost everybody does, or to stay. I knew from my brief phone conversation with Josie Cheramie, the island's director of tourism, that a few locals always stayed, including the police and a handful of self-proclaimed "storm riders." Amazingly enough, the storm riders were generally senior citizens. According to Cheramie, they were the last remnants of the old Grand Isle. Now, like most retirees on the island, they tended to hang out at a local diner called the Starfish—which is precisely where I was headed.

Continuing down the bayou, I fiddled with the dial on my car radio until I found a news update on an infant storm named Tropical Depression Fifteen (or TD Fifteen) that was currently soaking Honduras and Nicaragua. According to the radio, TD Fifteen was now threatening to spin out into the warm waters of the Caribbean and become a tropical storm. From there, if the conditions were right, it might even become a hurricane.

As my radio signal faded, I rolled down the windows, letting the warm air of the Gulf flap against my face. It was late October—Tuesday the thirtieth to be precise—the twilight of hurricane season.* For coastal dwellers it was a superstitious time of year when it was considered bad luck to breathe easy. And this year many people were

---

* Hurricane season is a six-month period that runs from June 1 to November 30.

doubly superstitious because the United States was riding a lucky streak in which not a single hurricane had hit the mainland in the past two storm seasons. If the luck held through November, it would be only the second time in a century that this had happened. No one liked statistics like these. They belied the nagging rule of odds: Two years was a long time — a storm was about due.

⚡

The unyielding flatness of the horizon was finally broken by what appeared to be a giant barstool way off in the distance. As I sped onward, the clumsy structure came into focus, and I recognized what it was: a water tower. This was the first landmark I'd spotted in miles, and it meant that Grand Isle was just around the corner. Moments later, I arrived on the sparsely settled peninsula of Cheniere Caminada, which ever so slightly rose from the marsh. I slowed my car as I passed the peninsula's lone cemetery. It was a forlorn lot, with a giant wooden cross and a dead oak tree whose skeletal branches swayed over the top of several crumbling tombs. A nearby sign commemorated the hurricane victims of 1893, most of whom were reportedly "buried in mass graves in this cemetery." The rest of Cheniere Caminada was just as spooky. Not a single person appeared anywhere near the handful of houses that lined the peninsula, and without hesitation I continued on across the low-lying steel bridge that stretched out to Grand Isle.

The moment I exited the bridge I felt a vague sense of relief. Unlike Cheniere Caminada, Grand Isle had a prominent central ridge that stood twelve feet in height and ran almost the entire length of the island. Although Grand Isle was just a sliver of land sticking out into the Gulf — seven miles in length and half a mile in width — its central ridge provided a sense of sturdiness, like a giant earthen backbone.

I turned onto Grand Isle's one main road and followed it down the length of the island. This road effectively splits the island in two halves—one facing the Gulf and the other facing the marsh. On the "Gulf side" there is a picturesque beach lined with a number of palatial summer homes that belong to people from New Orleans and Baton Rouge, and beyond are the roaring waves of the Gulf, which stretch out to the horizon, where the oil rigs lurk, rising together from the sea like some dark futuristic city. On the "marsh side" is a forest of oak trees that conceal most of the island's far more modest homes, belonging to the locals, and beyond the trees are the murky waters of the marsh, also known as Barataria Bay. Though I hardly realized it at the time, the main road is a very meaningful divide in Grand Isle. On one side are the summer people, who love the sea; on the other side are the locals, who know what it can do.

Two miles later, on the marsh side of the road, I came across a sun-bleached sign with blue lettering that read, THE STARFISH. I pulled into the parking lot and instinctively locked all my car doors, a gesture that certainly gave me away as an outsider. Almost immediately I was mistaken for a bird watcher. (This is a misconception that I am still rather sore about. Being a fact-checker I could handle — but a *bird watcher*?) "No," I told the man who had inquired, "I'm here for the hurricanes." He nodded his head skeptically.

Inside, the Starfish was a no-frills kind of place with a handful of wooden booths, a jukebox that played mainly soft rock, an aging waitress with a bottomless pot of coffee, and an electronic gambling machine in back that burped out a small jackpot of coins once every few days. I took a seat, feigned interest in a menu, and tilted my head toward a nearby table where a handful of seniors were sitting. In the coming days, I earned the nickname "plastic man," because as one regular explained, "Your ears looked like they could stretch all the way across the room."

My eavesdropping was soon interrupted when a skinny man in

hunting overalls and camouflage baseball cap walked over to my table. "I'm Ambrose Besson," he said in a garbled French accent that sounded more like "Ambroshe Bayzon." Like so many people on Grand Isle, Ambrose prided himself as a "Cajun," which is actually slang for Arcadian. The Arcadians were French pioneers who first settled the rocky shores of Nova Scotia in the 1600s and stayed there until the British began to expel them roughly a century later. Many of these hardy Frenchmen found their way down to southern Louisiana, where there was already a sizable French population. Here they resumed their lifestyle as pioneers, settling the outer fringes of the map and gleaming a hard, frugal life off the land. In Grand Isle, being Ca-

*Ambrose pauses to lean against a walkway that crosses Grand Isle's "hurricane protection dune."*

jun—or a "coonass," as the locals say—was a point of pride. Not only did it mean that you were keeping up the old tradition, it meant you were tough.

"Glad to meet you," he said. "Are you visiting? A student of some sort, eh?" He eyed my notepad and nodded vigorously, as if he'd hit the nail on the head. "I've had students interview me before," he boasted. "I believe they were from Iowa. In fact, I have the transcript if you're interested. Mind if I sit down? Where you from, Iowa? No, not from Iowa? Can't blame you. So, eh, what do you want to know?"

"You're Ambrose Besson?" I asked.

"That's me," he said with a rat-tat-tat-tat of his fingers on the table-top. He had a roughly shaved chin with a few breakaway curlicues and a face that was tanned and deeply creased from a lifetime of exposure to the wind and sun.

"Are you related to Roscoe Besson?" I asked him.

"Yes," replied Ambrose. "Did you know Roscoe?"

"No," I explained, "but I've read about him." Roscoe "the Rock" Besson was a legend on Grand Isle. According to one newspaper article that I'd found, the Rock had been riding out storms for seven decades and was "determined to carry that tradition to his grave."[4] Unfortunately, this is precisely what he had done. As Ambrose soon explained to me, the Rock had since died of cancer. Fortunately, the next name on my list of storm riders to track down was Ambrose Besson—the Rock's little brother.

The waitress refilled Ambrose's coffee and brought me a large bowl of gumbo with a bottle of Louisiana Hot Sauce. As I ate, Ambrose sipped his coffee and talked about storms. "I've never left for a hurricane," he told me. "I just figure nothing is going to happen to me. I'll get by, I'll make it, and afterward I'll start saving stuff."

"What kind of stuff can you save?" I asked him.

"Not much," he said with a laugh. "Believe me, not much. Your pictures, photograph albums—it's impossible to evacuate all that stuff—so you got to get it out of the water right away. And today you've got freezers with fish and meat, and you got to get the generator turned on so it doesn't spoil." Ambrose paused for a minute or so, then added, "That's one reason for staying, but that's not worth risking your life."

"So what *is* worth risking your life for?" I asked him.

"Well, I've been a police officer for forty-five years," he said. "I'm in the reserves now, pretty much retired, but when I was on active duty, dealing with storms was part of the job. We took care of people's property once they evacuated—drove around, did patrols, tried to stop the looting." Looting has always been a serious concern on Grand Isle, explained Ambrose. Back in 1965, in the wake of Hurricane Betsy, the looters came down the bayou by boat and rummaged through the debris for whatever they could find. There was probably looting after the hurricane of 1893 as well, speculated Ambrose. He may be right. According to one local legend, after the storm thieves scoured Cheniere Caminada for gold. Many of the old homes on Cheniere Caminada had mud-filled walls, and in lieu of a bank, residents allegedly stuffed their gold coins into the mud for safekeeping. When the wind ripped these walls apart, the gold coins were dispersed and the thieves were soon looking for them.[5]

"After Betsy we put an end to looting," said Ambrose. "We really stepped up our efforts to patrol the island directly before and after the storms." In the coming days, a number of residents told me how grateful they were for this heightened security. As one woman put it: "It's a terrible, sinking feeling to come onto the island after a storm and see the devastation, and then on top of that, find that someone has looted what you have left. And I think that's one of the things that makes our police and civil defense so strong in their hearts to stay."

"So you stay out of a sense of duty?" I asked Ambrose finally.

"Not really," he replied. "As a policeman I needed to be here, but not really for the storms themselves. I could have just come back afterward—they would have flown me in."

I suppressed an urge to sigh, stammered, began to ask another question, and then thought better of it. Ambrose had sensed correctly that I was looking for a story, or more precisely an answer, and he wasn't going to tell me everything all at once. We had begun a courtship of sorts, and if I wanted his story we would have to dance.

Ambrose turned around to face the table where he was originally sitting. A handful of seniors, who looked to be his friends, watched on eagerly. "Hey y'all," shouted Ambrose, "he's putting me on *The Young and the Restless*, and I am going to appear in a leopard-skin bikini!" The table erupted in laughter. "That's the gang," Ambrose told me softly. "I'll introduce you later."

Over the course of the next two weeks, I would meet the core members of the gang and a handful of other seniors who also hung out at the Starfish. There was "Leg," a burly, one-legged fisherman whose second wife had handicapped him with a blast from her shotgun. "She was shooting for my balls," Leg later told me. "I'm just glad she missed and hit my leg instead." There was Rosalie Trahan, a seventy-year-old woman who often spent her days cooking nightshade, a highly poisonous plant that she boiled eight or nine times to remove the toxins and turn it into a hardy Cajun dish called *merille*. There was seventy-six-year-old Ruby Mitchell, who grew up in a horse stable after her house was destroyed by a hurricane. "Back then, I wore flour sacks for clothing because that's all my family could afford," Ruby later recalled. A final regular worth mentioning (though he wasn't there that first day) was Bobby Santiny, a cantankerous former oil rig worker who claimed to be the most dedicated storm rider on the island.

According to Ambrose, the members of his gang were the last of a kind. Most of them were "old-time Cajuns," as he put it. Growing up, they learned the tricks of the marsh, like how to mend a fishing net, paddle a pirogue, or tiptoe over deep mud. They came of age in the 1950s, a time when the island was infiltrated by big oil companies, and almost overnight they had to adapt to a new way of life. They took jobs on oil rigs, or on charter boats, or looking after the many vacationers who had rediscovered Grand Isle. Nowadays members of "the gang" were mostly retired, and they spent their morning at the Starfish, drinking coffee and talking about storms and cooking and the way things used to be. Generally they spoke in Cajun French—a language that was quickly becoming extinct on Grand Isle—and when those from the younger generation came in to have lunch or grab a coffee on their way to work, they often didn't understand a word being said.

Ambrose's role in the gang was that of court jester, and he claimed it had been ever since he was born on April Fool's Day in 1934. "That's probably why I like to joke around so much," he told me. Moments later, Ambrose turned and addressed the gang. "Listen up," he told them. "The boy is writing a book about Grand Isle. It's called *Seven Miles of Sand and Sin*."

"That's a good one," replied someone.

"That *is* a good one," admitted Ambrose. Pleased with himself, he turned back to me. "So, what do you want to know?"

"I want to know what it's like during a hurricane," I said quickly. Ambrose smiled. I had changed my approach.

"Well, I was here for Betsy, did you know that?" he asked.

"No," I told him. "What was that like?"

"Well, we stuck it out at the Coast Guard station," explained Ambrose. "We had about ninety people in there for Betsy, because she came in fast and a lot of people got trapped on the island. The wind outside was breaking at about a hundred and eighty-five miles or so, and you could hear it coming like a freight train. The water came up six or seven feet over the island. You'd see houses, cars, even horses floating down the street. All the land on the island just went under. When I finally got to my house everything I owned was gone."

"And you rebuilt after that?"

"Yes," said Ambrose, "and I didn't have a nickel's worth of insurance either. Nobody did. They wouldn't sell it to us back then. It all came out of my own pocket."

"What if there is another big hurricane?" I asked.

"Oh, there definitely *will* be another big hurricane," replied Ambrose. "In fact, it could be out there right now. There's a little pressure area out over the Yucatan, and it might come this way."

Ambrose turned toward the gang for one last bon mot. "I am being interviewed about the storms," he explained, "because I've always stayed for them, unlike you pussies." Ambrose mumbled the last word, presumably so as not to offend any of the ladies at the table, but they definitely heard him, and several rolled their eyes. Ambrose smiled apologetically and then motioned his head toward the door. "Come on," he said to me. "Let's go have a look at the Gulf, see if we are in for some *mauvais temps*. Better write that one down," he added. "It's French for 'bad weather.'"

❧

Ambrose and I strolled out of the Starfish toward his big, green pickup truck. The inside of the truck was clean and almost completely empty, except for Ambrose's revolver, which he always kept above the emergency break. "I'm still a police officer," he explained. The town of Grand Isle has exactly eight police officers to watch over its 1,541 residents. Of those eight officers, four are on active duty, four are in the reserves, and all but one of them are in their twenties. That one, of course, is Ambrose Besson, who at the age of sixty-seven is the old man of the force. "I still know what I am doing when I go out there," he assured me. "Of course the laws have changed, and the techniques too. Now these young guys wear bulletproof vests." Ambrose grunted disgustedly and then laughed. "Like they're on *Miami Vice* or something."

Ambrose steered us onto the main road and back toward the bridge. From the comfort of the truck's passenger seat, I now had a chance to get a good look at many of the island's oversize seafront houses. Most had names that eliminated any trace of subtlety. There was The Children's Palace, Thanks Dad, Monee's Moments, Pappy's Dream, and How Lucky Can I Get. "Those are vacation homes," explained Ambrose. "Down here we usually call them summer camps. People have been coming to Grand Isle for a long time to vacation. It's kind of a tradition. They used to have some big hotels down here before the storm of 1893. You can read about it at the library."

The following day, I located the library and spent the first of many afternoons there, reading up on Grand Isle's history. A modern, spacious building on the Gulf side of the road, the library contained an excellent local history section. It was here that I read up on the vacation tradition that Ambrose had mentioned. I learned that the aristocracy of New Orleans used to summer in Grand Isle. They came to escape the diseases that ravaged the city, like malaria, smallpox, tuberculosis, typhoid, and especially yellow fever. Often the summer crowd was lured by enticing ads such as this one, which ran in the *Times-Democrat* in August of 1882: "Why Not Come Down? . . . Iced tea, and moonlight, lovevine and jasmine-flower, youth and beauty, surf costume, dances and song, and whatever else the wild waves may suggest or happy hearts incline to." Among those who came to visit was the novelist Kate Chopin, who used Grand Isle as the opulent setting for her masterpiece, *The Awakening*. There were a number of comfortable accommodations on the island, but the most extravagant of these was the Ocean Club, which was built in 1892 and featured 160 suites, 2 dining halls, 2 parlors, a billiards room, a card room, a children's dining room, an observatory, tennis courts, a bowling alley, and some 60 bathhouses on the beach. The contractors who built the Ocean Club allegedly boasted, "Nothing could blow it away." Roughly one year after its completion, however, the Ocean Club was destroyed along with the island's other hotels in the great hurricane of 1893.[6]

As Ambrose and I continued down the island, passing one gleaming seafront mansion after another, I couldn't help but wonder who was financing all of this new construction. Why were banks approving mortgages for these "summer camps" given the island's calamitous history?

"Insurance," explained Ambrose as we sped past a particularly large house called the Presidential Palace. "Today we've got government-backed insurance." Ambrose was referring to the National Flood Insurance Program, which Congress established in 1968 to provide coastal residents with affordable coverage. Before that, flood insurance was almost impossible to get. As a result, banks wouldn't provide mortgages, and people along the coast tended to pay in cash for rather modest homes. But when the National Flood Insurance Program went into effect, people began to build dozens of mansions along the beach, much like the Presidential Palace. There was an upside to all of this. In order to be eligible for this insurance, the government insisted on stricter building requirements. Today most homes on Grand Isle rested on stilts. The stilts significantly reduced the risk of flooding. Unfortunately, they did little to prevent wind damage.

"Have a look at this," said Ambrose as he pulled his truck off the road. We were now parked in a large dusty lot that offered a clear treeless view down to the Gulf. In the center of this lot stood a rectangular building high up on stilts with a sign in front that read, RICKI'S MOTEL. The motel was a very ordinary structure, except that it had no roof.

"We had a tornado come through here a few weeks ago," said Ambrose. "This motel got hit pretty bad. Now if there were some trees around it might have been a different story. You see, most of us around here live back in the trees because it's the trees that save you when the storm comes. The trees break the speed of the wind. This last tornado did a lot of damage, but at my house all it did was break a few branches."

Cutting down trees on Grand Isle was forbidden, explained Ambrose. In fact, as I would later learn, those who saved trees sometimes became heroes. Such was the case with François Rigaud Jr. The Rigauds were one of the very first families to settle Grand Isle in the 1780s. Sometime in the 1830s, François Rigaud Jr. allegedly encountered a wealthy newcomer cutting down some of the island's oaks. Rigaud drew his two pistols and persuaded the man to stop, thus forever securing his fame.

Unfortunately for the people of Cheniere Caminada, there was no equivalent hero or tradition on the peninsula. Instead, they cut down most of their oaks so that the breezes of the Gulf could reach their front porches. During the hurricane of 1893, the winds coursed across the peninsula unchecked—but this was just part of the problem. Eventually the tide rose and with it came massive logs that had floated down the Mississippi and washed into the Gulf. Under other circumstances, a good covering of oak trees would have caught these logs, but since there was none, the logs hammered the peninsula like a barrage of torpedoes. The few trees that remained on the peninsula proved crucial. A single oak tree caught a large house that had been uprooted and was drifting toward the Gulf. Inside were roughly eighty frightened people (all but two of them lived). Elsewhere, a desperate woman named Adelaide Crosby allegedly had her husband tie her long hair to a tree to keep herself from being washed out to the ocean. She was thrashed against the branches for several hours but, miraculously, survived. Adelaide's story is another celebrated legend on Grand Isle. Later in my stay I actually met Adelaide's grandson, Russell Crosby, who lived just a few blocks away from Ambrose. Russell claimed his grandmother's story was true and added that she was nine months pregnant at the time of her ordeal. The storm put Adelaide into a coma, but she recovered and had a healthy baby. "That baby was my aunt," explained Russell. Most of the peninsula's residents, however, were not as fortunate as Adelaide. All in all, roughly 820 people died on Cheniere Caminada. On Grand Isle, the number was just 27.[7]

Today, Grand Isle's tradition of preserving its trees is still visibly evident. The island's central ridge is lined with a narrow forest of oaks. The roots of these oaks go deep into the soil and hold the ridge together, and their branches stretch outward, offering shelter from the storms.

"Come on," said Ambrose as he started up his truck again. "Enough about trees. Let's have a look at the Gulf." Ambrose steered us back toward the Starfish, driving down the main strip for a mile or so, then veered onto a small dirt road that led to the Gulf. Just before we reached the beach, we came upon the island's "hurricane protection dune," which is intended to break big waves during a storm. The dune, built by the Army Corps of Engineers, is about ten feet tall and runs the length of the island. Ambrose scrambled to the top and I scurried after him. All that separated us from the Gulf was a narrow strip of beach.

"You see over there?" asked Ambrose. There was a steady wind, and he clutched his cap to keep it from blowing off. "Do you see those little shore birds going up and down the beach?"

"Yeah," I said. There were a dozen or so small, brown-feathered birds with long bills hopping and squawking at one another.

"They should be migrating south right now. That means they are not going to travel any further because the weather is bad farther on their migration route. That means something is going on in the Gulf," he said as he scanned the horizon. "Now if that storm out there right now—I don't know if they named it yet—if it comes this way, well, then, part of this dune will be gone."

The wind gusted again, muffling our conversation. The birds along the shore continued to frolic in the surf. "Of course," said Ambrose, "if we get the storm right here in Grand Isle, more than just this dune will be gone."

⚡

Around twilight I parted ways with Ambrose and paid a visit to the Gulf View Lounge, a nondescript little bar that sat just half a mile down the road from the Starfish. I had been warned that the Gulf View was the biggest dive on the island. "Nothing including the front end of a gun would get me into the Gulf View," one man from the Starfish told me. "Just look at the cars parked out front." I was also told that the Gulf View was a hangout for some of the island's harder-drinking seniors.

I parked my rental car alongside a badly dented pickup truck and headed into the Gulf View. The bar was situated in an old boarded-up building with a view of the Gulf that had long since been eclipsed by a number of newer structures, including Artie's Sports Bar, which looked almost extravagant by comparison.

Upon entering the Gulf View, I was greeted by Smitty, the establishment's eighty-five-year-old proprietor—a frail, white-haired man with light blue eyes, drooping earlobes, and soft, veiny arms. By his side was his daughter Paula, a pretty woman in her early fifties who later told me that she had given up a well-paying job in Texas in order to return to Grand Isle and help her father run the bar. Other than the three of us, the place was pretty much empty—except for eighty-seven-year-old Sid Santiny, who was here for his nightly beer with his wife, Mildred. "Up until recently, Sid and I used to shoot pool in the evenings," explained Smitty. "But I'm starting to get old."

"Who was the better pool player?" I asked.

"Well, I couldn't say," replied Smitty. "Though I don't think Sid ever beat me."

As Paula poured me a Coors, Smitty took a seat beside me and explained that he once also owned a casino, a restaurant, a dance hall, and a movie theater on Grand Isle. In 1965, Betsy destroyed it all. One of the few things left standing was the marquee on the movie theater, recalled. Smitty. So a day or two after the storm came through, Smitty instructed his daughter to climb up on a ladder and rearrange the letters to read, DOUBLE FEATURE TONIGHT . . . HIGH WIND IN JAMAICA & GONE WITH THE WIND. Smitty chuckled as he recounted this part of the story. "I lost everything in that storm," he said with a shake of his head.

"My father never could be defeated," Paula told me later in the evening. "After Betsy, when he told me to put a new sign on that marquee, he was making it clear—we got wiped out, but we're going back up *today*. That's just my dad. He's a testimony to the strength of the human spirit. It's just like William Faulkner said: 'I believe that man will not merely endure: he will prevail.'"

Over the next two weeks I enjoyed several visits to the Gulf View, where I sipped beers and chatted with Paula, Smitty, Sid, and Mildred. Usually I visited in the afternoons or early evening, but the place never seemed to close. Like Smitty himself, the bar was indomitable. "Even when a hurricane comes, we only shut down if the cops force us to," Paula told me. "We just keep serving beer."

After my initial visit to the Gulf View, I set out in search of a place to sleep. With TD Fifteen on the horizon, I decided against tenting. By now, my tent was becoming something of a joke. Despite my lugging it around for several months, I had hardly used it at all, other than as a stepping stone into people's guest bedrooms. For this trip, I even contemplated leaving it at home, but this seemed unwise, for the tent itself had become a good luck charm for me. It was my bulky, fifteen-pound rabbit's foot.

I briefly considered staying at Ricki's Motel but opted instead for the comforts of a solid roof overhead and settled on another seaside motel called the Sandpiper. Late that evening, I checked into a barren but clean room with a bed and a rickety table, flicked on the television for some news, and drifted off to sleep.

I awoke just after dawn with the television still on. It was Wednesday, October 31. Halloween. I sat up in bed and watched the TV as the weatherman pointed to a map on which a large white cloud was covering much of Central America. This was TD Fifteen, he announced, and it was on the verge of becoming Tropical Storm Michelle. Apparently, this whole weather system was headed for the warm waters of the Gulf of Honduras, which would provide the energy or "fuel" needed for a much bigger storm. Then it came down to prevailing winds. If they were blowing northward, the United States could be in trouble. "We should know more by this evening," the weatherman added.

I showed up for breakfast around nine o'clock at the Starfish. Unlike the previous day, hardly anyone noticed my entrance. The regulars were glued to the television, which was playing the Weather Channel. The news was TD Fifteen, which had battered much of Central America. Flooding was rampant. In Nicaragua, some 15,000 people had been forced to flee their homes. In Honduras, thirty villages were cut off from the rest of the country. The newspapers, which were scattered across the restaurant, told similar stories. In Honduras a two-year-old boy had drowned as his father tried to carry him across a swollen stream. So far, a total of nineteen people were missing.[8] But above all, the regulars in the Starfish wanted to know one thing: Where was it headed? On this matter, there was a great deal of conflicting information. Some meteorological computer models showed this weather system hitting the United States within three or four days. Others showed it turning west and hitting Mexico.

"I think it's too late in the season for it to come up here," one of the regulars told the waitress as she refilled his coffee. "The cold front coming down from Canada is going to save us." This seemed to strike a chord with people. It *was* very late in the season. The cold front *should* save them. There was a nodding of heads, a general feeling of agreement, but nothing too emphatic. And so, as the television droned on and began to repeat itself, conversation carried on almost as usual. Yet still there was an underlying tension—a gnawing, prestorm excitement—and perhaps nowhere was it felt more acutely than at the local high school.

In the spring of 1993, a freak tornado blew in from the Gulf and destroyed much of Grand Isle's high school complex. The roof came off, several walls caved in, and a set of lockers tipped over and killed that year's prom queen, a girl named Tracie Allemand. Ever since then, the school was especially sensitive to even slight fluctuations in the weather. "A lot of parents watch the Weather Channel," explained the principal, Richard F. Augustin, whose office I visited later in my stay. "If there's some bad weather coming, parents will just come and pick up their kids." Although much of the school had been rebuilt in the form of a giant concrete bunker and was now supposedly able to withstand 125-mile-per-hour winds, people still worried, according to Augustin. "For the first few years after the tornado struck, some kids would just start to cry when the weather got bad," he told me. "Even to this day, you've got kids in high school that when the sky gets dark, they don't freak out, but they are silent, thinking to themselves, just pondering."

Despite all the hubbub over weather, none of it seemed to have any effect on Ambrose Besson. When he strolled into the Starfish shortly after nine, he sat down at my booth and casually began asking me how I had slept and what I'd eaten for dinner the night before. "Tomorrow night you'll come over to my place for oysters," he announced. Sure, I told him.

Midway through breakfast I asked Ambrose if he was worried about the possibility of TD Fifteen becoming Tropical Storm Michelle and then heading our way. "Not really," he told me. "We've never had a hurricane hit here in the month of November. We had one in late October back in 1985. That was Hurricane Juan, and it arrived on Halloween night. Put four feet of water on the island. There was no wind damage, but a lot of water damage."

"But it's not November yet," I reminded him.

"That's right," replied Ambrose. "I almost forgot. It's Halloween, isn't it?"

The waitress brought Ambrose a cup of coffee, and as he sipped it he inquired about my schedule for the day. When I told him I would be visiting Bobby Santiny—another person on my list of veteran storm riders—Ambrose laughed. "Bobby is a good friend of mine," he told me. "Have you met him? He's a real short fellow. The problem with Bobby is that he could drown standing up in three feet of water."

Like Ambrose, Bobby Santiny had a reputation for refusing to evacuate during hurricanes. It was generally agreed that the two of them were the island's longest-standing storm riders, and naturally they were somewhat competitive with each other. They were distant cousins who had grown up playing in the marsh together, gone to high school together, and ridden out quite a few storms together (including Betsy). They were both well qualified in public safety—Ambrose as a captain in the police department and Bobby as the island's former director of civil defense. In their own ways, I think each of them aspired to don the mantle of Roscoe the Rock.

The Rock was a hard act to follow. Later in my stay, the Rock's oldest son (a former chief of police by the name of Roscoe Jr.) informed me that his father had missed only one storm. "At the time, he was sick with cancer and we wheeled him out on a stretcher," Roscoe Jr. recalled. "But he gave my mother such a hard time, and he was so belligerent, we decided never to do it again. In future storms we kept him down at the police station, in a jail cell actually, and he was happier there because at least he was on Grand Isle."

Ultimately, it was Bobby Santiny who came closest to exuding this kind of zealotry. Unlike Ambrose, he unequivocally dismissed the notion of evacuating. He was resolved to stay even if another Betsy was headed directly toward the island, or at least that's what he told me when I visited him later that afternoon.

Bobby Santiny lived back in the trees in what local historians estimate is the oldest house on the island. It was built around 1800 by Jacques Rigaud, the grandfather of François Rigaud Jr., the man who famously brandished his pistols to protect the island's trees. The house was constructed without the use of any nails, and its walls were doubly reinforced with oak and bricks. It was a squat structure with low ceilings and a narrow wraparound porch. According to one local historian, the interior was once decorated with six large steel engravings of paintings by the French painter Le Brun, depicting scenes in the life of Alexander the Great.[9] Nowadays, appearances were decidedly more modest. The porch was occupied by several trash bins, a cooler, some dangling Christmas lights, and a handful of lawn chairs.

Bobby Santiny was a short man in his sixties with narrow eyes and a receding tuft of white hair. When I arrived, I found him sitting on the porch with his wife, Joan. Apparently someone in the family had just returned from hunting, because Joan was now plucking a dozen or so dead doves, discarding their feathers into the trash bins around her.

*Bobby Santiny, veteran storm rider, stands in front of his house, which is believed to be the oldest on the island.*

As I took a seat on the porch next to Bobby, he offered me a Sprite. "That'll be a dollar," he told me. When his wife objected, he silenced her: "Come on, the boy is going to make a lot of money off my story." Nervously I began to pose some preliminary questions. "Can you talk me through a storm?" I asked.

"For you, I'd say to haul ass," snapped Bobby, "because you'd freak out, and I'd be laughing at you!" I blanched, but Bobby was just warming up. When we got talking about his brother, who was the town clerk, he was far less kind: "My brother leaves for storms because he's chickenshit! He's on the city council, and they all leave. I call them all a bunch of cowards!"

When I asked Bobby about his own storm-riding career, he told me his father used to own the local grocery store and that his family always stayed on the island to protect their business. Years later, Bobby became the island's director of civil defense. "I would look after people's stuff, check on their pets, and make sure there was no looting," he told me. Currently Bobby was retired. When the storms came he went to the fire station and cooked for the younger men whose jobs required them to stay behind. "I cook jambalaya, gumbo, chicken stew, potato stew, chili soup," said Bobby. "I get my rocks off when people like my food."

After an hour or so of conversation, Bobby abruptly excused himself. "I got to go," he told me, though he made no effort to get up from his chair.

"All right," I said. "One last question: Do you ever ride storms with Ambrose Besson?"

"No," snapped Bobby indignantly, "I don't." He pointed out that Ambrose had missed Hurricane Flossy in 1956 because of military service. He also alleged that Ambrose had evacuated for one or two storms (a claim Ambrose later denied). "No, I don't ride with Ambrose," reaffirmed Bobby. "But his brother, Roscoe the Rock." He paused for a moment, somewhat wistfully. "Now, we used to ride storms together."

⚡

Later that evening I attended the town's Halloween celebration, which was held at the firehouse. As the kids danced and gorged themselves on candy, the firemen hung out in the driveway. They were brawny, well-tanned men, and most of them were dressed in costume—one as a giant yellow bird, another as a Dalmatian, and a few others as wizards and warriors. They sat around sipping Bud Light, passing out plastic fire hats to the kids, and reminiscing about previous Halloweens. Along with the police and a few paramedics, these men were the island's modern-day storm riders, and I was eager to chat with them.

As I soon learned, the firemen were mainly part-timers and volunteers. To make a living, most of them worked on the oil rigs. It was here that many of them had had their most harrowing encounters with hurricanes. "I was stuck out in the Gulf for Hurricane Juan," one of them recalled. "They tried to evacuate us by chopper, but there were seventy-five-mile-per-hour winds." Someone else recalled a storm causing fifty-foot swells to crash into the side of the rig. "If you didn't hold on to your bunk, you'd get knocked out of bed."

When it came to riding storms on the island itself, few of them had stories to tell. Most of them had been working as public safety officials for less than a decade, and in that time no major storms had hit the island. When I asked who among them would stay on the island for the next major hurricane, there was no immediate consensus. "It's hard to say," one of them told me. "Whoever is on duty," said another.

⚡

The following day was November 1, and long before dawn ever broke TD Fifteen had become Tropical Storm Michelle. By the time I made it out of bed and over to the Starfish for breakfast, a slight breeze was picking up. The sky had turned cloudy and the waters of the Gulf grew rougher. Whitecaps crashed along the shore as creaky oyster boats wobbled in and out of port.

I spent most of the day at the Starfish, chatting with the gang and watching the news. According to the Weather Channel, Tropical Storm Michelle was working its way through the Caribbean, gaining strength by the hour, and heading toward western Cuba. Still, it was too early to say where it would hit. Everyone from Fidel Castro to Florida governor Jeb Bush was taking notice. Insurance companies were also on alert. Apparently, the storm had officially entered "the box"—a region demarcated by insurers, typically stretching from North Carolina in the north to Honduras in the south, and from Texas in the west to Haiti in the east. Once a storm enters "the box," many insurers will not sell new policies or change existing ones. In short, all bets were set.

Around six P.M. I went to meet Ambrose for dinner. As I drove down Santiny Lane, I noticed that the homes in his neighborhood were decidedly more modest than the ones on the beach. Many were just rectangular boxes on stilts, high above the ground, nestled in the swaying treetops—creating the surreal effect of a floating trailer park.

I found Ambrose in his back yard, lugging two heaving sacks of oysters out to a wooden carving table. When I tried to help him with his load he shooed me away. "I'm going to show you how to shuck an oyster," he grunted. Ambrose dropped one of his sacks to the ground with a thud, and emptied the other onto the table. The oysters that spilled out were still caked in thick black mud, and they looked more like coal than seafood. Ambrose grabbed one, washed it off, chiseled it open with a knife and hammer, sprinkled it with a bottle of hot sauce that he had ready, and then popped the whole slimy load down his throat. "We call these 'Cajun Viagra' down here," he told me with a gulp.

"So you just eat them like that?" I asked.

"Of course," said Ambrose, as he worked his knife along the inside of the shell. "In the old days—before the pollution—we used to walk down the street and eat oysters right off the shore. We used to go with a bottle of Louisiana Hot Sauce in our back pocket and eat them right there in the water."

"Really?" I asked.

"You don't know much about the old days, do you?" replied Ambrose.

"Not really."

"You know what hardtack is?" asked Ambrose.

*Ambrose Besson with his fishing partner, Ray Cheramie, and a friend, Jary Nacio, standing beside the boat on which they often fish for shrimp and oysters.*

"No," I replied.

"Hardtack was the only bread we had when I was growing up," he explained. "My mother used to make it, and it was harder than rock. You hit someone over the head with hardtack and you'd kill them. To this day I do not eat the crust on sliced bread—I only like the soft stuff." Ambrose ate another oyster, wiped his mouth, and continued. "And the coffee! We used to make one pot of coffee and it would last for the whole week. It was so thick, you could put a spoon in it and the spoon would stand up straight. And coffee was a luxury. For the most part it was mullet. Mullet for breakfast, mullet for lunch, and mullet for dinner. And of course, sometimes Mama and Papa would feed us and go to bed hungry. They never said a word, but we could see what was going on. It's not that we were poor. That's just the way it was on Grand Isle back then. That was the Cajun way. And it's not that I'm complaining or saying how hard it was, it's just that you need to understand these things if you're going to do this story right."

When I asked Ambrose to tell me more about the "Cajun way," he replied succinctly: "The Cajuns lived a hard life off the land." The history books more or less agreed. Ever since their expulsion from Nova Scotia in the 1700s, the Cajuns encountered one hardship after another. One particularly hardy band of thirty Arcadians, who arrived in Louisiana in 1770, did so only after a fifteen-month ordeal of shipboard starvation, mutiny, shipwreck, imprisonment, forced labor in Spanish Texas, and finally a 420-mile overland trek. Once they arrived, life was often just as hard. In the late 1700s, the Spanish governor of Louisiana noted with amazement that many Arcadian immigrants literally worked themselves to death in order to support large families, including widowed and orphaned relatives.[10] This seemed to be the legacy to which the Cajun trappers and fishermen of Grand Isle aspired. In truth, they were not pure Cajuns. Most of them were a mix of many ethnic groups, including Arcadian, Spanish, French, Italian, Irish, German, Cuban, and perhaps others. Nonetheless, they tended to identify themselves as Cajuns. Like the New Englanders who trace their lineage back to the *Mayflower* with a regal sense of pride, many on Grand Isle boasted toughly that their families had been expelled from Nova Scotia.

When Ambrose finished shucking a few more oysters, he handed me a knife and gestured for me to get busy. As I struggled to help him shuck, he talked at length about the old days. His father was a trapper, he explained, who went after a range of animals including mink, muskrat, raccoon, and otter. Like most men in his line of work, he made month-long trips to the mouth of the Mississippi, where he lived in a tent, set traps, and collected pelts. Some of the other trappers brought their families with them. The children lived along the trapping lines and returned to school for brief spells to "catch back" their studies. But Ambrose and his father agreed it was better for him to stay on the island and attend school full-time. There was still plenty of work to be done. Ambrose farmed cucumbers every day before and after school. He combed the beach for driftwood to fuel his mother's stove (cutting down an oak tree was out of the question). And of course, he fished. Above all, however, he dedicated himself to learning English. In the 1930s the dominant language on Grand Isle was still French. But like so many things, that was about to change.

In 1931, three years before Ambrose was born, a bridge to the island was built. It connected Grand Isle to Cheniere Caminada and — for all intents and purposes — the rest of the world. The effect was dramatic. Historically, Grand Isle was a place where pirates like Jean Lafitte and champion duelists like José "Pepe" Llulla came to seek safety and obscurity.[11] Even in the early 1900s, the island remained extremely isolated. Perhaps the most telling sign of this situation was the closeness of Grand Isle's families. Many of them were interrelated. According to Ambrose, children of his generation often addressed strangers as "Aunt" or "Uncle," because in many cases that's exactly what they were. Marrying family members was inevitable. A popular saying went, "If you were lucky enough to have a good-looking cousin, you also had a wife." In 1919, when the U.S. Coast Guard built a station on Grand Isle, some of the servicemen married island girls. Other than this, however, visitors were far and few between.

As soon as the bridge was completed, however, automobiles began arriving with groceries, fuel, and building supplies. New houses went up and old ones came down. Spoken English became more and more prevalent. In the early 1940s, following the outbreak of World War II, the Civil Air Patrol built a base on the island. With the base came electricity (until then almost everyone on the island was still using kerosene). Shortly thereafter, the oil companies arrived and began hiring island men to work on offshore rigs. Money began to circulate as it never had before. Television, refrigerators, and gas stoves became increasingly commonplace. Some of these innovations were startling to the island's older residents. "My grandmother didn't know what a television was," Ambrose told me. "I tried to tell her in French how it worked, but she didn't believe it. She would say, 'How can you be so stupid! Obviously there are people hiding behind that machine, playing a trick on you!'" Ambrose had a similar experience when he tried to comfort his uncle, who had been scared by the roar of a passing airplane. "I tried to explain to him that it was a jet," recalled Ambrose. "But he wouldn't believe me. He kept asking, 'How can a plane fly without a propeller?'"

"It's not that these people were stupid," explained Ambrose. "They had just led very isolated lives, and then suddenly, everything around them had changed." For better or worse, the bridge had brought a new world to Grand Isle, and Ambrose was among the first to be born into that world. His was the bridge generation—both literally and metaphorically, for it bridged the gap between old and modern. Between Cajun and American. And according to Ambrose, between the tough and the pampered. "Young people today live like kings!" he declared. "They don't know what it's like to hunt for food, gather rainwater to drink, or collect driftwood to burn. And they certainly don't know what it's like to stay for the storms."

"How about your kids?" I asked.

"My kids?" said Ambrose. "They never had to deal with that stuff."

"So they didn't stay for storms?"

"No," said Ambrose. "They left with my wife."

"How about your parents—did they stay?"

"Sure," said Ambrose. "How could they leave? Before 'thirty-one there was no bridge. The bridge changed everything. It allowed people to leave. But in the early days it was still a long drive to the mainland, and the weather reports weren't nearly as advanced, so most people continued to stay."

According to Ambrose, staying for storms was just another one of Grand Isle's antiquated rituals. I heard about this from a number of his contemporaries as well—fellow members of the bridge generation who remembered riding the storms of the 1940s and early 1950s, in the era just before evacuations became the norm.

From what I could gather, all storm-riding rituals began with a weather report. In lieu of the Weather Channel, people on Grand Isle used a number of different forecasting techniques. Some relied on the tide, others relied on the "storm birds" flying in from the sea, and still others relied on the *bouque d'ie*—a so-called eyebrow of clouds that gathered above the moon.

If it looked like a storm was coming, there were a number of things to do. The first order of business was usually cleaning the bathtub and sealing the drain with a good stopper. This way, a large quantity of drinking water could be safely stored in the house. Next, the livestock had to be tended. This meant tying up the horses on the high ground, collecting all the eggs from the henhouse, and killing as many chickens as could be eaten (because chances were, the rest would drown). Then it was time to board up the windows and put everything away, with the most valuable items on the highest shelves. Afterward someone had to tie up all the boats, making sure to leave one small pirogue nearby, to use once the island flooded. Finally, everyone gravitated toward the sturdiest house in the neighborhood and started cooking a big meal to pass the time before the storm arrived. Some households might even break out a bottle of wine and reminisce about storms from the past. But when the actual storm arrived, the mood sobered up quickly. If things got really tense, everyone would say the rosary together. Some of the older folks kept a rope nearby, as a last resort, in case they had to tie themselves to a tree. Eventually, the wind would soften and the tension would ease. This moment of calm was deceptive, for sometimes it was actually the eye of the storm passing overhead. To be safe, everyone waited it out. A few more hours would pass. At last, the wind would vanish, the birds would chirp, and then everyone knew: The storm was gone.

"In the old days, riding storms was just something everybody did," said Ambrose finally. It was almost dark by now, and Ambrose worked swiftly, shucking the last few oysters on the table. His hand movements were efficient and graceful. Eventually he set down his knife and reached for the Louisiana Hot Sauce, which he poured generously over the remaining half-shells. "Here," he said. "You can have the last of these."

In the dim light of dusk, Ambrose used a garden hose to wash himself off. He turned on the water and rubbed his hands together methodically, working over each finger until all the dirt was off.

When he finally finished he looked back up at me and smiled. "It's all just history now," he said.

"But you still ride the storms," I added.

"Yeah," said Ambrose. "But it's not like the old days."

"So what's it like, then?" I asked.

"It's no big deal," said Ambrose. "When a hurricane comes through, the road just kind of goes under. Sometimes the water connection goes, almost always the power goes, and then it's back to kerosene lanterns. So we light our lanterns, strap stuff down, sit around, maybe cook a meal."

"It sounds a little like the old days to me," I said cautiously. Ambrose laughed.

"I suppose it does," he said.

⚡

The following afternoon I met up with Ambrose at the Starfish around three. We sat in our usual booth, ordered coffee, and discussed plans for the rest of the day. "Why not visit the cemetery?" suggested Ambrose. It should be in top shape, he explained, because the graves were recently fixed up for All Saints' Day.

Sounds good, I told him. I then asked whether he had heard the news about Michelle. Ambrose nodded. "It looks like this storm is going to enter the Gulf, and it's definitely a hurricane," he told me. "They think that it's going to circle around and go back toward Florida. But you never know when it enters the Gulf. This is still a wait-and-see."

Of course, I already knew this. I had been listening to weather reports throughout the day, memorizing every last trivial piece of information about the storm. Hurricane Michelle was continuing on a northeast course toward western Cuba. From there, the National Hurricane Center was predicting that a trough of low pressure would sweep down through the Gulf and push the storm east through the Straits of Florida and out into the Atlantic. To test this theory, the National Weather Service was launching a series of weather balloons twice a day.

As for Grand Isle, the mayor wasn't ready to call an evacuation. I had met up with him earlier in the day for a brief interview. "It's not time for that yet," he told me from his office in the old Coast Guard station, which is now the city hall. Ever since he evacuated the island on four consecutive weekends back in 1997, the mayor had developed a reputation (at least among some people) as an alarmist. Over the years several local business owners had accused him of driving away the tourists, and one even demanded to be reimbursed for his losses. "That guy walked into my office and threw a bill down on my desk," lamented the mayor. "I told him, 'Look, I lost several hundred dollars on my snow cone business, but I can't worry about that—my job is to protect human life." As far as Hurricane Michelle was concerned, the mayor was determined to play it cool. "This one looks like it's headed for Cuba," he told me. "But I'll be watching it."

When Ambrose and I finished our afternoon coffee, we got into his pickup and headed down the main road toward the tip of the island. "I'm going to have to postpone my hunting trip," he said, somewhat annoyed. "I was supposed to go to Alabama. I got a hunting cabin up near the Florida panhandle, and I was planning to spend two or three months up there, but with this hurricane coming, I'll have to stick around for a bit."

Ambrose steered us off the main road and onto a small tree-covered lane that led to the cemetery. He pulled his truck off to the side of the road and the two of us got out. The sky was overcast and the wind was really gusting, which today had a decidedly foreboding effect. We walked down the lane under a swaying canopy of oaks until we reached the gate to the cemetery. Inside was a collection of aboveground tombs; most were freshly whitewashed and adorned with flowers.

"Around here we don't bury people in the ground," explained Ambrose as we continued into the heart of the cemetery. "If you go down more than three or four feet you hit the water table. That's why we use these big aboveground cement tombs. Still, sometimes we have problems during the storms."

"What kind of problems?"

"During Betsy a couple of these tombs washed away," explained Ambrose. "In fact, we found one of them thirty miles out in the marsh. It belonged to my niece. She was just a girl when she died. She was born with a physical defect. Really she was a twin, but the other child never developed on its own — it just grew off her side . . ."

"Like a Siamese twin?" I asked.

"That's it," said Ambrose. "We used to have some birth defects here on the island in the old days."

"I see."

"Well, anyway, as I said, this twin never fully developed. It was more like a large growth. So the doctors decided to cut it off, and my niece never really recovered from that surgery. She couldn't do anything but drag herself on the floor at home. Her arms would just fold up, she couldn't talk or anything, and eventually she died. I'm just glad we got her tomb back here in the cemetery."

As we continued strolling through the cemetery, Ambrose pointed out that several of the tombs were buckled down to the earth with thick canvas belts. "Those are hurricane straps," he explained. "They keep the tombs buckled down. A lot of people use them around here."

"How about the Rock?" I asked. "Is his tomb buckled down?"

"No, the Rock is buried over here in our family tomb," said Ambrose. He led the way to a large cement box, roughly the size of a minivan, with a small sliding door on front. "This tomb is big enough that it doesn't need hurricane straps," explained Ambrose. "All of my family is in here. There is a pit underneath, and you can stack plenty of people inside. We've got eight people in there right now, including my parents and my grandparents. The last one to be put in was my brother. I'll go on top of him and then the tomb will be sealed."

"So you're the last one?"

"Yes," replied Ambrose.

I spent the rest of the day with Ambrose, driving around in his green pickup truck, keeping an eye out for storm birds and listening to him gripe about the great deer-hunting trip that he would have to miss if the storm rolled this way. "The deer hunting in Alabama is *superbe!*" he exclaimed. "You know that spaghetti sauce we ate last night at my place? That had some of my deer sausage in it," he told me.

"Ambrose," I said finally.

"Yeah."

"What's your honest take on Michelle?"

Ambrose paused for a moment. "You know, we haven't had a bad hurricane since Betsy in 1965," he told me. "We're probably past due for a big one, but I'm pretty sure this isn't going to be it. The weather experts say it's headed for Cuba and then out into the Atlantic. And usually, well . . . those guys are right."

The following day Hurricane Michelle was upgraded to a category-4 storm, but it shied away from the Gulf and continued directly north toward Cuba. In response, Havana's mayor ordered the evacuation of 150,000 people from the city's flood-prone areas.[12] Meanwhile, the National Hurricane Center stood behind its prediction that from here Michelle would blow eastward out into the Atlantic. All signs indicated that a cold front was on its way. By Saturday evening, it arrived. The air began to chill, talk of hurricanes began to dwindle, and the waitress at the Starfish turned the TV from the Weather Channel to college football.

Around sunset I met up with Ambrose, and we walked down to the beach to have a look at the Gulf. We scrambled over the island's hurricane protection dune and continued right up to the surf. The sea had a slight chop to it, probably the same as it had all week, but it no longer seemed menacing. In the distance the sun was making its final descent, arcing downward into a tight pocket of sea between two oil rigs. The air was calm, and through it we could hear the chirping of those same little shore birds who had still not yet taken flight.

"Looks like I'll be leaving tomorrow to go deer hunting after all," said Ambrose. He looked out into the Gulf and smiled triumphantly.

As the sky darkened and the distant lights of the oil rigs began to glimmer, Ambrose turned to me and said, "You know what's going to get us in the end? Erosion."

"Erosion?"

"Yes," replied Ambrose. "You see, the barrier islands rely on the silt from the Mississippi. That's what keeps them built up. But when the Mississippi was channeled out into the Gulf of Mexico, we lost our silt. Now all that silt is just getting dumped out at sea. Meanwhile, the wave action is just eating up our little island. You see what I'm saying?"

"Grand Isle is disappearing?"

"Yes," said Ambrose. "The island is going."

I'd heard this assertion before. It was a serious concern throughout the region. In the last century alone, Louisiana's barrier islands had lost forty percent of their surface area. Sometimes as much as forty to sixty feet of land were lost in a single three-to-four-day storm. A bad storm could take a huge chunk out of an island, perhaps even fragment it. The most famous example of this was Last Isle, which once sat ten miles to the west of Grand Isle. In many ways, the histories of the two islands were eerily similar. During the mid-1800s, Last Isle was the choice vacation spot for the New Orleans aristocracy. The island's Muggah Hotel offered a range of luxuries, including a bowling alley, a billiards room, a card room, and a spacious ballroom. Advertisements boasted that "no pains [are] spared to insure the comforts of the guest." Then, in August of 1856, a hurricane swept in from the Gulf and leveled the island. Afterward, Last Isle began to erode rapidly. Between 1890 and 1988 the surface area of the island decreased by seventy-seven percent. Today, what was once Last Isle is now four separate islands known as the Isles Dernier. From a distance, observers report that they look like sandbars barely rising from the sea. Their erosion is an ongoing process, and like all of Louisiana's barrier islands, they have a PDD—a Projected Date of Disappearance. The Isles Dernier are slated to disappear in 2013. Grand Terre, the small windswept island off Grand Isle's eastern tip, is expected to be gone by 2033. With Grand Isle, it's more difficult to determine an exact PDD because the Army Corps of Engineers and the town of Grand Isle have been working feverishly to replenish the beach and build various protective structures.[13]

"They've been trying for years to keep the island from eroding," explained Ambrose. "They've built dunes, breakwaters, rock groins, and pumped in tons of sand from offshore. But sooner or later this island is going back to the water."

Neither of us spoke for a moment. Night had fallen. The sky was easing its way from purple to black, and Ambrose was squinting into the distance. He shook his head, then looked back at me. "You get another Betsy over here and there won't be too much left," he told me. "This island will be history."

The following day, Sunday, November 4, Hurricane Michelle made landfall in western Cuba. At around eleven P.M. the storm blew in across the Bay of Pigs, and what the CIA failed to achieve in 1961 Michelle did rather handily, destroying some 10,000 homes and damaging another 100,000 as it traveled northward across the island. It was a heavy blow, and Michelle proved to be the worst hurricane to hit Cuba in almost fifty years.[14]

By Monday evening, Hurricane Michelle had run its course. Having pummeled Cuba, the dying storm swept across the Bahamas and sputtered east toward the Atlantic, where it dwindled into a sea breeze. Back on Grand Isle, news of the storm's demise was most welcome. At the Starfish the mood was festive. Soft rock was playing on the jukebox, coins were clinking into the automated gambling machine, and quite a few of the regulars were stopping in to say hello. It was a good moment on Grand Isle. The Gulf coast was safe. Hurricane season was almost over. The whole island seemed to be settling in for a bit of peace. And somewhere far across the warm autumn night, Ambrose Besson was heading toward Alabama.

❧

After Ambrose's departure, I decided to stick around for a few more days. I enjoyed several afternoons of beer sipping with Paula and Smitty at the Gulf View, which by now had become my favorite bar on the island. "The only thing that I can tell you is that I might not be here tomorrow," Smitty remarked at the end of each afternoon.

"Does this worry you?" I asked him.

"No, son," he told me. "Worrying will kill you."

Besides hanging out at the Gulf View, I read at the library, loitered at the town hall, attended a church service, and even accepted an invitation to the island's American Legion dance, where I quickstepped with the seniors and drank whiskey late into the night. Before I departed, as I grabbed one last breakfast at the Starfish, the waitress handed me the bill and whispered: "I have a message for you."

"What is it?" I asked.

"Before you leave town, drive by the Gulf View."

I shrugged my shoulders, paid the bill, and thanked the waitress for relaying the message to me.

As I returned to my motel room at the Sandpiper, I began to make a quick list of all the things I needed to do in the next few hours: find my swimming trunks, pay my hotel bill, return my rental car. The list went on, and as it did I began to feel slightly depressed. I was tired of living out of a backpack—tired of waking up in the dead of night, disoriented and unable to remember where I was. This wasn't a sustainable way of life, and I knew it. I won't be so cavalier as to say that I wanted to settle down for good. Nor did I have any intense domestic epiphanies. I simply wanted to go back to the place I knew best. I never thought of myself as a Bostonian. I never got misty-eyed at the sight of Fenway Park or Quincy Market. I didn't like New England clam chowder, and I certainly didn't root for the Celtics. But in other ways, I missed the place. I missed the autumn leaves, the cobblestone sidewalks, the ivy-covered mews, and the Charles River, which wound its way westward to the small neighborhood where my brother, my girlfriend, and a few of my good friends lived.

There is something unavoidably sentimental about home. At the *New Republic*, where pundits and policy wonks reigned supreme, I felt foolish even considering such a notion. But now that I was safely out of the beltway, and somewhat wiser from many months of travel, I felt far less apologetic about this. After all, home is not just a place, but a vast amalgamation of human experiences. It is an unruly mix of scenery, smells, carpentry, family, memories, ambitions, hardship, and a million other things as well. It is a concept bursting at the seams. It is a vague and elastic word that we have stretched to the outer limit, and then tried to fill with almost everything that is dear to us. Therefore, how could it not be messy? How could it not be rife with emotion? Yes, I was glad to be going home. To be sure, it was not a home in the Thad Knight sense of the word, but it was a start.

As I drove down the island toward the bridge and the bayou beyond, it really started to hit me: My stories were reported, my flying pass was about to expire, my journey was over. Why, I wondered, were moments like this always so anticlimactic? Then, rather suddenly, I remembered the waitress's message. In all the hubbub of leaving, I had somehow forgotten her strange directive to drive by the Gulf View. Abruptly I pulled a U-turn and headed back down the main road toward Smitty's bar. Was someone waiting there for me? Perhaps I was really meant to stop in. Yet several minutes later, when I pulled into the bar's parking lot, there wasn't another car in sight. I tried the front door, but it was locked and no one answered my knocks. Maybe the waitress had gotten the message wrong. Then, as I turned to leave, I saw the signboard out of the corner of my eye. It was one of those tacky contraptions with blinking lights and moveable letters—only this particular signboard was mounted on the roof of a wrecked car that had been painted in a patriotic red, white, and blue. This was the Gulf View's marquee, and it usually announced various weekly specials. Today, however, it had an unusual message:

GOODBYE OUR EAST COAST BUDDY
MAY THE SEASONS OF YOUR LIFE
HAVE FEW HURRICANES!

I stood there for a good few minutes, staring at the marquee, wondering who on earth had put this together. Finally another car pulled into the parking lot and a woman hopped out. It was Paula Smith—

Smitty's daughter—and I realized immediately that this was probably her doing. Ever since Hurricane Betsy, she had been arranging the marquees for her father's businesses.

"Did you do this?" I asked her.

"Yes," she replied.

"Thank you," I stammered.

"I don't know," said Paula. "We just thought it would be a nice way to say goodbye."

# Epilogue

BACK HOME IN BOSTON, I finally settled down for a bit of rest. I moved out of my brother's place and into an apartment of my own, where I was soon enjoying the pleasures of a relatively stationary life—storing my clothing in a dresser, hanging photographs on the wall, and watering a few potted plants. Yet despite my growing domesticity, I often caught myself thinking about the people I had visited.

As fire season drew near I wondered how the Deckers were coming along on their brush clearance. When tropical storms swept across the Caribbean I thought of Ambrose Besson. Strange as it was, these faraway dangers suddenly had meaning in my life. And as I went about my daily routines, in the comfort and relative safety of my quaint residential neighborhood, I couldn't help but wonder: How close was the lava to Jack's house? Was the Tar River cresting the dike in Princeville?

I'd barely been home nine months when my curiosity got the best of me. I packed my bags, bought a few cheap plane tickets, and set out to revisit each place for a few days.

❧

As I drove across the Tar River into Princeville, I barely recognized the place. The old, forlorn ghost town had vanished. In its stead was a gleaming façade of new ranch homes, mostly doublewide prefabs that had been rolled in by truck and dropped off in almost the exact locations where the old houses once stood. With its new makeover, Princeville looked like a fledgling suburban development. There weren't many visible traces of the old Princeville—just the rotting remains of the town hall, a few old houses back in the woods, and the great overgrown cemetery behind Thad's house.

When I arrived at Thad's there were half a dozen guests already there. Now that life in Princeville was almost back to normal, Thad was rarely without a visitor, and often he had several. Today they were gathered on his new front porch, which had replaced the carport as his favorite hangout. When Thad saw me, he rose to his feet, gave me a bear hug, and introduced me to his guests. There were several people from church, an old neighbor, and Dennis, Thad's youngest son. Together we passed the afternoon, sipping water and talking over all that had happened in the last few months. Dennis told me that he had recently moved back into town. "It was because of my father," he admitted. "During the flood we really got a chance to hang out. It made us closer." Dennis wasn't the only one who felt this way. In the coming days, I heard the same sentiment from most of Thad's children and grandchildren. As his daughter Alvanie put it, "A lot of good came out of the flood."

Thad himself seemed to be doing better. Before the flood he could walk only with the help of two canes. Now he was getting by with just one, and sometimes he didn't even need that. "The flood gave Thad a new perspective on life," affirmed his younger brother, James. "It definitely gave him more self-confidence." As for his religious convictions, Thad remained an avid churchgoer, though attendance at his church seemed to be dwindling. "When the water was up the church was full, but when it receded the people went with it," lamented Jesse Williams, the church's pastor. When I inquired about Thad, Pastor

Williams simply smiled and said, "We can always count on Deacon Knight."

Princeville itself also seemed to be thriving. Thad's eldest living son, Sam Knight, was the town's zoning officer, and he could barely contain his excitement for all the new projects on the horizon. Celebrity donors like Prince and Evander Holyfield, along with non-profits like Habitat for Humanity, were making a big difference. "Right now we are getting ready to bring in a Boys and Girls Club, a recreation center, and a park that will have baseball diamonds and football fields," explained Sam. "So trust me when I say we are coming out ahead of the game."

But it wasn't Sam Knight that I mistrusted—it was the dike. Flooding remained a serious concern for the town, and whenever it rained, people worried. Even Thad, who appeared to be doing so well, had a recurring nightmare in which water was crashing down on him. Six or seven times he woke in the middle of the night, short of breath, disoriented, and unnerved by the workings of his subconscious. Unfortunately, his nightmare wasn't so far-fetched. Just several weeks before my final revisit, the Tar River had become bloated once again, and the nearby town of Speed was evacuated. Thad recalled the night well: "I asked Sam if we had to leave too. He told me he didn't think so. So I stayed."

"How was it?" I asked.

"It was a long night," replied Thad.

⚡

From the airport in Anchorage, I took a small rental car with steel-studded snow tires and headed down the Seward Highway for about an hour until I reached the turnoff to Whittier. From there it was another ten miles to the massive mountain tunnel that led the way into town. As I pulled up to the tunnel and paid the fifteen-dollar toll, the attendant told me that I would have to wait. "An alarm went off some-where in the tunnel," he explained. "It's just a glitch, you know, a ghost in the system." I nodded, unfastened my seatbelt, and stepped out of the car to chat with the attendant. I asked a few questions about the tunnel: What was its front door made of? How many cameras did it have? Where were its safe houses located? The attendant gave me several terse answers, eyed me suspiciously, and then retreated into his booth. Roughly half an hour later, when I emerged on the other side of the tunnel, there were two cop cars with flashing lights waiting for me. Now it was my turn to answer some questions. Was I carrying any firearms? Did I have any explosives? How about anthrax? The list went on. Then it was time to search my trunk. Finally the cop re-turned to my window and gave me a very close look. "Wait a minute," he said. "You're that writer from Boston, aren't you?" Yes, I replied. The cop laughed. "The guys on the tunnel crew thought you might be a terrorist. You know, everyone is still nervous from September eleventh." The cop shook his head, returned to his car, and gave me a police escort into town.

When I got to Babs's apartment and told her about my trouble at the tunnel, she began laughing. "That's the best story I've heard all week!" she boomed. "Whittier has its very first terrorist, and he's stay-ing here with me!"

Babs brewed some coffee and I deposited my sleeping bag on her couch, where I would be sleeping for the next five nights. Then, with-out wasting another minute, she launched into a tirade on the new road. "That road is killing this town," she told me. "It's so easy to leave now, people are no longer spending money here. In the old days, everyone had to wait for the train and buy a burger from me. Now they just drive on out. The tourists, the fishermen, the locals, every-one. They don't buy burgers here, they don't wash their clothes here, they don't use telephones here, they don't rent movies here, they don't do anything here. And that's not my only problem."

"What else is wrong?" I asked her.

"A girl opened an espresso stand next to my restaurant," she said. "I used to get a lot of tourists in the morning and now they all get her froufrou coffee and muffins instead of coming to me. Business is down by fifty percent."

"What's going to happen?" I asked.

"I'm going to make some changes," explained Babs. "I think I will offer a vegetarian menu for those kayak people that come up here. I don't know."

Babs and I talked through the afternoon, and after some time she finally remembered some good news. A private prison might be coming to Whittier. It wasn't definite, but with a little luck, there would soon be a 1,000-bed, medium-security correctional facility at the mouth of the tunnel. If everything went according to plan, a private company would come in to build and operate the prison; Whittier would finance the entire project with revenue bonds; and the State of Alaska would pay a fixed monthly fee for every man in custody. It was a foolproof business, insisted Babs.[1]

"Think about it," she said. "Right now we have loads of Alaskans being shipped to prisons in Arizona. I say, we might as well keep them here. It'll bring a lot of jobs to this town. We'd rent more movies, sell more burgers, get use of the prison's medical facility, and even have the tunnel open twenty-four hours a day. I think it'd be great."

"Would you have any worries?" I asked.

"Like a jailbreak?" said Babs. "No big deal. I'd just start packing my gun again. Besides, where are they gonna run to?"

Late in the evening, just before we settled down to sleep, I began to tell Babs about the other four home-keepers I had visited. All of them interested her, but Jack's story seemed to sweep her off her feet. "Oh, I like that one!" she said. "He's definitely one of a kind. I'd like to think that I am too. But that guy . . . he's something."

In the coming days Babs retold Jack's story to at least half a dozen people in town. She then called her best friend in Seattle and told her as well. "The volcano man is in the chapter after mine," she explained. When she hung up, I asked her again what she liked about Jack. "I don't know," she said. "His home just sounds like an off-the-wall and out-of-the-way place. The guy obviously doesn't give a rat's ass about anything. I'd have to say we're probably on about the same wavelength. And imagine, all that red lava. I just might have to visit him."

❧

After landing in Hawaii, I headed straight for a payphone and tried calling Jack on his mobile. No answer. I knew it might take a few days to get in touch with him, and luckily I had a friend who was working on a coffee plantation in Kona, so I stayed up with him. Meanwhile, I continued trying Jack on his mobile, and on the third day I finally got him. "Hey, I'm in Hawaii," I told him. "Can you meet me?"

"Sure," he said. "I'll meet you at the house."

"Which house?" I asked.

"The one in Royal Gardens," he replied. There was a brief, awkward silence. "You know the routine," he assured me. "Just walk across the lava."

A day or so later, when I arrived at the head of Jack's access road, I discovered a large fence with a newly constructed tollbooth blocking my way. "What's this?" I asked the tollbooth attendant.

"This is the County of Hawaii," he replied smugly, "and you owe us five dollars." Then he told me why: The County of Hawaii had set up a lava-viewing platform at the end of the access road and tourists had to pay five dollars a car. I tried to explain that I just wanted to park for a few days while I visited Jack Thompson, but the attendant quickly told me this was a bad idea and he wouldn't allow it. All right, I told him. So I shifted the car into reverse, parked a mile away, and headed back on foot. Casually I walked past the attendant. Everything was fine until I veered off the designated path, past a few DANGER! signs, and on toward the kipuka. "Wait, you can't go there! It's not safe!" yelled the attendant. I didn't look back.

My hike across the flats took about an hour, and luckily it was uneventful. I encountered smoke and some very warm rocks, but no fresh flows. When I finally arrived at Jack's I was pleased to discover that the lava had receded, the helicopters had stopped swarming, and his house was still standing. "It's really been pretty quiet ever since you left," said Jack. "The only problem I've had is with those damn pigs. They've gotten worse. My front lawn and much of my garden has been eaten up. I tell you, they're worse than the lava."

"How is your friend Don Bartel doing?" I asked eventually.

"He's fine," replied Jack. "He was here not too long ago, and was looking to buy a house here in Royal Gardens." Apparently, Jack had found him a place situated on its own little kipuka.

"Is he really going to buy it?" I asked.

"Well, I put him in touch with the owner, so we'll see what happens," said Jack.*

Later that evening, Jack and I grilled up two chickens that I had lugged with me. As we ate, I began to tell him about the other home-

---

* I later called Don Bartel at his home in California, and he told me that despite his many ongoing responsibilities, he had decided to pursue the possibility of having a second home on the volcano. As of the spring of 2002, he was still negotiating a price with the owner of the small house that Jack had found for him.

keepers. He was very curious, and as I described each place, he offered his opinions. I started with Babs. "She wants to visit me?" asked Jack excitedly. "Wow. I guess the grass is always greener—and at least we got grass!"

"Could you ever see yourself living in Whittier?" I asked him.

"Sure, why not?" he replied. "I'd go to Alaska just to get that sweetie back down here!"

Jack was adamant that he had a better deal than the Deckers. "Brushfires are unpredictable. The wind changes direction and it can kill you. With lava you just step out of the way." Jack did sympathize with the Deckers when it came to running roadblocks. "Yeah," he said with a sigh, "I've been running roadblocks for a long time too."

As the evening ended, I told Jack about Thad Knight and the story of Princeville. He listened attentively, and when it was over, he just nodded his head as if it all made sense. "What are you thinking?" I asked him finally.

"It just sounds like another person who really likes his home and is willing to put up with whatever might come along with it."

"What about his problems?" I asked. "How do they compare to yours?"

"It's not about the problems," replied Jack. "The problems could be whatever—drive-bys, wild dogs, pigs, hurricanes, lava, whatever—that doesn't matter. It's the home that matters."

⚡

The day I arrived in Malibu, a strong Santa Ana wind was gusting in from east, and it shook my little rental car as I cruised along the Pacific Coast Highway. High above it all, in her snug perch in Decker Canyon, Millie was sitting in her living room amid the many deer heads. When I found her, she was making Christmas wreaths and enjoying the heat of a roaring fire. I said hello, gave her a hug, and then eyed the fireplace uneasily. "Oh, don't worry about that, honey," said Millie with a laugh. "It's fine as long as it's in here and not out there."

We were soon making lunch and sharing bits of news. "Chip and Claire had a baby," Millie told me. "She's a beautiful girl named Helena." I offered my congratulations and we talked about her grandchildren for a while. Then, rather suddenly, Millie announced: "We have to go to the insurance office tomorrow."

"What for?"

"I have some questions about my fire insurance policy."

"You have fire insurance?" I asked.

"I just got it a few months ago," explained Millie. "I'm getting on top of my finances. I had to take out a new mortgage on the house, and the bank made me get it. Anyway, I got to go down there."

So the following day we dusted off Millie's old Lincoln Mark VII—and I mean we literally dusted it off, for it hadn't been used in some time—and together we went down to the insurance office. After waiting for almost an hour, a woman named Maria came out and talked to Millie. I made it a point not to listen, but I did notice Millie shaking her head quite a bit. Afterward, Millie was still shaking her head as we went for a cup of coffee. "It wasn't my idea to get fire insurance," she told me rather bleakly. "That woman wants me to get liability insurance too, but I told her, 'You can't get blood out of a turnip.'"

That evening as we sat in front of the fire, Millie inquired about the progress of my book. "Have you stayed with most of your clients?" she asked me.

"Yes," I replied, and began to tell her about the other home-keepers. Immediately Whittier fascinated her.

"Everyone is in one building!" She gasped. "Are there sidewalks or just hallways?"

"Just hallways," I told her.

"Well . . ." said Millie. She paused for a moment, as if she was considering the building's dimensions very carefully. "Now Mommy and Daddy used to have people living on the ranch, but they were in separate buildings and they came in and out as they pleased. That was different. All in one building, I couldn't stand it. I'd have claustrophobia. Not that I go to town much—I hardly go into town, actually—but at least I'm not locked in."

When I told Millie about Jack she was much more receptive. "I wouldn't want to deal with a volcano," she admitted, "but at least he gets to go to town once in a while."

As the evening wore on, the once blazing fire sank into a pile of embers, the room grew dim, and the many deer heads faded into the darkness. In this cozy setting, I told Millie about Thad Knight, and as usual his story brought out a warm response. "That's just beautiful," declared Millie. "We have houses washed away in Malibu too, down by the ocean. And for some reason, they just keep building back."

⚡

I found Ambrose just where I left him, sipping coffee with the gang at the Starfish. Within minutes of my arrival, Ambrose was heckling Bobby Santiny, his lifelong friend and storm-riding rival. "About the only thing that's changed around here is Bobby—he's about twenty pounds fatter," said Ambrose. The gang laughed, Bobby mumbled bitterly, and the waitress poured more coffee.

Later that afternoon, Ambrose invited me over to his house for a meal. As we sat in his kitchen, eating a very spicy shrimp gumbo, Ambrose pumped me for details on the other places I had visited. Jack's house on the volcano intrigued him immediately.

"I've never seen lava, other than in *National Geographic*, but it looks pretty nasty," said Ambrose. "So this guy Jack is surrounded on all sides? How does he do it? Does he have a woman up there with him?"

"No," I told him.

"No woman!" boomed Ambrose. "A Cajun would never be in a place like that without a woman. He must be talking to the trees."

Whittier didn't appeal to Ambrose in the least. Apparently, as a young man, he had joined the army and been stationed in a remote outpost in Keflavík, Iceland. "We used to stay in Quonset huts," recalled Ambrose. "There were about twenty guys to a hut, and the snow came up so high we used to crawl out through the ceiling. When the snowstorms came, we stayed in those huts for days. We used to play cards all the time—really, it was pitiful—but we had to psych ourselves into doing it. I'll tell you, it was a hellhole, and I could never see going back to anything like that."

In the end, the person who Ambrose related to most closely was Thad Knight. "My hunting camp in Alabama is situated in a flood plain also," explained Ambrose. "There is a house fifty feet from my camp that FEMA recently bought out. They bulldozed it, burned it, and buried it. I imagine FEMA was just tired of bailing those folks out."

"Has your hunting camp ever flooded?" I asked.

"Three times," replied Ambrose. "But I just rent it. I am building a place of my own down there, and it'll be on higher ground."

Late in the day, we hopped into Ambrose's pickup truck and paid a visit to the Grand Isle cemetery. By the time we arrived, the sun was low in the sky and the tombstones cast long shadows across the grass. The surrounding oak trees were all hung with Spanish moss, which draped downward and swayed slightly in the breeze. It was a haunting time to visit the cemetery, and I was glad we had come. The explicit purpose of our visit was to see the new grave of Ambrose's older

brother, Roscoe "the Rock" Besson. Apparently, the Rock had recently been exhumed from the Besson family tomb so that he could
be reburied with his wife. "They just moved his coffin a few weeks
ago," explained Ambrose as we strolled through the cemetery. "It
makes me feel a little funny that I won't be buried with my brother,"
he admitted. "I guess I always imagined myself down there with him,
you know, so we could play cards in the afterlife."

"Do you believe in the afterlife?" I asked.

"Not really," replied Ambrose. "To me this is heaven right here,
and so I'm just going to enjoy it while I can."

*If only I could bring them together in one room.* After returning from
my revisits, this was the fantasy that captured my imagination again
and again. I tried to picture all five of them in my small apartment,
sipping coffee and swapping life stories. I imagined Jack and Babs as
kindred spirits, sitting on my sofa, talking fondly of lava and snow,
and lamenting what a hellhole Boston was. I imagined Millie and
Ambrose on my back porch, amid my withered tomato plants, reminiscing about the old days when young people knew how to live off
the land. And I imagined Thad Knight showing off photographs of his
newly completed house, receiving congratulations from everybody
for successfully standing his ground. But what if it didn't go this
smoothly? Perhaps they would have nothing to say to one another.
Perhaps it would just be polite smiles and long, awkward silences. After all, what did the five of them really have in common, besides a
fierce devotion to home? Were they really linked in any other ways?

With my journey and revisits completed, I had an opportunity to
consider these questions more carefully. As I sifted through my notes,
I discovered a number of interesting similarities. To begin with, despite the various dangers that the fivesome faced, all of them had a

way out. Jack had a spare house on the outskirts of Hilo; Ambrose had one in Alabama; Millie could sell her place at the drop of a hat; Thad had already rejected a federal buyout; and Babs had some savings, a set of wheels, and even a road to leave on. These were people who chose to stay.

For the most part, they came from humble origins, lived hard lives, and worked tirelessly to build and rebuild their homes. None had graduated from college (except for Babs, who had completed a two-year program at South Seattle Community College), and most worked with their hands for a living. They were a hardy lot. All of them knew how to hunt or shoot a gun; Ambrose and Babs also fished, while Jack and Thad gardened. They were people who could live off the land if they had to, and sometimes that's what they did. Perhaps needless to say, none of them was a city person. Both Thad and Ambrose had been to New York City once, and they seemed to agree that once was enough. All of them regarded cities as dangerous places, far more dangerous than the homes in which they lived. This was a point several of them reiterated to me in the wake of September 11. "I'm safer up here on the volcano," Jack told me with a laugh. Humor was another common trait. All of them seemed to enjoy laughing, yet this was balanced by a definite stoicism. I never heard a minute's worth of complaining or self-pitying from any of them. They were strong, self-reliant individuals—loners, I would say. All of them were single and lived alone, except for Ambrose, who still resided with his wife.[2] None had plans to remarry. Both Thad and Millie claimed to be too old. Age was another commonality. The whole group was over fifty, and all of them were retired except for Babs, who vowed to flip hamburgers until the end.

In general, they now seemed determined to enjoy the simple pleasures in life. Thad would never chop wood or use an outhouse again. Ambrose no longer fished for mullet or even ate bread crust.

Babs could now sleep soundly without worrying about her maniacal ex-husband. Millie tended to her horses and let her children worry about brush control. And Jack never heard a peep from his neighbors. Despite all the reasons that it seemed impossible to do so, these people were enjoying their homes.

As for the differences, I noticed at least one major division within the fivesome. The way I saw it, there were two distinct subgroups. On the one hand, there was Millie, Thad, and Ambrose—all historically connected to the land on which they lived. They belonged to families, either by birth or by marriage, that had lived in a given area for several generations. Their roots ran deep. What's more, each of these families belonged to a unique historical group that had overcome considerable hardship before settling down. The Deckers were homesteaders; the Knights were freed slaves; and the Bessons were Cajuns. All had struggled bitterly to find a home for themselves, and once they had found it, they held fast. On the other hand, there was Jack and Babs. Both were transplants. They had picked up and moved to the outer fringes of the map: Hawaii and Alaska, the two most far-flung American states. From there, they had taken it a step further, secluding themselves on an active volcano and in a gated mountain hideaway. In these strange cul-de-sacs, they had found security and peace of mind.

Perhaps the greatest single difference between these subgroups was continuity. Jack and Babs had very little of it. Their homes started and ended with them—a point underscored by the fact that neither had any children. "I don't know who is going to take over this place when I'm gone," Jack told me on my revisit. Babs voiced a similar uncertainty: "I'm not sure what will happen with my apartment." This may have been depressing at times, but neither of them ever admitted this to me. Instead they focused on the prospect that some small part of their legacy would continue. Babs hoped that her burger stand would stay open, and Jack suggested that his house might make a good park ranger's outpost.

Meanwhile, Millie, Thad, and Ambrose all had children and grandchildren living nearby, whom they hoped would someday take over their homes. In this way, their homes were almost hereditary, passing from one generation to the next like a surname or a coat of arms. "I just want one Knight by my side," Thad's father had told him. On some level, Thad was obliged to stay. The same could be said of Millie and Ambrose. The onus was placed on them to maintain their family traditions. Yet in return, each of them became a part of something greater than themselves—something that would continue to exist even after they were gone. And perhaps this was the ultimate kind of permanence. Staying for a wildfire or a hurricane was one thing; but staying after death, now that was truly impressive.

Despite these subgroups—and all the innumerable differences among the fivesome—there was always that one overriding commonality: These people were devoted to their homes. Their devotion required considerable courage. Without a doubt, all five homekeepers were both tough and brave, but there was also something decidedly *not* brave about them. They each expressed considerable fears about the world beyond, and sometimes it seemed to me as if their desire to stay was as much rooted in fear as it was in contentedness.

I also wondered to what extent each of their lives had been limited by their devotion to home. Both Jack and Babs claimed to be at peace with the absence of romance in their lives, but what choice did they really have? Millie and Thad sang the praises of staying at home, but didn't they ever envy their siblings who'd moved away? (Incidentally, Thad's brother in Washington, D.C., became one of the first black FBI agents in the country.) Aside from all the hardships endemic to each of these places, was there not something suffocating about how all-important they'd become? Even Henry David Thoreau eventually left Walden Pond and wrote, "Thank Heaven, here is not all the world."

All of this begged the question: Under what circumstances would these people *ever* leave their homes? The odd thing was, despite the fact that all of them *could* leave, none of them even acknowledged this as a valid option. Their homes were not just dear, they were indispensable—a fundamental part of who they were. Primo Levi once wrote, "I live in my house as I live inside my skin: I know more beautiful, more ample, more sturdy and more picturesque skins: but it would seem to me unnatural to exchange them for mine."[3] It's worth adding that Levi's quote sounds a little bit like Professor Proshansky's theory of "place identity," which I mentioned briefly in the introduction. Both men suggest that our identities sometimes become irrevocably linked to places where we live. I agree. Thad Knight's story, for example, was inextricably linked with that of Princeville. He personified the town. Such was the case with all of them. They played important if not fundamental roles within the context of where they lived. Babs Reynolds mattered in Whittier, Alaska. Her two decades of living there had earned her acceptance and respect. If she left, all of this stood to be lost. Babs claimed the "lower forty-eight" didn't appeal to her because she didn't "know any of those people down there"—but perhaps the real drawback was that none of those people knew her. In Utah she would not be the institution that she is in Whittier. She'd just be another drifter, one of many, coming in across the salt flats for a bit of winter sunshine.

I think the final question to consider is whether the hardships themselves appealed to these home-keepers. Did the actual raw, punishing elements heighten their resolve to stay? Perhaps in the tradition of the American pioneers, like Daniel Boone and Davy

Crockett, they were drawn to the high adventure of the American wilderness. Perhaps, over the years, their intimacy with danger and their ability to survive created a deep sense of pride and belonging. This certainly seemed to be the case with Millie and Ambrose, who knew the tricks to fighting wildfires and riding storms. Indeed, all of them had struggled fiercely to maintain their homes, and this struggle had imbued their lives with a commanding sense of purpose.

The drawback to these places was undeniable, but the reward was a unique and invigorating existence. By staying in Princeville when it was still just a ghost town, Thad had embarked on a personal odyssey that redefined his family relationships, his faith in God, and his view of the world. Babs Reynolds had become a legend in Whittier by lasting more than twenty years in a place where people usually cracked in three. Jack Thompson had witnessed and lived alongside one of nature's most spectacular occurrences. Millie Decker was a last bastion of the Wild West, and Ambrose Besson was among the hardy few who still stayed for hurricanes. In a nation dominated by highways, strip malls, and cookie-cutter houses, these people had distinguished themselves, and over the years their lives had become as extraordinary as the places in which they lived.

Perhaps, in the end, Babs said it best in a conversation we had during my revisit. We were sitting in her kitchen drinking coffee, and outside the wind was blowing wickedly. "You know," she said, "as unpleasant as that wind is, it says something for the people who stay here."

"What does it say?" I asked her.

Babs thought for a moment as the gusts continued to whistle through the minute crevices in her apartment. Finally she replied, "It just lends a certain dignity to the whole operation. It says you're tough. You're different. You're not like everybody else."

# Notes

## Introduction

1 United States Census Bureau, *Report on Geographic Mobility from March 1992 to March 1993*, 20–481.

2 United States Census Bureau, *Report on Geographic Mobility from March 1999 to March 2000*, 20–538. Compiled by Jason Schacter, demographer.

3 Ibid. The information on rural inhabitants was actually not included in this report, but was provided to me by its author, Jason Schachter, from an unpublished study that he compiled.

4 Harold M. Proshansky, "Place Identity: Physical World Socialization of the Self," *Journal of Environmental Psychology* 3 (1983): 57–83. Robert Gifford, *Environmental Psychology: Principles and Practice* (Needham Heights, Mass.: Allyn & Bacon, 1997).

## The Underwater Town

1 There were a number of articles describing Princeville as abandoned, including Richard Lezin Jones, "Hurricanes Leave Princeville Like a Waterlogged Pompeii," *Philadelphia Inquirer*, October 23, 1999, and Chris Burritt, "N.C. Town's Fu-

ture Murky," *Atlanta Journal-Constitution*, October 27, 1999.

2  Joe A. Mobley, "In the Shadow of White Society: Princeville a Black Town in North Carolina 1865–1915," *North Carolina Historical Review* 63, no. 3 (July 1986). I gathered additional information by interviewing Joe Mobley several times during the summer of 2002. Joe Mobley is a retired historian and administrator at the North Carolina Office of Archives and History. He is also a lecturer on North Carolina history at North Carolina State University in Raleigh. He has distinguished himself as the leading scholar on Princeville.

3  According to the U.S. Army Corps of Engineers (Engineering and Planning Branch), Princeville flooded seventeen times between 1908 and 1965. The Corps speculates that periodic flooding occurred before this as well, but there are no records from this time.

4  Robert Kilborn and Lance Carden, "USA: News in Brief," *Christian Science Monitor*, September 14, 1999.

5  Patrick J. Fitzpatrick, *Natural Disasters: A Reference Handbook* (Santa Barbara: ABC-CLIO, 1999).

6  Ricardo Alonso-Zaldivar, "Weakened Floyd Leaves Legacy of Heavy Flooding, Record Evacuations," *Los Angeles Times*, September 17, 1999.

7  Linda McNatt, "The Entire Town Is Gone," *Virginian-Pilot*, September 20, 1999.

8  Frederick Olmsted, *The Cotton Kingdom: A Traveller's Observations on Cotton and Slavery in the American Slave States* (New York: Mason Brothers, 1861).

9  Horace James, *Annual Report of the Superintendent of Negro Affairs in North Carolina, 1864: History and Management of the Freedmen in this Department up to June 1st, 1865* (Boston: W. P. Brown Printers, n.d.), as quoted in Joe A. Mobley, "Princeville:

A Black Town in North Carolina, 1865–1981," an unpublished research report, North Carolina Office of Archives and History, 1981, Raleigh.

10  Mobley, "In the Shadow of White Society."

11  Bonnie Rochman, "Reburying Unearthed Caskets," *Raleigh News & Observer*, November 1, 1999.

12  Peter T. Kilborn, "Landmark for Ex-Slaves Felt Brunt of Storm," *New York Times*, September 21, 1999; Emily Yellin, "Town with Fabled Past Facing Uncertain Future," *New York Times*, November 22, 1999.

13  Yellin, "Town with Fabled Past."

14  White House Press Office, "President's Council on the Future of Princeville," February 29, 2000. Executive Order EO 13146.

15  Chris Burritt, "Historic N.C. Town Standing Pat," *Atlanta Journal-Constitution*, November 24, 1999.

16  It's worth noting that I was not present at this vote. My recreation of events is based on multiple personal interviews with Delia Perkins, Anne Howell, Linda Worsley, and Sam Knight, as well as several newspaper articles, including Burritt, "Historic N.C. Town Standing Pat"; Lynn Bonner, "Town Picks Dike Repair over Buyout," *News & Observer*, November 24, 1999; and Associated Press, "Flooded Black Town Decides to Rebuild," *New York Times*, November 24, 1999.

17  Thad's son Sam Knight, who oversaw the distribution of many charitable donations in Princeville, says that he gave his father less than his fair share. "I didn't want people to think there was any favoritism going on," he told me.

18  George Howe Cult, *The Enigma of Suicide* (New York: Summit Books, 1991).

19  Michael T. Aubele, "Flood Issues Rise on Opposite Side of Princeville Dike," *Daily Southerner*, December 14, 1999.

20  Thomas McDonald, "Princeville Imposes Gag Order on Tarboro Council's Decision," *Daily Southerner*, December 16, 1999.

21  "Republican Floyd Plan Includes More Money, but Leaves out Princeville Dike," Associated Press, March 7, 2000.

22  Natalie Phillips, "Road Warriors," *Anchorage Daily News*, June 8, 1997.

Tower of the Arctic

1  The town of Sweetwater, Texas, has an annual rattlesnake roundup that attracts as many as 30,000 tourists: "Rattlesnake Roundup Time," *Houston Chronicle*, March 12, 1998.

2  Just as my editor said, the *Los Angeles Times* ran this article on Whittier: Kim Murphy, "Alaskans Find New Road Paved with Uncertainty," *Los Angeles Times*, June 7, 2000.

3  *The Strangest Town in Alaska: The History of Whittier, Alaska, and the Portage Valley* (Seattle: Kokogiak Media, 2000). United States Army, *Building Alaska with the U.S. Army, 1867–1965*, Pamphlet No. 360–5 (Seattle: Headquarters U.S. Army for Alaska, 1965). "Alaska: The Elegant White Elephant," *Time*, February 21, 1964, 27.

4  "Alaska: The Elegant White Elephant."

5  Whittier's 250 inches of snow a year is an average (from October 2, 1950, to December 31, 2001) based on data from the Western Regional Climate Center.

6  Jon Little, "Sterling Poodle Becomes Prey," *Anchorage Daily News*, March 30, 2001.

7  The school also relies on peer tutoring. When I visited, the students were preparing for a schoolwide research project on salmon, in which high school students worked side by side with first- and second-graders. The older students were expected to

record detailed scientific data, while the younger students counted fish or learned to read a thermometer.

8  I interviewed Elena Meyers again the following afternoon. Her remarks as rendered in this section of the book are actually a compilation of quotations from both of these interviews.

## THE LAVA-SIDE INN

1  Robert I. Tilling, *Eruptions of Hawaiian Volcanoes: Past, Present, and Future* (Washington, D.C.: U.S. Department of the Interior/U.S. Geological Survey, 1993). *Volcanic and Seismic Hazards on the Island of Hawaii* (Washington, D.C.: U.S. Department of the Interior/U.S. Geological Survey, 1997).

2  Dr. Don Swanson, Scientist-in-Charge at the Hawaiian Volcano Observatory, personal interview, May 2001.

3  In the past Kilauea has experienced some explosive eruptions, most notably in 1790 and in 1924, but this is atypical.

4  Tilling, *Eruptions of Hawaiian Volcanoes; Volcanic and Seismic Hazards.*

5  Robert Nilsen, *Moon Handbooks' Big Island of Hawaii: Including Hawaii Volcanoes National Park* (New York: Avalon Travel Publishing, 2001).

6  George Cooper and Gavan Daws, *Land and Power in Hawaii* (Honolulu: University of Hawaii Press, 1990).

7  Henry David Thoreau, *Walden* (Oxford: Oxford University Press, 1997).

## CANYON OF THE FIREFIGHTING HILLBILLIES

1  Mike Davis, *Ecology of Fear: Los Angeles and the Imagination of Disaster* (New York: Henry Holt, 1998).

2  Ibid.

3  Bob Pool, "Fires Rage, Torch Malibu Area," *Los Angeles Times,*

November 3, 1993; Jack Cheevers, "Help Gone Awry," *Los Angeles Times*, November 3, 1993; Richard Colvin, "Following the Flames on Path of Destruction," *Los Angeles Times*, November 7, 1993; George Gordon, "Death Toll 3, Arson Suspected," *Malibu Times*, November 11, 1993.

4   Daniel Hernandez, "7 Wildfires Burn 80,000 Acres," *Los Angeles Times*, August 14, 2001; Jeff Barnard, "Firefighters Attack Western Wildfires," Associated Press Online, August 15, 2001; Craig Welch, "Hundreds of Fires Blaze Across NW," *Seattle Times*, August 14, 2001.

5   Raymond Chandler, *Red Wind* (Cleveland: World Publishing Company, 1946).

6   There is conflicting information on whether the arrival of the Santa Ana winds actually coincides with heightened crime. Some reports (Gregory McNamee, "Breezy Stories," *Tucson Weekly*, November 15, 1995) assert that homicide rates double on bad Santa Ana days. Other investigations (Paul Young, *L.A. Exposed: Strange Myths and Curious Legends in the City of Angels* [New York: St. Martin's, 2002]) suggest that the homicide rate actually goes down during the weeks of peak Santa Ana activity.

7   For information on Chumash Indians and the Spanish governor (José Joaqín de Arillaga), see Thomas C. Blackburn and Kat Anderson, *Before the Wilderness: Environmental Management by Native Californians* (Menlo Park, Calif.: Ballena Press, 1993). For information on Cabrillo and the French traveler (Eugene Duflot de Mofras), see Stephen Pyne, *Fire in America: A Cultural History of Wildlife and Rural Fire* (Princeton: Princeton University Press, 1982).

8   The most accurate historical information about Marion Decker, including his date of arrival, comes from court records

in the case *The People v. May K. Rindge*, 174 California (April 1917).

9  For background on the Rindge family in Malibu, see Luanne Pfeifer, *The Malibu Story* (Malibu: Malibu Lagoon Museum, 1985). For information on the movie colony fire of 1928, see Davis, *Ecology of Fear*.

10  The quote from Laura Ingalls Wilder, the reference to Alfred Jacob Miller's painting, and most of the historical information relating to evolution of firefighting comes from Pyne, *Fire in America*. Additional background information comes from a personal interview with Stephen Pyne in August of 2002. Pyne, one of the nation's leading "fire historians," teaches at Arizona State University.

11  Information on plant life comes from Margaret Huffman, *Wild Heart of Los Angeles* (Niwot, Colo.: Roberts Rhinehart Publishers, 1998). Additional information comes from a personal interview with Margaret Huffman in August of 2001. Huffman is an expert on California native plants and serves as a docent at Topanga State Park, Charmlee Park, and the Ballona Wetlands.

12  Kathleen Kelleher, "Devastating Fire Helped Bring Malibu Together," *Los Angeles Times*, December 4, 1994.

13  Richard Lillard, "Mountain Men and Women in the New West of Los Angeles," *South Dakota Review* 19 (spring/summer 1981).

## ISLAND OF THE STORM RIDERS

1  State of Louisiana Department of Culture & Recreation & Tourism, *Birds of Louisiana* (Baton Rouge: Office of Tourism Publications).

2  Betsy Swanson, *Historic Jefferson Parish: From Shore to Shore* (Gretna, La.: Pelican Publishing, 1975).

3  The number of people who died on Grand Isle and Cheniere

Caminada is an estimate derived from two sources: Rose C. Falls, *Cheniere Caminada: The Wind of Death* (New Orleans: Hopkins' Printing, 1893); Dale Rogers, *Cheniere Caminada: Buried at Sea* (Thibodaux: self-published, 1981).

4  David Maraniss, "Grand Stand on Grand Isle: 1 Percent of the Population Wouldn't Budge," *Washington Post*, August 28, 1992.

5  Rogers, *Cheniere Caminada: Buried at Sea.*

6  Sally Kittredge Evans, *Grand Isle on the Gulf: An Early History* (Jefferson Parish Historical Commission, 1981).

7  Falls, *Cheniere Caminada: The Wind of Death*; Rogers, *Cheniere Caminada: Buried at Sea.*

8  I later verified these reports in the following newspaper articles: "Storm Still Battering Nicaragua, Honduras," *Miami Herald*, November 1, 2001; "Tropical Storm Ravages Central America," *Los Angeles Times*, November 1, 2001.

9  Evans, *Grand Isle on the Gulf.*

10  Carl A. Brasseaux, *Scattered to the Wind: Dispersal and Wanderings of the Arcadians, 1755–1809* (Lafayette, La.: Center for Louisiana Studies, 1991).

11  Both men actually resided on Grand Terre, the small windswept island just several hundred yards off the eastern edge of Grand Isle.

12  "Cuba Braces for Impact of Hurricane Michelle," *New York Times*, November 4, 2001.

13  All scientific information and statistics about erosion from Shea Penland, *Louisiana Barrier Island Erosion Study: Atlas of Shoreline Changes in Louisiana from 1853 to 1989* (prepared by the USGS in cooperation with the Louisiana Geological Survey, 1992). Historical information about Last Isle and its hotels

from James M. Sothern, *Last Island* (Houma, La.: Cheri Publications, 1980).

14  Jack Beven, "Tropical Cyclone Report: Hurricane Michelle," a report for the National Hurricane Center, January 23, 2002.

EPILOGUE

1  According to the *Anchorage Daily News*, as of the spring of 2002, plans for a private prison in Whittier had passed in the Alaska House of Representatives but stalled in the Senate. Despite this setback, the prison's backers remained optimistic. (Tom Kizzia, "Private-Prison Push Likely to be Revived," *Anchorage Daily News*, May 23, 2002.)

2  It's worth noting that Ambrose and his wife, Sissy Besson, have been married for more than forty years. In my time on Grand Isle, however, I hardly ever saw them spending time together. They seemed to have a strong but independent marriage.

3  Primo Levi, *The Periodic Table* (New York: Schocken Books, 1984).

# Acknowledgments

Without the help of Thad Knight, Babs Reynolds, Jack Thompson, Millie Decker, and Ambrose Besson, this book would simply not exist. Any credit that I get for this project truly belongs to them. These are their stories—I merely did my best to retell them.

I would also like to thank a handful of other key people in each of the places I visited: Sam Knight and Anne Howell in Princeville; Brenda Tolman, Carolyn Raye Casebeer, and Jan Latta in Whittier; Don Bartel, Chuck Humphries, and Dr. Don Swanson in Hawaii; Bonnie Decker, Chip Mandeville, and his wife, Claire, in Malibu; and Sissy Besson and Josie Cheramie in Grand Isle. Time and again, these people welcomed me into their homes, returned my calls, and did their best to help me recount these stories as accurately as possible. I am greatly indebted to all of them.

As far as the actual writing of this book goes, I would like to start by thanking Joseph Finder—the best mentor a young writer could hope to have. If it were not for his sustained, brotherly concern, I doubt I would have had the nerve to embark on this journey. I am also so grateful that he put me in touch with my literary agent, Tina Bennett, who helped me mold, polish, and produce this work. Her keen advice and tireless encouragement have made her an invaluable partner with whom I hope to work for a very long time. Many thanks also go to her dynamic assistant, Svetlana Katz. At Houghton Mifflin I would like to thank my editor, Heidi Pitlor, whose vision for this book has been far-reaching. Over the course of the last two years, she has helped me improve my writing on an almost daily basis. Her devotion to this book has been astounding, and I hope I am lucky enough to work with her in the future. Additionally I would like to thank a few others at Houghton Mifflin: Megan Wilson, Carla Gray, Melissa Grella, and Alison Kerr Miller, all of whom worked diligently and shrewdly on my behalf.

I would also like to thank my friends and coworkers at the *New Republic*, who encouraged me to pursue this project, gave me valuable leads, and helped me refine my prose. They include Brian Groh, Ben Soskis, Negar Akavi, Martin Peretz, Andrew Sullivan, and Will Lippincott. A number of other friends also helped me greatly along the way, including Elaine McArdle, Mike Bowden, Meaghan Rady, Christian Manders, Charles Wachter, Phil Blix, Beverly Sanford, Jane Levin, and Micah Nathan.

Finally, I would like to thank my family. My stepsister Robyn most generously gave me her "flying pass," for which I am still incredibly grateful. My mother and father believed in this project from the start, never once questioning if it was feasible or practical. Their love and encouragement have been the wellspring of my every success. My brother Greg, who is a gifted photographer and oral historian, inspired me and counseled me on numerous occasions. Last, but by no means least, I would like to thank my fiancée, Kasia Lipska, whose unwavering friendship ushered me through my lowest moments and helped me carry on.